# Joy and the Objects of Psychoanalysis

SUNY series in Psychoanalysis and Culture
Henry Sussman, editor

# Joy and the Objects
# of Psychoanalysis

## Literature, Belief, and Neurosis

## Volney P. Gay

State University of New York Press

Published by
State University of New York Press

© 2001 State University of New York

All rights reserved

Printed in the United States of America

For information, address the State University of New York Press,
90 State Street, Suite 700, Albany, NY 12207

Marketing by Anne Valentine
Production by Bernadine Dawes

Library of Congress Cataloging-in-Publication Data

Gay, Volney Patrick.
    Joy and the objects of psychoanalysis : literature, belief, and neurosis / Volney P. Gay.
        p. cm. — (SUNY series in psychoanalysis and culture)
    Includes bibliographical references and index.
    ISBN 0-7914-5099-6 — ISBN 0-7914-5100-3 (pbk.)
        1. Psychoanalysis. 2. Joy. 3. Neuroses. 4. Parent and child. 5. Object relations
(Psychoanalysis). 6. Psychoanalysis and literature. I. Title. II. Series.

RC506 .G39 2001
616.89'17—dc21

                                                                        00-053798

1   2   3   4   5   6   7   8   9   10

*To the memory of*
*Pietro Castelnuovo-Tedesco, M.D.*

# Contents

# Preface

## ANOTHER VIEW FROM NASHVILLE

I write this preface on a cool spring morning in Nashville, Tennessee, in an office at Vanderbilt University where I've taught some twenty years. About thirty years ago as a philosophy major at Reed College I read Sigmund Freud's *The Interpretation of Dreams* (1900a). Although I didn't understand it fully, I decided to become a psychoanalyst. After a long journey I did so and also became a professor at McMaster University, then at Vanderbilt. Among my blessings are colleagues in religious studies, psychiatry, and anthropology who take psychoanalysis seriously. By teaching psychoanalysis in each department, I learned more about its limits and about the limits of the academic enterprise. For each department has its own culture and distinctive notions of what counts as valid evidence. For example, when Freud says that myths are like dreams, anthropologists and psychiatrists agree and find this equation confirmed in their own fields. Religionists, however, find this equation reduces the social value of myths to mere personal psychology. Who is right? How can we decide between these competing claims? We can't. Hence, we conclude that each discipline is correct with regard to its domain of inquiry and its methods. Each discipline and its practitioners partake in a limited discourse: none of us knows fully and precisely what dreams are and why they're important. This agnostic affirmation harms no one. Disciplines that study the mind, which includes neurosciences, persist independently of one another. Knowing that we don't know everything about dreams or about other mental events, we sleep soundly.

In contrast to the easy world of the university is the uneasy world of children raised in chaotic circumstances. As I show in the following chapters, these children cannot remain calm in the face of not knowing the nature of the mind, especially other minds. Because their happiness depends upon chaotic moods of their parents or siblings, tasks like predicting an uncle's rage or cajoling a depressed mother, become unavoidable. Because these tasks are impossible to accomplish fully, like Sisyphus these children cannot relent. They struggle continuously and so have no room for joy.

## JOY AND THE OBJECTS OF PSYCHOANALYSIS

For a hundred years, psychoanalysts have applied their clinical theories to objects of culture. This has created entire libraries of insights, discovery, and debate. In this book I reverse field and use literature to reevaluate psychoanalysis. I argue that neurosis occurs when one cannot recollect joy. Dramatic and literary accounts of joy, therefore, are essential to contemporary psychoanalysis because these accounts illuminate the nature of our analytic "objects."

Humanistic insights about joy predate psychoanalysis. They help us address a central puzzle of contemporary analysis (and literary-critical theory): the multiplicity of points of view. I focus upon the nature of joy as articulated by literary artists because they apprehend an object that, when absent, produces a form of human suffering that Freud named "neurosis." The absence of joy, I suggest, evokes in children a lifelong quest for repair and restitution. Because they are children, they believe that only a concrete, actual thing, like money or sexual victories or self-inflicted pain, can replace this lost object. Confronting this form of human pain and self-repair, analytic theorists grapple with the same puzzle and often name a particular thing, such as "oedipal fears," or "low self-esteem," as the cause of neurosis. However, if neurosis is primarily the *absence* of joy, all such specific solutions will prove limited. None will prove sufficient; new observers name new objects and this multiplicity of objects produces a multiplicity of theories.

Given these kinds of objects, theories of psychopathology must be similar to children's theories of the mind. Consequently, the objects of psychoanalysis (and similar psychotherapies) are structured like narratives, not like organisms or other natural objects. This means psychologists cannot use the machinery of scientific reduction to dissect psychoanalytic—and literary—objects. In the Introduction, I show how Henry James's novel, *Washington Square*, parallels a patient's story. What James shows indirectly through masterly understatement, clinicians rediscover directly, that patient narratives have their ancestry in archaic beliefs about the minds of others.

# Acknowledgments

Like many authors, I realize that what I sometimes call "my" book is more accurately named "our" book. This is evident when I note the many scholars and scientists cited in my references and I remember the clinicians, teachers, editors, students, and patients who have helped me.

I acknowledge my home university, Vanderbilt, and Dean Jim Infante, College of Arts and Science, for granting me a sabbatical leave to work on this project; my colleagues in the doctoral program in Religion and Personality, Professor Liston Mills, especially; my doctoral candidates, and my research assistants, Karen Stroup, Marilyn McCabe, Wendy Jones, Lori Patton, and Eileen Campbell-Reed; and my secretary, Betsy Cagle.

At the St. Louis Psychoanalytic Institute, Eric Nuetzel has long been a valuable partner. In quiet moments I hear the echoes of countless hours of case conference and supervision, and I thank all my instructors at the St. Louis Institute. I think Steven Humble and Philip Chanin, from Nashville, for sharing their clinical work and clinical insights with me for many years now.

I also knowledge the help I've received from SUNY Press, especially James Peltz, Bernadine Dawes, and three anonymous reviewers whose comments and careful reading of the original manuscripts were subtle, friendly, critical, and encouraging all at once.

Finally, I thank those patients who most recently have challenged me to examine myself and who helped me understand a little more about joy.

# Introduction

## THE OBJECTS OF PSYCHOANALYSIS

What do psychoanalysts study when they study their patients? When I meet a new patient in my consulting room, to what do I attend? To this apparently simple question, there are many interesting (perhaps excellent) answers. One might say, for example, that analysts study their patient's illnesses, examine their causes, and "analyze" these illnesses back into their constituent parts. What are these parts? A short list, which I discuss below in more detail, might include: free associations (Freud 1900a), transference reenactment (Freud 1914g), the ego and its struggles with the id and superego (Freud 1923b), unconscious fantasy (Fenichel 1945), the personal myth (Kris 1956b), core conflictual relational themes (Luborsky 1984), microstructure of free association (Teller and Dahl 1986), maladaptive patterns in personality disorders (Benjamin 1993), self-conscious life plans (Schafer 1992), and pathogenic beliefs (Weiss and Sampson 1986).

A puzzle about psychoanalysis, often noted by Sigmund Freud and others, is that its objects are remarkably similar to the objects of the great novelists. One might use this against Freud and psychoanalysis, arguing that this proves psychoanalysis cannot be a science because artists, who have no scientific training, have examined its objects and anticipated its conclusions. I address this issue at length in chapter 1, "Psychoanalysis as a Science, Again." For now, I exploit these similarities to illustrate my basic assertion. The objects of analysis are similar to the objects of novelistic reflection because both

1

psychoanalysts and novelists reflect upon the consequences of a peculiar mix of beliefs about a person's "destiny." I shall describe this
peculiar mix as one part pathogenic beliefs and one part horror of
overwhelming feelings or affects.


### ON THE PLEASURES OF HATRED: TWO ILLUSTRATIONS

To illustrate my claims I summarize a psychoanalytic case, "Taking
Care of Daddy's Feelings," and then compare it to a story by Henry
James. One might describe my case using various analytic languages;
from Freud's to Ego Psychology to Self-Psychology. Each offers
elaborate models of the mind and the deformations of yearning and
wish. While respectful of each, throughout this book I use a variation of contemporary "cognitive" psychoanalysis associated with the
work of Harold Sampson and Joseph Weiss. They help us see better
why being neurotic is so common and why it feels, from the inside,
like one is living in a prison or Möbius strip or Escher print and that
one is condemned to live there forever. I follow this case with comments on another father-child pair portrayed in Henry James's novella *Washington Square*, published in 1881. Uniting these two stories is their shared theme: a narcissistically enraged parent enjoys
secretly hating his child. Dimly perceiving this awful truth, then denying that perception, each child acquires the conviction that life
affords her or him little beyond misery and defeat.


### "TAKING CARE OF DADDY'S FEELINGS"

My patient, Reverend A, was a young middle-aged man who sought
treatment many years ago. To use Freudian terms, he revealed numerous masochistic features, guilt over incestuous sexual play, and
chronic castration anxiety. While these terms are relevant to his life,
I suggest that the causes of Reverend A's suffering derive from his
intense and inverted relationship to his father (though, of course, in
a longer case study we would wish to know about Reverend A's
mother). An intelligent and verbally gifted man who puts effort into
being charming, with self-deprecating humor, Reverend A is also
open, emotional, and engaging. While trained in a demanding and
intellectual career, he is not aloof and obsessive in ways typical of his

research profession. He presented for analysis after he had failed an oral examination by senior professors. He had passed the written part on his first attempt, but struggled continuously with the oral section. Realizing that something prevented him from clearing this last hurdle, he sought an analysis to prepare him for a final effort.

In the nine months prior to the exam, Reverend A recited in vivid detail the sequence of failures that constituted his life, beginning with a still embarrassing scene when he was about six. While riding to school with his father (who had died a few years before Reverend A consulted with me), other boys forced him to lie on the car's floor. One day his father discovered this arrangement and shouted at his son that he'd make him fight back or he'd attack him himself. In response, my patient jumped up and started swinging wildly. From Reverend A's point of view, he was now branded as a double failure: he could not fight back when picked on and he had embarrassed his idealized father. From my point of view, this scene reveals his father's ferocious vulnerability and narcissistic terror that his son was being treated in a way that embarrassed him. The boy's *internal* reasons for accepting the harassment, reasons generated out of previous experiences with his father, failed to emerge into consciousness.

The father's manifest devotion to his son took on exaggerated concern for the boy's physical well-being carried to ludicrous extremes: Reverend A recalled with a shudder an event at age eight or so when his father insisted that he wear a baseball catcher's protective gear (mask, shin guards, chest guard) while playing a sandlot game with his cousins at a family picnic. (Reverend A treated his son with similarly exaggerated concerns of potential danger.) Not only was my patient the only child dressed that way, he had to wear the gear at all the positions, and the gear was far too large for him. Reverend A's father made numerous protestations of "love" for his son followed by equally numerous predictions of his future inadequacy.

One can reconstruct these events a number of ways and explain their role in my patient's life in a number of ways as well. One might emphasize the father's obvious castration imagery, symbolized by his phobic attitudes toward his son's physical well-being. More central, though, was the father's chronic concern about anyone in his environment showing pride, of being too smart, or revealing similar narcissistic yearnings in themselves. For example, the father delighted in pointing out a newscaster's errors of fact or pronunciation to as many people as would listen. When he forced his son to play ball with a ridiculous amount of padding, he not only made the sport seem dangerous, but also communicated his need to deny his aggressiveness toward his son. That denial and the acute anxiety my patient saw in his father became another reason for Reverend A to fail constantly at any project involving self-assertion. For by failing at these tasks my patient drew his father back into his orbit, pleased his father, and so repaired temporarily his father's psyche.

Failing at manly tasks, especially sports like baseball and ice hockey, became an elaborate drama between father and son: the father was disgusted at his son's failures and delighted in pointing them out. The son became hooked on failing and giving his father the pleasure he seemed to need; for a pleased father was at least an involved father, and separation between the two would not occur. The exchange rate, establishing which behavior would gain his father's love, was set high. Having failed from junior college (he was deemed unfit for regular college), the boy made sure he slept in late, ate breakfast late, and thus provided his father many opportunities to lambaste him for being lazy compared to the fireball of energy his father said he would be in the same circumstance. (Family legend had it that his father had sped through his college and three advanced degrees in record time). When Reverend A's father beat his chest over his own achievements, he quoted Freud and expatiated upon Freud's theories about "those ruined by success."

In the opening phase of treatment, Reverend A showed a rueful sense of inevitable defeat, defeat he brought upon himself through overt and covert means. Although these defeats were humiliating and painful to him, he arranged to make them known to his professors, especially those who seemed to dislike him. When they obliged and let loose a volley of criticism, they joined his internal attacks, and he burned with humiliation, an affect he knew well.

In some versions of the classical theory of masochism, it is the strength of certain part instincts and derivative wishes that leads to sexualization of physical or psychic pain (Fenichel 1945, 72–73; Brenner 1982, 124). Does my patient's lifelong urge to harm himself, to fail college, and to fail professional school many times reveal an upsurge in such a part instinct? Was there a constitutional element, perhaps magnified by poor parenting, that accounts for his masochism? If the term "constitutional factor" designates an unfathomable, not quantified, and unknowable force, then we might say, yes, there was such a factor, but such a factor has no explanatory value. It begs the question of the origins of masochism to say it originates in masochistic tendencies.

An alternative way to think of my patient's behavior is to follow the lead of Joseph Weiss (Weiss and Sampson 1986) and the implications of his theory of pathogenic beliefs. Weiss and his colleagues clarify how children and adolescents adopt a pattern of behavior that seems to please their parents and so (I would add) retain their parents' availability as emotional affordances. Weiss suggests that patients must bring these expectations to the analysis and there test their pathogenic beliefs, such as "Mother will die if I separate from her." Through numerous such tests of the therapist's actual intentions, the patient slowly comes to see the possibility of a new kind of relationship. With increasing trust comes increasing revelation of suppressed and repressed materials, increasing commitment to therapy, and increased testing and then rejection of the pathogenic beliefs responsible for the patient's neurosis.

Reviewing the first 150 hours of analysis of Reverend A, the following observations emerge that support Weiss's general claims about the pattern of reconstructive therapy. As Weiss (Weiss and Sampson 1986) predicts, constant transference testing made it possible for Reverend A to modify his sense of destiny. For example, he would come late to the analytic hour, wear a torn shirt, then describe some foolish error he'd made with his son or wife. Passing these tests, that is, not joining him in his attacks on himself and forgoing the dozens of opportunities he gave me to best him, made it more likely for him to describe other aspects of his life about which he felt ashamed. For example, in therapy hours just before the examination my patient (1) described sexual play with a brother, about which he had remained intensely guilty, (2) resumed his golf game, which father had been ambivalent about, (3) made many overtures to me to slam him if I wished to. Repeating the "sins" of TV broadcasters, he made obvious grammatical errors then waited for me to pounce on them and shoot him down. When I did not correct his grammatical errors, he pointed them out to me. When I responded that he was challenging me to treat him as father did, he wept for a few minutes (he brought two cloth handkerchiefs to the sessions and often used both to cover his eyes).

These series of transference tests permitted him to explore areas of his life of which he was ashamed, such as sexual play with his brother, to begin to work through his guilt, and therefore to decrease his unconscious guilt—for his sexual games and for his sexualization of his anxieties by compulsive masturbation. These new discoveries, in turn, permitted him to wish to succeed openly, and not seek to fail as he had in the past.

On the weekend of the exam, for dinner partners he sought young male instructors there for the same exam. These professors-to-be represented, like me, new objects who would make him feel less alone, share his anxious anticipation, compete without too much aggression, and so indirectly help him resist the urge to masturbate, an activity of which he was deeply ashamed. Their nonrejection and their goodwill, like mine, gave him new ways to respond to the examiners (who replicated father's power to eject him from the game of life).

For example, on learning that one of the examiners was a former college professor, who had not noted this herself, my patient reminded her of their previous acquaintance. This additional act of confidence was another test of his new sense of ability: "I thought she might be nice to me and let me pass, but then I thought maybe I don't need that." When he presented himself at the exam room the senior professor said, "Well, a new victim! Too bad, we were much nicer yesterday!" My patient could hear this as probably *not* a wholehearted wish on the examiner's part to hurt him and he discerned that the professor might wish him to succeed. In the oral exam he was far more assertive, talkative, and revealing of the extent of his knowledge than he had been in any previous effort. He showed them that he "was smart." After the exam, but before he learned its outcome, he vowed that even if he failed, he would continue to work in analysis and to do extra tutorials readying himself to take the exam next year. In other words, it would not be a catastrophic failure from which he could never recover.

In the next session he immediately told me he had passed the exam. He was elated, yet it felt partly unreal; he recalled his father's voice—"Now don't be so smart!"—and then wished to tell senior male colleagues and his friend who had referred him for analysis. He placed his acceptance letter under his pillow, wrapped in its envelope, like a child who puts a new toy under a pillow: "I know it sounds silly." Weeping, dabbing at his eyes with his two handkerchiefs, he said, "I realize you will not make fun of me for doing that."

*Castration anxiety and castration guilt*

Having passed the exam, and having made other assertive gestures (for example, he wore better clothing, he got a better computer) one would expect castration anxiety and dread of punishment to appear—as retaliatory consequences. Both feelings and fantasies did appear but within a context determined by a central experience of guilt over separating from his beloved (and needy) father. On the one side, my patient recalled seeing a father and son business, the son using the title of "Junior." Surely, this angered the son; a grown man called "Junior"? On the other, he recalled that a senior person in his field had offered him an additional title, honorary of his new status, but still inferior to what he might achieve later. So many things were clicking for him. He recalled his father's use of Freud's expression "those ruined by success." In turn, he recalled Joseph Heller's novel, *Something Happened* (1974). The narrator, an aggressive executive, says "Click" to himself when one of his schemes for advancement falls into place. In the novel things really happen *after* the narrator's favorite son dies. The father-narrator had two boys; one who was retarded and whom the father despised because he demonstrated that the father had produced a monstrosity, the other, his favorite, who was a bright boy and the apple of his father's eye. The beloved son suffers a bloody, but superficial, wound when he collides with a window. Seeing this accident, the father rushes to his son's side. Viewing what seems to him, a non-physician, a sure sign that this son will also be damaged, that is, scarred for life like the other son, he quietly suffocates the boy.

My patient heard himself saying "click" just like the Heller character. I suggested that this meant he equated passing the test with the murder of a child, a child who failed to measure up to his father's self-centered needs. My patient laughed ruefully and noted that before he would torture himself with scenes of his son damaged or ill. Now, after having passed the exam, he added another, even more horrible, thought that he had murdered his boy. Does my patient really wish to murder his child? No, but that this is one way to get ahead and to garner praise and pity for oneself is an idea with which he struggles.

My patient identifies both with brutal fathers (as he often experienced me) and with sons, junior partners, and newcomers. He is both the bright son and the retarded son: his father demanded a bright boy he could be proud of, yet consistently found ways to show my patient he was a retarded boy and would remain so forever. In *Something Happened* the father's mood and his corporate star rise *after* the bright boy has been sacrificed. The father starts saying "click" *after* he has made sure that he will not be humiliated by having two damaged sons and no adequate object to carry on his greatness. This is inverted oedipal rivalry carried out to its bitter, Shakespearean end. Yet, my patient's associations to the Heller novel manifest his accurate assessment that his father also required him to sacrifice himself in order that *father* could feel better (narcissistically secure) about himself.

Following these hours, Reverend A reported a trip home to visit his mother and his older brother Z, whom A feels is doing poorly, emotionally and financially. Z is unmarried, lives in an isolated rural location, and is overweight and depressed. After a tense discussion about their father's will, A realized that because he has a child and the medical expense of psychoanalysis, he would receive much more money than Z. They played golf, and when he found himself doing well Reverend A stopped himself in mid-swing so quickly that his back "went out." He had to ask Z to help him off the course. His back continued to hurt him in the analytic hour. I suggested he felt guilty about his success, about passing the exam, about surpassing his brother, and about having an analysis, and then being rewarded for it. In response to these differences he was afraid that his brother was angry and jealous. By damaging his back Reverend A stopped himself from hurting Z even more by beating him at golf. (Reverend A had been playing excellent golf for two weeks prior to this match with his brother.) He laughed, saying he had thought of that idea driving home, but mainly because he believed that I, his analyst, might point out the linkage between his feelings of elation and his hurt back. As the hour ended he rolled off the couch, with a small laugh, struggled to sit up and then stand. In obvious pain, he hobbled to the door.

In mythic terms, Reverend A enacted the role of the damaged and wounded hero; he inflicted pain upon himself for triumphing over his brother, for changing the family's equilibrium, for surpassing his father and brother, and for charging ahead in his career and life. Naturally, in a more complete account of this case one would like to know about Reverend A's mother and ask why he depended so much upon his father for emotional support. However, my account is brief and, as I noted, illustrative. My patient introduced into the analysis a relevant novel, Joseph Heller's *Something Happened*, and helped us both understand him better. I now turn to a relevant story by Henry James.

## HENRY JAMES'S *WASHINGTON SQUARE* (1881)

That my patient's story is similar to Heller's novel and James' novella proves nothing interesting about psychoanalytic theory. That these stories turn on the same theme, though—a depressed father demands caretaking from a child whom he secretly despises—is interesting, for what my patient lived through accidentally and inadvertently, James's heroine, Catherine, lives through deliberately and, from the author's point of view, consciously. What my patient and I had to discover slowly, James portrays directly and, by constant reapplication from the same palette, deepens as the story evolves.

James portrays four people: a wealthy and esteemed physician, Austin Sloper; his daughter, Catherine; her Aunt Lavinia, who is Sloper's sister; and his daughter's suitor, Morris Townsend. In brief, because he had lost his beloved first born son to disease and then lost his beloved wife (he had treated both) after she bore Catherine, Dr. Sloper hated the little girl passionately. This profound emotional truth he registered constantly in his actions and denied in his words. Trading on his status as a brilliant physician, he was able to convince himself that he wished only the best for Catherine, and so he fooled most of the people most of the time. Like my patient's father, Dr. Sloper discovered that hating a child who fails to maintain one's narcissistic requirements has unexpected benefits: one can "love" the poor thing, extend all manner of care to its maintenance, and extract from it repayment for the suffering it has brought upon one. (I use the third person pronoun "it" because it captures the parent's actual feelings more exactly than the usual personal pronouns.) Sharp-witted outsiders who only glimpse these relationships may swallow the charade; dimwitted insiders, like Catherine's aunt, cannot see through it. The unhappy child, no matter how gifted, cannot but imbibe these lies from the beginning. Eventually, the child grows up, fails at the usual things, and then comprehends to differing degrees the parent's secret triumph.

James establishes an oblique tone in his first sentence when he uses the adjective "exceptional" to put the first pin into our specimen: "During a portion of the first half of the present century, and more particularly during the latter part of it, there flourished and practiced in the city of New York a physician who enjoyed perhaps an exceptional share of the consideration which, in the United States, has always been bestowed upon distinguished members of the medical profession."[1] This physician, Dr. Sloper, is exceptional (excellent) in that he is bright and has married very well but also, James says, receives an exceptional (aberrant) share of praise. Though well rounded with flourishes and softened by the word "perhaps" we understand, to use more pedestrian language, that Dr. Sloper suffers from a big head. He thinks his good fortune is deserved: "He was an observer, even a philosopher, and to be bright was so natural to him, and (as the popular voice said) came so easily, that he never aimed at mere effect, and had none of the little tricks and pretensions of second-rate reputations. It must be confessed that fortune had favored him, and that he had found the path to prosperity very soft to his tread." This common bit of hubris and its attendant narcissistic style goes unchallenged until a tragedy: "His first child, a little boy of extraordinary promise, as the doctor, who was not addicted to easy enthusiasm, firmly believed, died at three years of age, in spite of everything that the mother's tenderness and the father's science could invent to save him."

Failing the grandiose demands he has made upon himself, and believing that he is the "brightest" physician in a huge city, Dr. Sloper takes refuge in exactitude and science. However, he suffers an even worse loss when two years later his beloved wife gives birth, and then, under his care, dies. James recounts the Doctor's internal monologue: "For a man whose trade was to keep people alive he had certainly done poorly in his own family; and a bright doctor who within three years loses his wife and his little boy should perhaps be prepared to see either his skill or his affection impugned. Our friend, however, escaped criticism; that is, he escaped all criticism but his own, which was much the most competent and most formidable." By taking this line Dr. Sloper prevented anyone else gaining an advantage over him: his censure was greater than theirs and thus, James says, everyone else—perceiving this—left him alone. He remained idealized and grand, if not now tragic and ennobled.

James describes Dr. Sloper's daughter, she whose birth "caused" his wife's death, with masterful indirection: ". . . Mrs. Sloper gave birth to a second infant—an infant of a sex which rendered the poor child, to the doctor's sense, an inadequate substitute for his lamented firstborn, of whom he had promised himself to make an admirable man." This second infant is a nonboy, a partial entity, who cannot be made into an admirable man and who, by definition, cannot show the brilliance Dr. Sloper ascribed to his three-year-old son. Because, one suspects for reasons of propriety, Dr. Sloper cannot give away the baby girl, he pretends to love her. While he announces his wishes that his daughter become a worthy and accomplished person, he entrusts Catherine to his dimwitted sister, Lavinia. Agreeing with Dr. Sloper that Catherine ought to be raised by a "brilliant" woman Lavinia nominates herself for that role. A widow of a poor preacher, and thus verging on desperation, she moves into her brother's luxurious home claiming that she wishes to remain for only six months. She quickly assumes the role of mistress of the house, becomes Catherine's confidante and Catherine's model of female domesticity, and stays forever. (Of Lavinia Penniman, James says, "She was romantic; she was sentimental; she had a passion for little secrets and mysteries—a very innocent passion, for her secrets had hitherto always been as unpractical as addled eggs.")

Dr. Sloper's complicity with his sister's lie is thus complete: he can tell himself and others that he wished only the best for his daughter, but entrusts her education to a silly woman whom he despises. With beautiful economy James notes that in another act of supposed piety Sloper names the little girl after her dead mother: "She had been named, as a matter of course, after her poor mother, and even in her most diminutive babyhood the doctor never called her anything but Catherine." No need to call her "Cathy," "Kate," or a dozen other nicknames, for each would reinforce her individuality in her own eyes, thus detracting from her servile role in the family. To her father, Catherine is a poor reflection of thc only woman he really admired, her mother, and for Lavinia she is a vehicle of security and social standing. For both persons she becomes an essential bulwark against anxiety: Aunt Lavinia need never fear being destitute; Dr. Sloper need never mourn his dead son and dead wife nor acknowledge his narcissistic rage that he, "the best doctor in New York," could save neither. Sloper's pathogenic assertions about Catherine, that she was dimwitted and inadequate, even as a baby, bind her to him: "She grew up a very robust and healthy child, and her father, as he looked at her, often said to himself that, such as she was, he at least need have no fear of losing her."

Regarding Catherine's independent existence, James illustrates again Dr. Sloper's rage at her and Sloper's narcissistic core: "[H]e contented himself with making known, very distinctly, in the form of a lucid ultimatum, his wishes with regard to Catherine. Once, when the girl was about twelve years old, he had said to [Lavinia]: 'Try and make a clever woman of her, Lavinia; I should like her to be a clever woman.' Mrs. Penniman, at this, looked thoughtful a moment. 'My dear Austin,' she then inquired, 'do you think it is better to be clever than to be good?' 'Good for what?' asked the doctor. 'You are good for nothing unless you are clever.'"

In another version of inverted self-object relationship, again, typical of my patient's father, while lamenting his unhappy fate to have had such an inadequate child, Dr. Sloper glows with self-satisfaction. Like Reverend A's father, Sloper muses with a studied superiority upon his suffering that God should have saddled him with a defective child: "He smoked a good many cigars over his disappointment, and in the fullness of time he got used to it. He satisfied himself that he had expected nothing, though, indeed, with a certain oddity of reasoning. 'I expect nothing,' he said to himself, 'so that, if she gives me a surprise, it will be all clear gain. If she doesn't, it will be no loss.'"

James pursues these "certain oddities" with precise attention to Dr. Sloper's self-justifications and elaborate defenses against loss: "He had moments of irritation at having produced a commonplace child, and he even went so far at times as to take a certain satisfaction in the thought that his wife had not lived to find her out." This marks the triumph of narcissistic defense: in the face of his terrible losses and profound narcissistic wound that two beloved patients died under his care, Sloper reverses his feelings. He finds satisfaction that his wife's death must, now, be seen as a blessing because death spared her the unimaginable horror of parenting a less than brilliant child.

Sloper's capacity for seamless denial and projective defenses remains unblemished when his other sister, Mrs. Almond, a clever woman, confronts his attacks upon Catherine's suitor, young Morris Townsend. The latter is both uncommonly handsome and clever (in other words, the young man whom Sloper imagined his three-year old boy would have become). Mrs. Almond asks:

"What do you think of him as a father?"

"As a father? Thank heaven, I am not his father!"

"No; but you are Catherine's. Lavinia tells me she is in love."

"She must get over it. He is not a gentleman."

"Ah, take care! Remember that he is a branch of the Townsends."

"He is not what I call a gentleman; he has not the soul of one. He is extremely insinuating; but it's a vulgar nature. I saw through it in a minute. He is altogether too familiar—I hate familiarity. He is a plausible coxcomb."

"Ah, well," said Mrs. Almond, "if you make up your mind so easily, it's a great advantage."

"I don't make up my mind easily. What I tell you is the result of thirty years of observation; and in order to be able to form that judgment in a single evening, I have had to spend a lifetime in study."

Like Reverend A's father, Dr. Sloper uses his superior training, his age, his cleverness, and his paternal authority to project his struggles into his child. (The social truth that Morris Townsend can claim the title of gentleman is denied when Sloper claims to look into his soul and see there a nongentlemanly essence. This irrefutable, transcendental judgment condemns Townsend with no hope of appeal.) Like King Laius, Sloper is preternaturally sensitive to competition from younger men who might draw his child away from him and her lifelong task of remaining by his side, absorbing his hatred and disappointments. Sloper's paranoid system is complete in its reversals and denials: "It must be deucedly pleasant for a plain, inanimate girl like [Catherine] to have a beautiful young fellow come and sit down beside her, and whisper to her that he is her slave—if that is what this one whispers. No wonder she likes it, and that she thinks me a cruel tyrant, which of course she does, though she is afraid—she hasn't the animation necessary—to admit it to herself. Poor old Catherine!" mused the doctor, "I verily believe she is capable of defending me when Townsend abuses me!"

To love her father means to adore him and to reflect continuously upon his superiority. By exaggerating Townsend's interests in Catherine's estate, Sloper pictures him as interested merely in Catherine's money, not in her (though, again, ironically, since Sloper had also married a woman he loved and who brought with her a large fortune, entrée into all the right circles, and wealthy patients). When Sloper speaks, using his superior mind and vocabulary,

Catherine is mesmerized even when his words condemn her: "The doctor delivered himself of these remarks slowly, deliberately, with occasional pauses and prolongations of accent, which made no great allowance for poor Catherine's suspense as to his conclusion. She sat down at last, with her head bent and her eyes still fixed upon him; and strangely enough—I hardly know how to tell it—even while she felt that what he said went so terribly against her, she admired his neatness and nobleness of expression."

The complex weaving of love for her father, his denial of his hatred, and a feeling of inexorable logic aligned against Catherine emerges in the narrator's aside, "—I hardly know how to tell it." In clinical jargon, Catherine acts masochistically: in the moment she is losing what she most desires for herself, a future of being loved by her young man, she feels the pleasure of her father's cleverness.

One last morsel from James's feast is another moment of projection in which Sloper, having tormented Catherine, ascribes death wishes to her and then using her proclivity toward guilt, tightens the noose. Catherine pleads with her father to let Townsend court her and so give them time to demonstrate their goodwill and compatibility:

> "I may see him again?"
> "Just as you choose."
> "Will you forgive me?"
> "By no means."
> "It will only be for once."
> "I don't know what you mean by once. You must either give him up or continue the acquaintance."
> "I wish to explain—to tell him to wait."
> "To wait for what?"
> "Till you know him better—till you consent."
> "Don't tell him any such nonsense as that. I know him well enough, and I shall never consent."
> "But we can wait a long time," said poor Catherine, in a tone which was meant to express the humblest conciliation, but which had upon her father's nerves the effect of an iteration not characterized by tact. The doctor answered, however, quietly enough: "Of course; you can wait till I die, if you like." Catherine gave a cry of natural horror.
> "Your engagement will have one delightful effect upon you; it will make you extremely impatient for that event." Catherine stood staring, and the doctor enjoyed the point he had made.

To be caught up in a parent's desperate plea for mirroring, slavish devotion, and hatred is to be in a topsy-turvy world. What is puzzling to the narrator (though not to the author), that Catherine somehow finds pleasure in her father's tormenting speech, make no sense to her either (though James records Sloper's pleasure in attacking his daughter's hopes). On the contrary, like Catherine's father and Reverend A's father, the parent who is superior in authority and "logic" wins all arguments:

> It came to Catherine with the force—rather with the vague impressiveness—of a logical axiom which it was not in her province to controvert; and yet, though it was a scientific truth, she felt wholly unable to accept it.
>   "I would rather not marry, if that were true," she said.
>   "Give me a proof of it, then; for it is beyond a question that by engaging yourself to Morris Townsend you simply wait for my death."

Attempting to answer her father's distorted logic and believing that he actually wished her independent happiness, Catherine retorts to Sloper's challenge (with "her own feebler reason"):

> Suddenly, however, she had an inspiration—she almost knew it to be an inspiration. "If I don't marry before your death, I will not after," she said. To her father, it must be admitted, this seemed only another epigram; and as obstinacy, in *unaccomplished minds*, does not usually select such a mode of expression, he was the more surprised at this wanton play of a fixed idea. (Emphasis mine)

The battle is engaged, Dr. Sloper is excited, his bitterness and narcissistic pleasures are heightened; as in previous conflicts with Catherine, he smells victory and savors self-justification. Catherine's struggles into womanhood become an elaborate contest of strategy, moves, and countermoves. His clever sister, Mrs. Almond, challenges Sloper's attack upon Catherine and his gloating over her defeat:

> "She's going to stick, by Jove! She's going to stick."
> "Do you mean that she is going to marry him?" Mrs. Almond inquired.
> "I don't know that; but she is not going to break down. She is going to drag out the engagement, in the hope of making me relent."

"And shall you not relent?"

"Shall a geometrical proposition relent? I am not so superficial."

"Doesn't geometry treat of surfaces?" asked Mrs. Almond, who, as we know, was clever, smiling.

"Yes, but it treats of them profoundly. Catherine and her young man are my surfaces; I have taken their measure." . . .

"Say it amuses you outright. I don't see why it should be such a joke that your daughter adores you."

"It is the point where the adoration stops that I find it interesting to fix."

Sloper's disguised fear of losing his daughter's adoration reappears systemically when James describes his delight in Catherine's suffering at his hands. It amuses him, he says, for it affords him pleasures of intellectual combat he never thought she could rouse in him. In contrast to Freud's first efforts to locate a single traumatic instance that produced neurotic character, James's novella portrays dozens of instances of the systemic malformation of love. In an actual family thousands of interactions occur, each with the same theme: the child is wrong, the parent, out of love, must correct the child and draw the child's attention to the parent's superiority.

Reverend A's father required my patient to watch televised baseball games with him, then corrected the umpire's decisions and challenged the home team's manager who clearly needed a lesson or two in baseball strategy. Using her adoration against her, Dr. Sloper binds Catherine to him for as long as he will live. With exquisite attention to her yearnings and her most primitive fears he challenges her ability to distinguish her wishes for independence from her wishes to leave her father; to distinguish her love for Townsend from her (much justified) terror of her father. This she cannot do. A brilliant instance of predator and prey occurs on a mountaintop in Europe where Sloper has taken Catherine to keep her away from Townsend. Reaching a lonely summit, Sloper disappears and then suddenly reappears. Catherine wonders why:

What was the plan? Catherine asked herself. Was it to startle her suddenly into a retraction—to take an advantage of her by dread? Dread of what? The place was ugly and lonely, but the place could do her no harm. There was a kind of still intensity about her father which made him dangerous, but Catherine hardly went so far as to say to herself that it might be part of his plan to fasten his hand—

the neat, fine, supple hand of a distinguished physician—in her throat. Nevertheless, she receded a step. "I am sure you can be anything you please," she said; and it was her simple belief.

"I am very angry," he replied, more sharply.

"Why has it taken you so suddenly?"

"It has not taken me suddenly. I have been raging inwardly for the last six months. But just now this seemed a good place to flare out. It's so quiet, and we are alone."

"Yes, it's very quiet," said Catherine, vaguely looking about her. "Won't you come back to the carriage?"

"In a moment. Do you mean that in all this time you have not yielded an inch?"

"I would if I could, Father; but I can't."

The doctor looked round him too. "Should you like to be left in such a place as this, to starve?"

"What do you mean?" cried the girl.

"That will be your fate—that's how he will leave you."

Lest we ascribe Catherine's belief that her father might kill her to an exaggerated, "hysteric" sense of danger, James underscores Sloper's rage at Catherine and Townsend when he speaks again with Mrs. Almond. In a vastly cruel moment Sloper ascribes a kind of perverse (masochistic) pleasure to Catherine's troubles:

"I suspect that, on the whole, she enjoys it."

"She enjoys it as people enjoy getting rid of a leg that has been crushed. The state of mind after amputation is doubtless one of comparative repose."

[Mrs. Almond:] "If your leg is a metaphor for young Townsend, I can assure you he has never been crushed."

"Crushed? Not he! He is alive and perfectly intact; and that's why I am not satisfied."

"Should you have liked to kill him?" asked Mrs. Almond.

"Yes, very much. I think it is quite possible that it is all a blind."

"A blind?"

"An arrangement between them. Il fait le mort, as they say in France; but he is looking out of the corner of his eye. You can depend upon it, he has not burnt his ships; he has kept one to come back in. When I am dead, he will set sail again, and then she will marry him."

"It is interesting to know that you accuse your only daughter of being the vilest of hypocrites," said Mrs. Almond.

As a physician in the 1870s to 1890s, Sloper would have seen, if not performed, numerous amputations. If observant, he would have noticed the absolute terror amputation arouses in most people—men and women alike. There is no "comparative repose" afterward, only loss, shame, and eventually mourning (if not rage, denial, and self-destruction). Sloper is a doctor who can invert a patient's horror following an amputation, and a father who, having severed his daughter's love for her young man, inverts her suffering, hallucinating in its stead his own glow of satisfaction. Unable to separate from her father and perceiving how much pleasure her suffering afforded him, Catherine does what love commands.

# CHAPTER 1

# Neurotic Suffering as
# the Absence of Joy

## PSYCHOANALYSIS AS A SCIENCE, AGAIN

A characteristic problem emerges when a group of analysts ask themselves questions like "What is the core of our discipline?" or "Upon what psychoanalytic facts can we all agree?" or "Is psychoanalysis a science?" The problem is that among the psychoanalytic elite one finds little consensus about the best answers to these questions. In response to this difficulty hostile critics might note triumphantly, we told you so, the entire theory is bankrupt. There is no consensus because there are no observational facts and thus there is no science. Optimistic analysts might claim that our lack of consensus means merely that while we can cite numerous facts, we have not yet consolidated our science and that someday a ruling paradigm will emerge to which many or most expert analysts will give assent. Between these two responses lie many others, including mine.[1] I take seriously our failure many times to reach consensus. I suggest that we can understand it, in part, as the consequence of *what* we study, rather than how we study it, or any accidental features of analysts as persons or as scientists.

What we study are the patterns of feelings and thoughts that emerge when two persons create the intense, ritualized form of relationship known as psychoanalysis. Commentators both friendly and hostile to psychoanalysis have long noted how similar these feelings and thoughts are to those of religion and mythology. Freud made this parallel explicit when he named many of his ideas, like his notion of the oedipus complex, for characters long familiar from Western myth. For some critics, this peculiar dependency upon myth renders psychoanalysis at best an interesting version of primitive forms of thought. At worst, it renders psychoanalytic thought and practice merely another form of religion and hence obscurantism. Given Freud's apparent affinity for mythic thought and mythic categories, the scientific status of his discipline is quickly ascertained: namely, zero.

For others, this peculiar dependency upon mythic categories reflects accurately the very things or "objects" about which psychoanalysts speak. Nicolas Abraham, for example, says that psychoanalytic terms, no matter how well defined, are always "anasemic" (Abraham and Torok 1994, 84–88). That is, they are without fixed meanings according to ordinary usage. They are so, he argues, neither because Freud's language is a new form of speech nor because it is obscure but because Freud discovered *new things*. These new things are the objects of analytic reflection: "In fact, the anasemic structure, proper to psychoanalytic theorizing, does not exist in any known mode of language. It proceeds entirely from Freud's discovery" (85). Abraham notes correctly that his own remarks are hardly lucid; in fact they verge on what he terms the "rhapsodic" (97). I return to his claim below in chapter 2, where we will consider to what degree psychoanalytic terms refer, in an ordinary sense of that term, to "anything."

Here I note merely that for descriptive scientists this "anasemic" feature of psychoanalytic terms proves frustrating. Hence, in the third iteration of the major diagnostic manual of American Psychiatry, *Diagnostic and Statistical Manual of Mental Disorders* (1980) or the DSM III, its authors discarded the central concept in psychoanalytic discourse, "neurosis." While everyone used the term and while it names a core feature of Freud's theory, it proved difficult if not impossible to come up with a single, straightforward definition suitable for the tasks of DSM III labor: cataloguing the variety of psychiatric diseases and offering researchers a shared, descriptive vocabulary.[2] There might be excellent reasons for jettisoning the term "neurosis," but doing so begs the question: what are the objects of psychoanalysis? The answer, according to the authors of DSM III, is, roughly, we do not care because whatever these objects might be they do not permit rigorous, objective definition.

To approach this question from yet another angle, we turn back to the issue of neurosis and its definition. For example, we can locate a relatively clear portrait of neurosis by considering some of its typical features. One feature is that neurotic persons have little joy. Before assessing theories of neurosis it may be useful to recall moments in our own histories when we were joyful. For to be neurotic is, perhaps, to be the opposite of joyful. It is to be miserable and suffer in a special kind of way. To be neurotic is to say "I'm my own worst enemy," "I'm always working against myself," or as the song puts it, "I can't get no satisfaction." Freud denotes a common neurotic presentation in the first paragraph of his case history, "Rat Man" (1909d). His patient complained about fears, compulsive impulses, and prohibitions (159). Each of these neurotic behaviors contributed to the misery that drove him to seek Freud's help.

To name these forms of human misery psychiatrists and psychoanalysts reach into the bag of medicalized Latin and draw from it technical terms such as anxiety disorder, dysthymia, and character pathology. These terms often become entombed in textbooks, like DSM III and DSM IV. While such terms are valuable for some kinds of research, they may obscure how common neurotic misery is. More importantly, these scientific terms tend to collapse neurotic suffering into a type of pain and thus it becomes a "medical problem." Because in our time medical problems are further reduced to the mechanics of the body, a too obedient adherence to theories and world views like those proffered in diagnostic manuals reduces neurotic suffering to mere sequelae, the end products of biological events.

Yet, this seems extreme. For when we examine neurotic suffering and its counterpart, joy, we find no simple "structures" from which they arise. We can locate no specific mechanisms, either physiological or psychological, that produce them. Neurotic suffering is not the product of a thing that normally operates within the psyche and which, unfortunately, sometimes goes awry in the way that heart valves sometimes go awry. "Joy" and "neurosis" name real things. These real things, though, do not happen to be objects that can be manipulated the way scientists can manipulate faulty body parts. At least this is the thesis I pursue in this book.

Further, if neurotic suffering really is nothing more than the product of invisible biochemical processes, then there seems little value in trying to understand patients' interior views of their suffering. Nor would there be much value in attempting to alter neurotic suffering by either psychotherapy or the modes of care rooted in folk culture and folk religion. Questions about the ontological status of neurotic suffering, whether or not it is all reducible to biological events, evokes an ancient debate about what "essentially" a person is, what medicine ought to be and what cures patients of their suffering. I address this debate below and in chapter 2. There I compare the objects of scientific medicine, in this instance diabetology, with the objects of psychoanalysis. I suggest throughout this book that the core of neurosis is not a biochemical event but is much more like an error of judgment. Just as simplistic religion is an error (as is simplistic atheism, one might add), so too neurosis seems to be an error. A profound metaphor about the self, some intricate part of the interior maps of oneself, particularly about one's mind and other peoples' minds, is systematically misshapen. As a consequence, one suffers pain that ought to have ceased many years earlier.

Indeed, a common feature of neurotic suffering is that it remains as powerful, as controlling, and as debilitating twenty or thirty years *after* the particular events that may have precipitated it. As Freud discovered, in these moments the "unconscious" appears timeless. Unlike physical pain, the "now" of an acute neurotic moment is as sharp and disabling as the original suffering. Early in his work (1900a), Freud reaffirmed the ancient phenomenological insight that to the dreaming ego there is no "flow of time." During dreams we may find ourselves "being" at any time in our past (or our future) and believe fully that what we experience is real. Freud made the startling discovery that precisely the same experience of time typified his neurotic patients. Then he discovered that the essence of his mode of therapy, the creation and exploration of the transference of past relationships onto the current relationship with the therapist, is yet another instance of timelessness. For example, an educated patient whom we know as the Rat Man, struggled against his horror at a peculiarly distressing fantasy of attack upon his anus. (It derived from having heard of a form of torture in which hungry rats supposedly ate their way through a prisoner's buttocks.) As he unfolds this fantasy he repeatedly calls Freud "Captain," referring to a cruel captain whom he associated with the rat torture. At other times when he was caught up in transference reenactment the Rat Man roamed around the room trying to escape the violence he was sure Freud would visit upon him.

A brilliant cinematic example of neurotic inhibition occurs in Akira Kurosawa's film *The Seven Samurai* (1954). A samurai warrior, played by Toshiro Mifune, witnesses a woman murdered while holding an infant and, in the midst of a ferocious sword fight, he freezes. He receives the woman's baby and screams out "This is me!," meaning that his mother was murdered in a similar way. The neurotic significance of this action is that by freezing in place the hero is vulnerable to attack from the villains chasing after him. In full-fledged neurotic moments and transference reenactments, one lives in alternating, dissociative states. Like the samurai warrior caught in the throes of reenactment, or the Rat Man pacing Freud's study, persons caught in a neurotic moment alternate between belief and unbelief, between one set of convictions and another. We lurch between these states of mind like someone caught between cars on a fast moving train. At such moments even intelligent persons may appear stupid. When Sir Arthur Conan Doyle plunged headlong into the murky world of spiritualism and other questionable belief systems, he did so, we know, because he was devastated by his losses (Gay, 1989). Ironically, this left him, the creator of the immortal detective, Sherlock Holmes, unable to detect the cheapest frauds in spiritualist humbug. His great counterpart and friend Ehrich Weiss, better known as "Houdini," recorded sorrowfully Doyle's struggles and his wild approval of nonsense like "fairy photographs" and "ecotoplasmic apparitions."[3]

## THIRTEEN (OR SO) FEATURES OF NEUROTIC SUFFERING

The previous summary of Freud's insights into the timeless quality of neurotic suffering lets us name some of the odd features of neurotic behaviors. We begin with the problem of definition, because here Freud and psychoanalysts part company with those who affirm that only what is seen (or measurable or countable) counts as data suitable for scientific discourse. On the side of Freud's critics are the majority of normal sciences, the majority of philosophers of science and, indeed, common sense. Opposed to them are all schools of contemporary psychoanalysis. For all psychoanalytic schools affirm Freud's initial claim: essential parts of everyone's motivational system are unconscious.

To say that part of my motivation is unconscious is to say that I cannot comprehend an important aspect of my self. To do that I need the help of another. This basic Freudian claim rules out two plausible routes for the investigation of unconscious motivation: direct observation and introspection. Because my unconscious motives are "within" my mind, they are not available to external examination. Neither are they available to introspection, since this means to "look inside myself." While introspection sometimes provides important clues as to who I am and how I feel, this knowledge is conscious, not unconscious. For example, I alone can know if I have a headache. There are no "unconscious headaches" because the concept "headache" means that I can report and introspect accurately how I feel. However, according to psychoanalysis there are also unconscious motives and unconscious struggles within me. By definition, these are not available to introspection: unconscious motives are "deeper" in the mind than objects like headaches that are open to introspection. (The objects of which Freud speaks are analogous to "unconscious headaches," a phrase that captures the oddity of psychoanalytic concepts.)

By asserting the existence of unconscious motives (or beliefs or thoughts or self-representations, etc.) which cannot be known directly, either by the patient or by an external observer, Freud requires us to deduce their structure indirectly. We cannot observe analytic objects directly with the usual appeal to public evidence and mutual, scientific critique. We cannot ask fellow psychoanalysts to look through our analytic scope and confirm or disconfirm what we see. We cannot take microphotographs of an "unconscious fantasy," for example, to a scientific meeting and ask the group there assembled to examine the "same thing." We can bring videotapes of analytic hours and call it "data," but since Freud claims that these data are merely manifest contents, the task of elucidating the nature of the latent contents (their "meanings") remains paramount. Generations of psychoanalysts have struggled with this problem and proposed sometimes brilliant strategies, beginning with Freud's elaboration of the technique of free association. This and other strategies help us triangulate the content or "meaning" of unconscious entities which, again by definition, are always beyond the direct reach of the patient and ourselves.[4]

In response to these problems with the concept of unconscious motivation (and similar Freudian ideas), it might seem reasonable, to some, to abandon the psychoanalytic enterprise altogether. Alternatively, perhaps, we should abandon it until laboratory science makes it possible to match observable brain states with reports of mental activity.[5] This would permit mapping patients' reports onto detailed maps or scans of a person's brain, for example, and thus supply to clinical psychoanalysis its missing metapsychological science. With that in hand we could begin to choose between competing theories of unconscious mentation. That would make a certain kind of progress and the homogenization of psychoanalysis more likely. Clinically, we would be less dependent upon heuristic strategies, politically we would have fewer schools of analysis, and structurally our discipline would not depend so precariously upon the brilliance of individual practitioners. Psychoanalysis (and other forms of psychological and interpretative theory) might leave the hermeneutic wilderness and join the basic sciences.

Before wishing too strongly for this to occur it may be useful to examine features of behaviors labeled neurotic. We begin with the problem of definition, because it provides our first clue as to the nature of that thing called "neurotic behavior." For example, the Rat Man (Freud 1909d) reports that his father had died some time before he met Freud. Yet upon hearing some new joke the patient would note to himself, "I must tell Father that" (174). An educated man who grieved his father's death, the patient also believed that his father still lived and that he might see him. Freud adds, "And although he had never forgotten that his father was dead, the prospect of seeing a ghostly apparition of this kind had no terrors for him; on the contrary, he had greatly desired it" (174–75). These and the hundreds of similar beliefs and actions typical of neurotic life are peculiar. For while patients know that they suffer, and while we can observe their suffering, neither they nor we can easily delimit it. This is doubly peculiar since although we agree that their suffering is among the "objects" of psychoanalysis we cannot tell our patients what their suffering is. In fact, to designate what their suffering is we need to tell a story. Using concepts supplied by their folk culture some religious persons designate suicidal guilt as "God's punishment," while some analysts designate it as the expression of "repressed thoughts," and still others might see it as the product of "failed self-object relationships." With each new or distinctive theory of suffering and designation of its objects one finds a new school of psychoanalysis.

This makes it difficult to define precisely neurotic behavior. Among features common to neurotic suffering are the following. Neurotic behaviors are:

1. Painful and "real" but difficult to define operationally.
2. Not fully products of somatic events.
3. Not susceptible to reason and instruction.
4. Not easily modified by external demands, including all the modes of therapy.
5. Based, in part, upon beliefs, but when examined these beliefs yield neither a simple structure nor simple logic.
6. While comprehended by gifted persons, not easily formulated, even by panels of expert psychiatrists and psychologists.
7. Along with neurotic fantasy, subject to multiple, diffuse, and seemingly endless readings.
8. Centered upon stories uncannily similar to those of public mythology, e.g., Oedipus, Jesus' birth, Superman, the Virgin Mother, and the Temple Prostitute.
9. Able to be cured sometimes by emotional reorganization, which may include religious convictions and spiritual renewal.

If we grant these first items, we can add additional claims:

10. These religious cures depend upon assertions that, logically, must be false. For example, the religious affirmation that God loves me even though God slays me may represent the height of Hebrew and Christian spirituality, yet logically it is false since in ordinary parlance to love someone is *not* to slay them. In brief, while religious solutions may "cure" neurosis, they do so by affirming contradictions, rather than uncovering and resolving conflicts.
11. These affirmations are parallel to, if not identical with, the kind of affirmations that typify the "good-enough mother" and her affirmation of essential paradoxes. In a famous paper Donald Winnicott says, for example, that the good parent does not challenge an infant's use of "transitional objects": "[W]e will never ask the question: 'Did you conceive of this or was it presented to you from without?'" (1953, 12).[6]
12. When examined logically (or obsessively) religious solutions to neurotic suffering and the good-enough parent's affirmations do not name identifiable contents. Strictly speaking,

neither religious affirmations nor the parent's affirmations of the infant's imagination denote meaningful utterances.[7]

Finally, we note a seemingly trivial point:

13. Neurotic behaviors are the opposite of joyful.

This last claim may seem the oddest of the list. For it hardly seems to answer demands for rigor and clarity to announce that we should understand neurosis not merely by a set of measurable behaviors or a checklist, but by another, equally vague concept of "joy." While granting this point, I suggest there is some value in reflecting upon joy, especially since religious cures typically issue in a sense of joy. I am agreeing with Freud's lament that religious conversion often cured patients of their neuroses, but did so in a "crooked manner" (Freud, 1927c). Given this insight, we hazard the guess that these religious conversions might be structural analogues to the diseases of which they were the cure.

There are far less grand instances of joy, too. I consider breaking through an inhibition or comprehending what actually happened *just before* one dissociated or claiming a bit of pleasure for oneself all instances of "joy." Patients typically use this term or other terms like "balance," "wholeness," "integrity," "peace," or "playfulness," "spontaneity," and so forth to name their experience. Like the word "joy," these terms are always after the fact, retrospective efforts to label experience. They are usually inadequate to convey the depth and range of feeling. We might say that such terms are *always* inadequate as complete definitions of joy for they attempt to name "the quality without a name." An English-trained architect, Christopher Alexander, puts this thought concisely when he describes a quality he claims is both universally evident in all great architecture and incapable of being named. It is a "quality which is the root criterion of life and spirit in a man, a town, a building, or a wilderness. This quality is objective and precise, but it cannot be named."[8]

I return to Alexander's claims below, after we consider two other important routes toward reflection upon joy. These are to focus upon the joyful subject, and to reflect upon the object that brings joy. To focus upon the person who is joyful tends to reduce joy to a set of sensations and internal states. At an extreme, this reduces joy to mere hedonism which, since the Greeks, we know reduces further to endless searching after new, more intense sensations. In the *Gorgias* (ca. 370 B.C.E), Plato says that hedonism is wrong because it requires a person to increase the amount of excitement in order to keep alive the sensation of change and novelty. This we cannot affirm without affirming the nonsensical claim that a life of scratching and sensuousity would constitute the highest form of human existence.

## Three Instances of Joy

Joy contrasts to neurotic suffering because it rests upon a different sense of temporality and connectedness. If it is reasonable to view neurotic suffering as the opposite of joyful, then it may be useful to explore more fully what it is like to be joyful. I suggest we consider three instances: religious joy (since it is often an antidote to neurosis), ordinary joy, and joy as presented in some Western texts.

### Religion and joy

Readers dedicated to some form of modernist thought will tend to agree with Freud and dismiss this route to overcoming neurotic suffering. Yet, apart from one's own theology or antitheology, it is scientifically interesting that this route works. In his classic study of how religion (sometimes) cures, William James notes in *The Varieties of Religious Experience* (1902) that religions have always provided versions of what we would call psychotherapy.

A more recent example is a worldwide theatrical event, *Les Misérables*, derived from Victor Hugo's old fashioned novel *Les Misérables* (1862). The saintly priest, Monseigneur Bienvenu, responds to the theft of an expensive item with Christian charity and thus sets in motion the central story, the rehabilitation of a criminal. Hugo compares Bienvenu's faith to the brilliance of theologians and philosophers. Monseigneur Bienvenu is a person immersed in religious joy that contrasts sharply with the agonizing of philosophers and theologians. Of them Hugo says:

> Human thought has no limit. At its risk and peril, it analyses and dissects its own fascination. We could almost say that, by a sort of

splendid reaction, it fascinates nature; the mysterious world which surrounds us returns what it receives; it is probable that the contemplators are contemplated. However that may be, there are men on the earth—if they are nothing more—who distinctly perceive the heights of the absolute in the horizon of their contemplation, and who have the terrible vision of the infinite mountain. ([1862] 1987, 56)

In contrast to them is Monseigneur Bienvenu, who "was not a genius. He would have dreaded those sublimities from which some very great men even, like Swedenborg and Pascal, have glided into insanity. . . . But for his part, he took the straight road, which is short—the Gospel" (56–57). Bienvenu reverts to the injunction, love one another.

### Ordinary joy

Ordinary joy, I hope, is available to the reader. I ask you to remember one or two moments of joy and to reflect upon the ecology of the moment, especially upon your sense of yourself in a world of particular feelings and thoughts. To do this properly the reader should be comfortable. Sitting in an overstuffed chair, say, observing a view, or riding in a car (not driving a car), or walking along a meandering path are helpful ways to recall such moments. Our goal is to let a gradual hypnotic-like state develop in which there emerges a thicker kind of memory. Some people achieve this type of joy through meditation, others through self-analysis, others by mulling over a cup of coffee or staring into a beer. Some employ personal rituals, like prayer, that they have chanced upon and use to achieve this state almost automatically. Still others draw upon a culturally sanctioned form of spiritual exercise. In all cases, it is very important to forgo impulses to solve problems and to control time.

Done properly, you will enter a peculiar state of mind. All true hobbies, especially the supposedly useful ones like fishing, hunting, and woodworking, have this as their secret goal. The honest hobbyist confesses that the last thing relevant to hobbies is relevance; the point of fly fishing, for example, which is a demanding form of self-discipline, is to "be fishing" not to catch fish. Sometimes the point of fishing is to redeem one's soul and to attain "right discipline," tasks that transcend completely the mundane and sacrilegious idea that one fishes in order to catch dinner. As Norman Maclean says in *A River Runs Through It,* "In our family, there was no clear line between religion and fly fishing" (1976, 1).

A similar moment of freedom from the restraints of normal demands and the forced organization of time occurs on "snow days" in North America when children's prayers are answered and God makes it snow sufficiently that school closes. The sudden sense of deliverance, of unexpected grace, the open road, the cessation of pressure and examination, makes most children thankful and joyful.

Obeying my injunction to examine a moment of joy, I recall a certain morning on a vacation about ten years ago. With another family we rented a large house overlooking Lake Michigan. A converted barn, it was comfortable but rough and not too refined, the kind of place one might drop a wet bathing suit just about anywhere and not worry too much. Our two families numbered about eight, give or take a visitor or two, and so the house was usually noisy. One day it happened that I was left alone. Suddenly the house was quiet, and in contrast to the usual hubbub, peaceful. I spied a window seat in the living room. It faced east. At ten o'clock on a summer morning the sunlight filtered through the highest part of the trees and then flooded down onto the window seat. The owners had covered the seat and wall surfaces with a thick pad of some sort. I grabbed a book and arranged myself in the space.

When I look back at that moment I struggle to find the right words to portray accurately my experience. I felt secure, shielded by the wooden frame and the large beams of the old barn and yet part of the outside world. I felt like I was steering a ship through the trees; sitting neither too high nor too low. Alone but not lonely, knowing that later the house would fill up with my family and friends, I was invested in the book but not compelled to read it—I was not studying it for an exam or as a project for one of my classes. Sometimes I read and became oblivious to my surroundings. At other times I looked out the window or looked to my left, across the room and contemplated the door facing west. Through it I glimpsed a stone patio. Beyond the patio, I knew, was Lake Michigan, which I could hear lapping the shore. A large field rolled up to the base of the house, about six feet below the window's ledge. I recall looking at the book's pages, maybe two feet from me, and then out to the field that stretched half a mile further.

What made my time there so enjoyable? What continues to make it important to me some ten years later? Are there qualities in the window seat itself that produced this pleasure or were there idiosyncratic and unrepeatable qualities in me, in my "mood," that account for this pleasure? When I recall the window seat in Michigan I recall different parts of it at different times. Sometimes I focus upon the view from the window, other times on the thick, homemade cushion. At other times I remember a rainstorm that beat against the windows a day later. This memory of the rainstorm in Michigan evokes images of the rainstorm in a movie, *Rashomon*. Thinking of *Rashomon* reminds me of another movie we saw during that vacation. One day, after struggling with where to go on a blustery afternoon, the adults and older kids declared that they would not be caught dead seeing one particular film, a cartoon epic about the Care Bears. Joining the public denunciation of the Care Bears was my four-year-old daughter. A minute later, after the crowd of adults and older kids dispersed, she whispered to me that indeed she wanted to see the Care Bears but was afraid to contradict the public declarations against it. So she and I saw the Care Bears movie while the older kids and adults saw another film. I was a bit bored but happy my child had confided in me her *actual* wishes: that she wanted to see the Care Bears and to eat Junior Mints. Each of these memories branches off to other memories and to other relationships. The rainstorm reminds me of another rainstorm in Chicago, when the sky turned green and I met a certain woman.

Sometimes psychoanalytic patients tell similar stories about themselves. Ideally, as therapy progresses they tell more and more such stories. When these accounts follow analytic hours in which we have focused intently upon some portion of their inhibition, I take them to be signs of analytic progress. A patient, for example, tells me that, contrary to his former compulsive need to obey instantly every authority, he asked his boss to wait two minutes while he used the bathroom to relieve his overburdened bladder. I interpret his choice to reduce his suffering and relieve himself as a victory for our work.

Another patient, in the midst of mulling over her "failed" marriage, describes her breakfast at a modest restaurant, an event she hesitates to relate to me since it seems so trivial. For the first time in her life she ordered her food exactly as she wished it: coffee just so, waffles just so. Rather than obey the condemning, internal voices that harangued her about the starving children in China she engaged herself fully with eating and enjoying her food. No waffle ever tasted better. As she savored the joy of that moment she noted that she was not anxious. Then she recalls that she has often harangued her husband and her children in exactly the way her father harangued her when she was little. This insight shames her. She wants to avoid that feeling, especially because it evokes (what I think is exaggerated) guilt about the times she has criticized her husband. Yet, because we have dealt with her shame many times before, she does not condemn herself and she does not avoid this new, intense feeling. She forgives herself and wonders why it hurts so much and how she might be kinder to her husband. Then she breathes easier and she seems to enjoy our work together. I do too.[9]

*Joy in romantic poetry*

In his "Defence of Poetry" (1821) Percy Bysshe Shelley mounts a vigorous defense of the values of poetry, claiming not only that it sustains human beings but that without it there could be no other arts and public institutions. For example, he says, "In the infancy of society every author is necessarily a poet" ([1821] 1921, 26); and "Poets are the unacknowledged legislators of the world" (59). We might dismiss these claims as special pleading by a romantic poet who was too softheaded and too softhearted for his own good. Yet, among Shelley's often quoted lines are many both rhetorically and psychologically valid. For example, he notes the poverty of narcissism: "The great secret of morals is love; or a going out of our own nature, and an identification of ourselves with the beautiful which exists in thought, action, or person, *not* our own" (33, emphasis mine).

The presence of loss, the recognition that a source of pleasure is gone and will not return evokes both dread and, when surmounted, joy. For when loss evokes dread it carries with it a sense of unrelieved awfulness, best described as death. To fully express both sides of loss, suffering, and the hope for resolution makes a kind of mourning possible.

In romantic poetry are frequent reflections upon joy as a response to nature and as response to the inevitable suffering love brings with it.[10] A superficial reading of these poems might suggest that they are "purely subjective" and assert that the source of joy lies within the poet. Yet, romantic poets say joy arises out of one's *rela-*

*tionship* to nature which they portray as a source of solace even though it is the source of our destruction. In "Ode on Melancholy" (1819), John Keats enthrones "Melancholy" as a dominating presence in the poet's life. The poet's task is to respect the presence of loss. This capacity to welcome melancholy makes joy possible.

> She dwells with Beauty—Beauty that must die;
>     And Joy, whose hand is ever at his lips
> Bidding adieu; and aching Pleasure nigh,
>     Turning to Poison while the bee-mouth sips:
> Ay, in the very temple of delight
>     Veil'd Melancholy has her sovran shrine,
> Though seen of none save him whose strenuous tongue
>     Can burst Joy's grape against his palate fine;
> His soul shall taste the sadness of her might,
>     And be among her cloudy trophies hung.
>
> (Keats 1973)

The celebration of nature as immanent salve for human suffering and a source of joy is, of course, a chief claim in William Wordsworth's earliest poems. In response to the ever-present reality of death is nature and her promise of a certain, limited kind of immortality. In his most famous poems, such as "Ode: Intimations of Immortality from Recollections of Early Childhood" (1807), joy does not occur except in the face of loss:

> Thou Child of Joy,
> Shout round me, let me hear thy shouts, thou happy
>         Shepherd-Boy!
>     Ye blessed Creatures, I have heard the call
>     Ye to each other make; I see
> The heavens laugh with you in your jubilee;
>     My heart is at your festival,
>     My head hath its coronal,
> The fulness of your bliss, I feel—I feel it all.
>
> ·  ·  ·  ·  ·  ·  ·  ·  ·  ·  ·  ·  ·  ·
>
>     The Pansy at my feet
>     Doth the same tale repeat:
> Whither is fled the visionary gleam?
> Where is it now, the glory and the dream?[11]

In poems that our callused age makes almost impossible to hear,
Wordsworth proclaims that joy arises out of our ability to sustain
the tension that obtains between our recognition that death dominates us and our demand for some form of immortality. Agreeing with
Freud's earliest reflections upon poetry, one might wish to reduce
such poetry to *mere* wishfulness and these verses to *mere* infantile
thought. However, this would be an error since Wordsworth, like
Keats, recognizes these wishes and these infantile thoughts precisely
for what they are. As the poet says, "Heaven lies about us in our
infancy." Keats often and explicitly links the pleasure of poetry to
those of drinking, eating, and suckling (Gay 1992). But these are
transitory too. These poetic declarations predate Freud by a hundred years but proclaim the same insight: joy arises out of transience
and affirmation of the ego's integrity in the face of certain destruction, namely one's own death and the ineluctable pull of time.

Are Wordsworth and Keats replacing one form of theology (folk
Christianity, perhaps) with another, more aesthetic version, romantic ideology? If we reduce these lines to their manifest theological
declarations it would seem that these poems are blatantly regressed
yearnings, mere fairy tales to which no grown-up, modern person
should give credence. Both of these moves seem to me mistaken
and grotesque. For both overlook the fact that these poems are aesthetic objects, that they work by way of tension, contrast, metaphor,
language, and the other technical achievements without which they
have no value. But what is this value? One answer is that they give
one joy to read.

A more resolved version of the same sentiment appears in
Wordsworth's "Tintern Abbey" (1798).[12]

> For I have learned
> To look on nature, not as in the hour
> Of thoughtless youth; but hearing oftentimes
> The still, sad music of humanity,
> Nor harsh nor grating, though of ample power
> To chasten and subdue. And I have felt
> A presence that disturbs me with the joy
> Of elevated thoughts; a sense sublime
> Of something far more deeply interfused,
> Whose dwelling is the light of setting suns,

And the round ocean, and the living air,
And the blue sky, and in the mind of man:
A motion and a spirit, that impels
All thinking things, all objects of all thought,
And rolls through all things. Therefore am I still
A lover of the meadows and the woods,
And mountains; and of all that we behold
From this green earth; of all the mighty world
Of eye and ear, both what they half create,
And what perceive; well pleased to recognise
In nature and the language of the sense,
The anchor of my purest thoughts, the nurse,
The guide, the guardian of my heart, and soul
Of all my moral being.

It might be embarrassing to recall Wordsworth. For after all, according to modern (and postmodern) sensibilities his poetry is sentimental, deriving from woods and trees and such and not pertinent, therefore, to the cities. But Wordsworth anticipates the reductive, psychological reading when he notes that he praises "the mighty world / Of eye and ear, both what they half create, / And what perceive." Wordsworth and Keats acknowledge fully the subjective origins and the illusory quality of their wishes. Neither poet meanders in occult promises, neither affirms a theological or religious claim, such as "We have immortal souls," without also affirming its antithesis, "We create this need for immortal souls."

So central is joy to poetry that some authorities of the nineteenth century align all poetry with the capacity for joy. In *Representative Men* (1850), Ralph Waldo Emerson notes "One more royal trait properly belongs to the poet. I mean his cheerfulness, without which no man can be a poet, for beauty is his aim. He loves virtue, not for its obligation but for its grace: he delights in the world, in man, in woman, for the lovely light that sparkles from them. Beauty, the spirit of joy and hilarity, he sheds over the universe."[13]

Are these poems and Emerson's sentiments not merely reflections of one person's or one culture's idealized representation of "joy" and irrelevant, therefore, to the vast array of other forms of joy? These poems, while focused upon "joy," seem limited to mere nature worship, pertinent, perhaps, to the early nineteenth century. Have we not moved beyond them? We in modern European-American cultures are post-Freud and post-Marx, and have no ear for such niceties.[14] At least we have no ear for them if we merely focus upon the word "joy" and seek in it its hidden meanings. Gustave Flaubert describes this error when Emma, the heroine of *Madame Bovary*, reasons about the nature of joy:

> Before she married, she thought she was in love; but the happiness that should have resulted from that love, somehow had not come. It seemed to her that she must have made a mistake, have misunderstood in some way or another. And Emma tried hard to discover what, precisely, it was in life that was denoted by the words "joy, passion, intoxication," which had always looked so fine to her in books.[15]

Opposed to a child's imaginings are the experiences of an adult who has suffered through the errors of initial idealizations. In *Ethan Frome* (1911), Edith Wharton portrays a young man first waking to his fascination with a young woman, Mattie, whom he should not love: "The fact that admiration for his learning mingled with Mattie's wonder at what he taught was not the least part of his pleasure. And there were other sensations, less definable but more exquisite, which drew them together with a shock of silent joy."[16]

Ethan struggles to control himself: "The next morning at breakfast Jotham Powell was between them, and Ethan tried to hide his joy under an air of exaggerated indifference, lounging back in his chair to throw scraps to the cat, growling at the weather, and not so much as offering to help Mattie when she rose to clear away the dishes. He did not know why he was so irrationally happy, for nothing was changed in his life or hers."[17] We can guess that he was happy because he glimpsed relief from his loveless marriage. Through Mattie his depressive conclusions, that he would remain miserable forever, were dissolved. Ethan's idealization of Mattie's commonplace observations merely underscores his hunger for relief. That hunger made joy possible.

Ordering exactly what one wants to eat at a restaurant does not guarantee joy. Many people are always demanding about their food and not, for all of that, any happier than my patient in her former habits. On the contrary, for finicky gourmets *not* worrying about being exact and not dominating the waiter might constitute *their* moment of freedom and thus joy. Some people make a point of never responding to the demands of authority. For them, making a boss wait while they use the bathroom is part of their neurotic life. The secret lies, then, not in the action itself, taken in isolation from the patient's life, but the action *in contrast* to the patient's compulsive sense of what he or she must be. Neurotic suffering, I suggest, is a state of being in which one *cannot* experience these forms of joy.[18]

FRAMING THE STORY, INDUCTION IN
RITUAL, THEATER, AND PSYCHOANALYSIS

Neurotic life rests upon obsessive struggles over certainty and objectivity. Neurotic life is filled with absolutes and "either/or" expressions. Either something is "real" or it is "unreal." If "unreal," as defined by a child's sense of "real," it is useless and a problem. A poem or dream, for example, either means something fixed and ascertainable or it is so much junk. Opposite this neurotic demand for certainty and "objectivity" are ancient realizations that "meanings" are cocreated and that there are multiple forms of reality. Among these multiple forms is the world of play, both those things that children do by themselves and their more organized variants, the worlds of sport, competition, and make-believe. To capture this dimension of human behavior theoreticians like Donald Winnicott and the anthropologist Victor Turner, who seek to illuminate the intermediary spaces of cocreation, always stress the element of play.[19] The late Paul Pruyser, a religionist and psychoanalyst, entitled his major work *The Play of Imagination* (1983). He rightly noted the centrality of play to investigating the space in which artistic and analytic processes take place.

Religious ritual, a theater performance, and psychoanalysis are places in which "mere" stories become especially powerful and capable of transforming those who engage in them. To tell a proper story, though, requires a "frame" before anything interesting can occur. To frame the story in each of these three modalities one must first make an *induction*. An induction is a set of proscribed actions and explicit rules that makes possible the scene of action. In ritual these actions are typically announced by senior members of the culture. Victor Turner records that among the Ndembu people, for example, when the group feels that they require ritual aid they consult a diviner who makes a diagnosis based upon his culture's theory of psychopathology. If, for example, a woman suffers what we would call a gynecological disorder a husband or kinsman seeks out a diviner. Then the diviner "denominates the precise mode of affliction in which the shade, as Ndembu say, has "come out of the grave to catch her." Dependent upon that mode, the husband or kinsman employs a doctor *(chimbuki)* who " . . . 'knows the medicines' and the correct ritual procedures for appeasing the afflicting shade . . ." (1969, 13).

An induction is what Turner calls "a common diachronic profile or processual form" (13). In Western theater, which has its roots in ancient ritual, the induction is the complex learning required of audience and actors who must obey its proscriptions before the play can materialize. The magic proper to theater is illusory in this sense. But it is not therefore false. Rather, it is like other complex performative actions. Like the actions of a priest whose proper words create a marriage, the induction creates a new social fact: we are engaged in a drama. Since this drama emerges out of complex, often hidden social realities, by viewing it on stage it assumes visible form.[20]

Theater and other forms of mantic expression are essential to a culture's self-understanding. Precisely because it permits projection, that is, the externalization of internal conflicts and internalized perceptions, theater is a public form of self-revelation and potential self-diagnosis. The good play says *these* are our conflicts, *these* realties and *these* unknown forces are what terrify us most. Even political theater is more than merely a harangue. Even when it is polemical and claims to reveal the truth, the artists who create its illusions do more than propagandize and advertise their political judgments. They do not enclose hidden messages to their work; they seek to disclose forces and realities that would otherwise remain hidden. In theater that has achieved lasting status dramatists are valued for illuminating struggles and anxieties that would otherwise remain invisible. They do not also offer ready-made answers to these anxieties. In this sense, good theater is the opposite of advertisement: ads seek to create, or at least heighten, one's discomfort with the status quo and then offer, as the perfect answer, the product unfolded in its glory in front of us.

A case in point is Shakespeare's *The Taming of the Shrew*, first performed about 1594. To an ideologically minded critic this story of a domineering man who tames a stalwart woman, Kate, is nothing more than an illustration of injustice and misogyny. Yet the play is a particularly rich reflection upon both injustice and misogyny. We see this clearly in the "Induction," the odd little story that begins the play. A lord and his servants decide to trick a drunken tinker, Christopher Sly. Upon waking from his latest stupor Sly is confronted by the lord, who convinces him that he is really a nobleman who has suffered a disease in which he thought he was a poor tinker. The lord and his servants supply Christopher with fine clothes, money, and a comely wife played by one of the young male servants. To demonstrate further Sly's status they suggest he watch a play mounted especially for him, *The Taming of the Shrew*. In some productions Sly and his supposed wife then take their places among the audience who, having watched the Induction, now watch the play seated next to characters from the play. The Induction leads us to consider to what degree all titles, gender distinctions (after all, the women's roles, including Kate's, in Shakespeare's time were played by young men), and the arbitrary disposition of power dominate life both on stage and off: "Through this jest the Induction also instructs readers/viewers on exactly what privilege means" (Dolan 1996, 7). Shakespeare, though, is not writing a critique of privilege. He is exploring the nature of power and its construction. He does not designate one class as victims and another as oppressors without also ascribing to the oppressors a self-conscious unease with the ideologies of the state and its institutions.

A famous cinematic instance of framing and induction is the opening scene in Kurosawa's film *Rashomon* (1950), set in eleventh-century Japan.[21] Vast torrents of rain pound the decrepit gate at Rashomon, once the magnificent entrance to Kyoto, Japan's capital city. Scampering under it are three ragged men, a woodcutter, a priest, and a commoner. Framed by the huge, tilting gate, they seek shelter from the rain. One of them shouts, "I refuse to believe it! This is the most terrible story I've ever heard!" He adds something about the story being too evil to be true. This arouses our interest and we want desperately to hear the story, which turns out to be about a bandit on trial for raping a woman and killing her samurai husband.

As the film unfolds we witness four versions of the same event; one told by the priest who has observed the trial, and three others told by the main actors in the rape and killing. (The dead husband speaks through the mouth of a medium.) Each participant's version contradicts the others' versions. Either one participant is telling the

truth and the other two are lying or each participant is lying and
there is no truthful account available. The storm that drives the men
together drives us to feel their claustrophobia, which, in turn, mimics the ethical dilemma the priest suffers when he realizes that even
ghosts lie (a wonderful conceit since it suggests that self-centeredness
and narcissism persist beyond the grave).

Having heard this bloody and comic story the priest is distressed.
What is truth? he asks imploringly. What is the good? Upon what
constant truths can he ground his religious faith in the meaningful-
ness of human life? The priest's questions and his despairing mood
are mirrored by the water pounding against the ancient, leaking roof.
With this beautiful cinematic frame in place Kurosawa presents these
clichéd metaphysical questions and then answers them indirectly by
making an abandoned baby appear. The three men debate how to
respond to this new problem. The least wealthy among them, the
woodcutter simply rescues the infant. An answer to religious despair is the woodcutter's compassion for this new life. The right
gesture echoes a well-known technique of the Zen koan: the stu-
dent is presented a conundrum and asked to give the right intellectual response. Students who offer intellectual formulae are repri-
manded, commonly with a sharp slap, because they fail to see the
error of the question itself. Intellectual questions like "What is the
meaning of life?" merit a big fat kick from Zen masters because, in
psychoanalytic language, they are obsessional demands. So too questions like "What does the poem (or dream, film, ritual, dance) *really*
mean?" are nonsensical. To these demands there are no simple answers because as Isadora Duncan and Kurosawa note in their own
ways, if one could say what it all means why bother to dance or make
a film? These intellectual, obsessive questions blunder by reducing
art to statements, actions to ideas, and lived tension to ideologies.

Does God exist? What makes life worth living? What is truth?
Kurosawa sidesteps these intellectual struggles through his art, using what Orson Welles called the best toy set ever made, to re-present
these struggles, not to solve them. The woodcutter's compassionate
act is neither rational nor irrational. He notes simply that he and his
wife already have many children at home, another will not be that
hard to feed. We might ask what values are here represented. What
religious or ethical injunction is the woodcutter fulfilling? (Of course,
if ethical actions flowed directly from religious knowledge we would
expect the priest, not the uneducated laborer, to act correctly.)

Can we deduce the reasoning that led up to the woodcutter's action? Perhaps, but then this kind of question presupposes that values and such are based on principles, and these principles derive from fully explicated formulae, perhaps universal and categorical imperatives, as Kant tells us ([1796] 1964). Perhaps the woodcutter's gesture derives more from his immediate perception that greater joy will derive from rescuing the baby than joining those who abandoned it.[22]

Without disputing the value of Kant's efforts to locate the source of values in an eternal realm of truth, we note that Shakespeare had already considered this question with his profound empathic sense. We recall Hamlet, Lear, and Macbeth who struggle to comprehend their ethical natures including their propensity toward evil. Rather than distance us from these persons, as sermonizing does, Shakespeare pulls us into their struggles. Having been inducted into the story, he seduces us with his gorgeous language and we pity Macbeth, for example, when our more primitive response might be to deny our capacity for evil, project it onto others, and enjoy hating Macbeth. Shakespeare affords us a peculiar form of joy: we gain genuine pleasure by contrasting our ordinary dullness (our repressive obliviousness) with this shock of recognition, much as we gain relief when, having focused upon ourselves as victims, our analyst says calmly and accurately, "You also hated and you wished to harm the other person."

In a similar way, regarding anti-Semitism in *The Merchant of Venice* and other, equally dark topics, Shakespeare fails to satisfy our urges to simplify and thus distort human complexity. While Christians, for example, know that the essence of Jesus' teaching is mercy, this does not prevent some of them from also hating Jews with robust pleasure. Shakespeare illuminates this range of complicity in hatred even among the noblest of his characters. For example, even when he celebrates supreme victories of his beloved English kings he also records their less than ideal actions: "[W]e notice how the hero of Agincourt [Henry V] gives the order to cut the throats of the French prisoners *before* he is provided with a suitably heroic reason or excuse for such an order . . ." (Bradshaw 1987, 24, emphasis his).

In contrast to Shakespeare's willingness to assign good and evil to his characters, folk religion typically assigns evil actions to entities that possess us and assigns grace to the work of entities like "God's will," which may be equally alien. This fits well our wishes that heroes exhibit our idealized self-representations and villains exhibit their inverse. Hence, heroes must obliterate villains who merit destruction, not re-integration into an original unity. Thus, the plotlines of science fiction and fantasy, aside from differences in technologies, seem especially repetitious and uninformative: we know that Luke Skywalker must confront the Dark Side and must, eventually, destroy it in a gigantic battle between Good and Evil. The paranoid pleasures this affords us are undeniable for we can finally name the enemy and isolate it "out there," in the horrible shapes that bombard us from the outside. Yet, are paranoid pleasures identical to joy?

Joy differs from the pleasures of projection and imagined violence because it requires us to keep in mind the duality of affective life. In sharp contrast to projective devices, which dominate science fiction, Shakespeare's are unitary and unifying. He willingly explores the conventions of personhood, especially our wishes to split off parts of ourselves and to project these binary, split-off pairs into imaginary worlds

This radical impulse toward unity, a feature echoed in Freud's demands upon himself and upon his analytic patients, challenges the concrete operational notion of "the transcendent" as the out there, heavenly, other. It also calls into question the ontological status of the moral law. Before the Renaissance, Western religious authorities could locate moral rules in an out-there, timeless, and eternal realm ruled by a transcendent deity. But what if this medieval theology, with its comforting sureness and absolute convictions about the "out there," no longer merited belief? Bradshaw notes, "If values are not objective, or supernaturally sanctioned, what follows? For many people, including most Christians and many of Shakespeare's characters and critics, the answer is only too clear: cynicism, nihilism, or despair. But these are not necessary consequences; other things may follow, including different kinds of self-commitment and affirmation." (1987, 37) The issue is not should one "be a Christian" or "be an atheist" but how can one live in a modern world where these questions, such as "Does God sanction tyranny?" cannot be answered. "This makes the crucial distinction between *dogmatic* scepticism, as represented by the terminal, materialistic nihilism of a Thersites, Iago, or Edmund, and *radical* scepticism, which turns on itself—weighing the human need to affirm values against the inherently problematic nature of all acts of valuing. Shakespeare's scepticism is radical in this sense" (39).

Agreeing with this skeptical view of values and the artistic disclosure of their subjective origins are authoritarian intellectuals. Once they and other elites have acquired insights from the mantic arts they must then control their subsequent expression. For the power of art and other passionate expressions, including dreams and neurotic enactments, is their ability to portray human passions, to evoke joy and therefore to persuade. Plato makes this explicit in *The Laws,* written just before his death in 348 B.C.E. Precisely because artists reveal what is otherwise hidden and split off, the well-run state cannot tolerate them roaming freely, for their works induce feelings of joy and sorrow. Because these feelings are spontaneous and powerful they are potential sources of revolution against the established order:

> The inference at which we arrive for the third or fourth time is, that education is the constraining and directing of youth towards that right reason, which the law affirms, and which the experience of the eldest and best has agreed to be truly right. In order, then, that the soul of the child may not be habituated to feel joy and sorrow in a manner at variance with the law, and those who obey the law, but may rather follow the law and rejoice and sorrow at the same things as the aged. . . .

If the elite and aged leaders fail to control the feelings of young persons, god alone knows where those feelings might lead. While affirming the power of the arts, Plato nevertheless asserts that states invented them. This seems unlikely, for he had already said that children might go astray precisely in ways that are *contrary* to the law. If ritual, chants, and other arts were merely inventions, like traffic lights, why should the authoritarian state worry about spontaneously created alternatives? Plato's anxiety about art emerges in his rhetorical efforts to reduce it to technique and planning:

> —in order, I say, to produce this effect, chants appear to have been invented, which really enchant, and are designed to implant that harmony of which we speak. And, because the mind of the child is incapable of enduring serious training, they are called plays and songs, and are performed in play; just as when men are sick and ailing in

their bodies, their attendants give them wholesome diet in pleasant meats and drinks, but unwholesome diet in disagreeable things, in order that they may learn, as they ought, to like the one, and to dislike the other.

Respecting and fearing the transformative power of art, Plato issues a directive:

And similarly the true legislator will persuade, and, if he cannot persuade, *will compel* the poet to express, as he ought, by fair and noble words, in his rhythms, the figures, and in his melodies, the music of temperate and brave and in every way good men. (Laws 2:659d–660a; emphasis mine)[23]

In *Dangerous Voices: Women's Laments and Greek Literature,* Gail Holst-Warhaft (1992) makes a similar point about the intensity with which Solon and other classical Greek authorities sought to restrict mourning rituals: "[T]he new social order at Athens and a number of other city-states in the classical period involved, even necessitated, the careful control of women in their prominent role as mourners of the dead" (118).[24]

*Induction into the treatment*

Like all other aspects of analysis, the induction of psychoanalysis is subject to debate and dispute as to its precise requirements. Yet there are requirements and rules, for without them there can be no analytic events. Freud noted this in his papers on technique published between 1911 and 1914. How to best conduct an analysis and who should do it are questions that turn on the more fundamental issue: What are its objects? Searching for the best way to answer each of these questions, Freud offers a typically complex response. In one sense psychoanalysis is a kind of medical treatment, in another it is a kind of game, in another it is a kind of education, or confrontation.

In "On beginning the treatment" (1913c), he says explicitly that there are parallels between beginning an analysis and the game of chess, adding that only the beginning and end games admit of "exhaustive systematic presentation" (123). Cautioning against a purely mechanical approach to treatment, he carefully delineates rules that are useful "on the average" (123). Indeed, while these papers are filled with rules, generalizations, and advice on technique, Freud's most consistent admonition is that the analyst cannot conduct therapy by relying solely upon manifest rules and intellectual understanding. For example, while some laboratory psychologists might insist upon the exact wording of patients' dreams, the analyst need not (1911e, 95).

The demand for simple, straightforward rules for conducting the treatment, for what would now be called "manualized therapy," stems from a theory of neuroses that sees them as relatively straightforward problems that can be solved or errors that can be corrected or diseases that can be treated. Even though he sometimes speaks about neuroses these ways, this is not Freud's most considered view. As he notes, even skilled therapists, accustomed to seeing in others manifestations of unconscious processes, cannot escape the pull of their own unconscious organization. At the same time they too misconstrue the depth and tenacity of neuroses. As I have noted above, this seemingly everyday bit of human suffering has not yet, Freud says, "found a proper place in human thought . . ." (1913c, 129). Rather, both laypersons and physicians incorrectly treat neurosis as if it were a simple entity: "Doctors lend support to these fond hopes. Even the informed among them often fail to estimate properly the severity of nervous disorders" (1913c, 129).

The most famous of Freud's rules for inducting into treatment is that of "free association." Like other central Freudian concepts this appears at first to be an oxymoron. For the rule, the "fundamental rule," of free association is that we *require* the patient to report "literally everything that occurred to his self-perception and not to give way to critical objections" (1925d, 40). We bind the patient, as Freud says, to this odd kind of freedom. Of course, given the general theorem of unconscious forces that drive neurotic behavior, this rule is merely another way to demonstrate to the patient the patient's utter lack of freedom. In other words, the fundamental rule is essential to the proper induction into treatment. It makes it possible for both patient and analyst to discover, without undue influence, the particular patterns of wishes, impulses, and defenses that cocreate the patient's character. Free association (and the patient's failures to honor the injunction) provides a grid against which the analyst and patient can denote the patient's resistances, chief among them, the transference: "[I]f a patient's free associations fail the stoppage can invariably be removed by assurance that he is being determined at the moment by an association which is concerned with the doctor himself . . ." (1912b, 101). The relationship is, of course, the transference: "a universal phenomenon of the human mind, it . . . dominates the whole of each person's relations to his human environment" (1925d, 42).

Freud's admonitions and his apparent oxymorons are reasonable if one agrees with his more basic claims, that (1) the objects of analytic reflection are not structured by intellectual arguments or beliefs, (2) mechanical rules of analytic technique are easily parodied into something nonanalytic, and (3) the core of the analytic relationship, the transference, is both real and unreal. It is unreal in the sense that the patient brings to contemporary relationships expectations and wishes tied to earlier relationships. This amazing and ubiquitous capacity thus confuses the temporality of two, separate moments. But the transference is perfectly real in its tenacity and its consequences. It determines all of the patient's significant relationships, which are dominated by neurotic conflicts, and it dominates therefore the therapeutic relationship.

Using proper technique and wishing to ameliorate those external conflicts the analyst creates a condition in which these external conflicts curve back and center upon the analyst. These conflicts take the form of a two-person drama. The analyst calls internal conflicts "out" of the patient's mind and reconstitutes them within the frame of the analysis and into battles with the analyst: "The unconscious impulses do not want to be remembered in the way treatment desires them to be, but endeavour to reproduce themselves in accordance with the timelessness of the unconscious and its capacity for hallucination" (1911e, 108).

One might object to this line from Freud, for it suggests that he ascribes personal attributes to unconscious impulses as if they had intentionalities separate from that of the patient. This would seem to throw us back into medieval folk psychology since it explains an individual's internal strife by populating the patient's mind with invisible sub-personalities. Freud is not guilty of this error. He does not say we confront unconscious alter egos, each pushing for a hearing, but rather, analysis lays bare an illusion, our sense of personal unity and integrity, that we are a unified self.

NEUROTIC SUFFERING AS THE ABSENCE OF JOY

Did Freud discover new things? I think so. Using new devices—the analytic hour and analytic relationship—he located boundaries within the mind that had not been hitherto established by science. True, great artists like Aeschylus and Shakespeare had denoted them before Freud but one might dismiss even their works as entertainment, not the stuff of knowledge. Freud, in this sense, was, as he wished to be seen, an explorer of new territory for science. How to name properly this territory and how to map it are the central questions of this book. Here we note that because there are boundaries within the mind, increasing the scope of self-understanding carries with it a certain dread. There is in Hamlet's words an undiscovered country, but it resides within the mind itself. On this reading of Freud's discovery, though, we stress again the striking parallels that he noted between the content of his discoveries and the insights of artists like Aeschylus and Shakespeare. We can add that there are, in addition, striking similarities between these theatrical processes and those of the analytic venture.

This is most notable in the induction required for proper ritual, theater, and therapy. The first two require breaks in ordinary time and the cessation of ordinary work. These requirements reappear in psychoanalysis when we ask the patient to suspend normal problem solving, normal thinking, and the intellectual control that attends these modes of thought. The couch, the darkened room, and the relative quietness of the analyst are not merely holdovers from Freud's early training in hypnosis. Rather, psychoanalytic technique includes our efforts to make reflective, less controlled states of mind more likely for our patients and for ourselves and so encourage both participants to discover the suture lines that run throughout the psyche.

Religious studies scholars and anthropologists have long noted that the efficacy of ritual processes increases when ritual experts, such as the shaman, lay out the frame of ritual space. In ritual space we make it possible to suspend ordinary time consciousness and to invoke ritual time (Gay 1996).[25] Ritual time refers to an experience of contemporaneous occurrence. For Christians, for example, each correct performance of the Eucharistic meal, eating the wafer and drinking the wine, invokes the precise moment when Jesus conducted the ritual of the Last Supper. This notion of the simultaneity of ritual occurrence matches what Bradshaw describes as Shakespeare's "double vision" (1987, 24). For both in theater and in correct ritual performance we are asked to take part in a dual process. Since, according to Freud and Shakespeare, we are ourselves dual beings this demand upon us is more realistic, more accurate, and more empathic to our natures than are any other evocations.

I am not suggesting that therefore the content of Christian preaching is true. Rather, it is no more and no less true than a proper performance of *The Taming of the Shrew*. When the actor playing Sly leaves the stage and takes a seat beside us to watch the play "put on for his benefit" is he now an actor or a patron? Is he still in role? Shakespeare says that the play is for Sly and so within the frame of the play's world Sly *is* a patron. This makes us oddly enough patrons "on the outside" and we wonder if Shakespeare means us to feel uncomfortable. (When Alfred Hitchcock wanders through one of his films devoted to murder and sadomasochism it is a comic, odd, and compelling moment that underscores our seduction into his art.) Echoing Cartesian doubt, can we prove that our current notion of who we are is the only way to understand our identities? To what degree are *we* also living a dream scripted by unseen and unknowable forces?

In response to these profoundly upsetting questions philosophers have elaborated often ingenious solutions. In doing so they ascribe cardinal virtues to an ego function, namely, doubting, which we recall was the Rat Man's principle symptom. Science requires discrimination and method, hence Descartes (1596–1650) is rightly celebrated for his treatises on method and its celebration of doubting. Like Aristotle and other ancients Descartes proffered hierarchical theories of the mental life. Also like the ancients Descartes devalues mere passions in favor of the higher values of thinking.

In sharp contrast to the demand for hierarchy and organization is the capacity for play and imagination. Of the latter Descartes notes that it can mislead us and might, theoretically, be the product of a demonic Other. Reason alone can guarantee clarity and thus sobriety is necessary for true knowledge. The first step in achieving this kind of clarity is, again, to separate "mental" functions from those of the body. This step also makes joy unlikely. For to sustain emotions like joy we must be able to reflect upon *two relationships* that obtain in the same moment. The first exists between the subject (well delineated by romantic poetry, for example) and the aesthetic object, the object that inspires joy. The second exists between one sensory experience and its contrasting opposite. To perceive this contrast one must retain the memory of each, side by side and simultaneously. This claim, that joy resides in the relationship between a subject and that subject's surroundings, assumes that we *cannot* rank the passions, nor set one kind of ego function as higher than all others. On the contrary, joy, according to this reading, is the product of aesthetic contrasts.

These aesthetic contrasts reside in the relationship between persons and their environments at a specific time, in a specific way, with a specific person or with recollection of specific persons. Sitting by the window in Michigan the contrast between noisy family life and sudden quiet was part of *my* pleasure at that time. If I had been alone for many days that aesthetic (and quite real) contrast would not have been present and my pleasure would have been less. The window seat would not be joyful with intense early morning sunlight glaring straight into the room. Nor would it be pleasant if it looked out onto a brick wall, three feet from the windowpane. Nor would it be pleasant for a tall person, say six foot eight inches, who could not sit comfortably against the back cushions. In saying this I am verging upon the cliché "Different strokes for different folks," which implies there is no point in pursuing the aesthetic question since everything reduces to idiosyncrasy. But this is the opposite error of examining the window seat itself for the secret. This antiestablishment cliché errs by rejecting the possibilities of finding regularities in the patterns or sets of contrasts that occur in the good house or the good hour.

We attempt to do this in the dramatic encounter of transference reenactments where we can speak about both patient and analyst experiences as culminating in a new creation: "The celebrated good analytic hour," Hans Loewald writes, " . . . tends to proceed by virtue of the momentum of the process in which analyst and patient are engaged at a propitious time . . ." (1975, 296–97). This process he likens to a form of art: "In this complex interaction, patient and analyst—at least during some crucial periods—may together create that imaginary life which can have lasting influence on the patient's subsequent life history" (297).

Loewald's reflections upon the flow of complex moods and multiple registrations of time represent the kind of experience not

available in neurotic experience. In sharp contrast to the dual consciousness offered in ritual process and the good hour, neurotic processes are like hypnotic states because they are dissociative. Because
joy depends upon a unified contemplation of diverse experience and
diverse aspects of the self, hypnoid states cannot be joyful. For in
neurotic time the past is experienced as *present* just as Rat Man experienced Freud as if he were the cruel captain of his imagination.
While transference reenactment is required for analytic process, it is
hardly joyful. Freud calls it "this school of suffering" (1909d, 209).
On the contrary, the genius of Freud's method is that it gives therapists the ability to permit controlled regression, via the frame, and
controlled suffering that seems destined to occur in any form of
transference repetition. To be a patient is to feel, necessarily, "I am
here again. I am caught and I must resort to my old defenses. I am
little and powerless: I cannot leave this place of suffering except
through some attack upon myself or upon another person."

*The analytic moment: From manifest incoherence*
*to latent coherence*

Opposed to beginning hypnotic or directive therapies, induction into psychoanalysis requires obedience to the basic rule, free
association. This peculiar rule distinguishes analytic therapy from all
others. It is peculiar in that by obeying it the patient produces a
seemingly irrational flow of thoughts and experiences that would
strike a third person as chaotic: "In complete contrast to what happened with hypnotism and with the urging method [of the 1890s],
interrelated material makes its appearance at different times and at
different points in the treatment. To a spectator, therefore, —though
in fact there must be none—an analytic treatment would seem completely obscure" (1925d, 41). Why does it not seem completely
obscure to the analyst?

Analysts welcome the appearance of these apparently chaotic
materials because, theory tells us, they will eventually reveal repeated
patterns of themes and typical conflicts. By examining these patterns
Freud says the analyst can ascertain "the unconscious material itself"
(41) or deduce its character from the patient's associations. I stress
patterns, not "ideas," or "unconscious wishes," because Freud clearly
tells us to note that *everything* the patient does and feels counts as

free associations. Esteeming a patient's words over a patient's feelings, for example, is wrong because it grants privilege to language and other highly organized behaviors over affects and internal processes, the amazing assortment of tinglings, buzzings, rumblings, and other nonverbal chatter that present themselves to consciousness. This error is typical of philosophers and, indeed, most patients who believe that the "highest" forms of thought are linear, conscious, verbal, and rational. Because this is not true, because thought entails nonverbal and irreducible affects, the "art of interpretation" (41) is essential to analytic work.

The purpose of analytic rules is to create a private theater analogous fully to the public theaters of other, less individualistic, cultures. What the Greek dramatists put on their stages, Freud's patients brought into their dreams and into his office. Proper analytic technique is analogous to proper technique in the theater, at least at its inception. We set the stage, create a ritualized space, and observe. Sometimes we get drawn into the play, but if we forget we are acting we err and all the joy disappears into the automaticisms of neurotic reenactment. We are then like those naive viewers who, we are told, ducked down in terror when they first saw movies in which actors drew their guns and fired at the camera.

In Winnicottian language, analysts set up an intermediate arena. In it we stage an induction and hope to persuade patients that this novel arena, situated between ordinary reality and the patient's inaccessible mental states, is a good place to be. Why? Why put patients and us through these struggles? Why put them into a place where they "expect love while the analyst, in Freud's words, plans to provide a substitute for it?" (Friedman 1997, 26). In more technical language, why foster a transference expectation, induce sometimes painful regression, and remain ambiguous to the patient for years on end? Lawrence Friedman's questions bring us back to this book's central topic, the objects of analysis. That is, what are the goals of analysis, what are its objectives, and upon what things does analysis focus? When patients raise these questions, technique requires us to see them as resistance, and thus extremely interesting. When nonanalytic colleagues and others raise them outside the analytic hour we take them as bona fide challenges that merit full disclosure.

I can offer one simple response at this time, and a longer response later. By creating ritual space and suspending the rules that govern ordinary time and ordinary social intercourse, we make possible a new kind of joy. In contrast to neurotic states, states of joy *mediate* between wishfulness and regret, between dream-like states and wide awake consciousness. These moments are transitional, in both Winnicott's and Wordsworth's sense, because we are *not* compelled to choose between two (or three) quite different realities. Most people enjoy the luxury of the between time that makes movies, theater, and art so compelling. While the range of possible responses to art is vast, it typically evokes in us not hallucinatory wish fulfillment (we are aware that we're in a movie) but the pleasure of dual registration.

When Freud says that the goal of psychoanalytic technique is to permit the transference to develop as a "playground" (1914g, 154) he describes a similar pleasure available to the analyst, and later, we hope, to the patient. Because patients, initially, have no vantage point from which to view simultaneously two (or more) modes of existence available to each of us they careen between them. Like Sir Arthur when he fell into the hands of spiritualist frauds, forgetting his own lessons, neurotics cannot bring with them into these alternative universes skills and knowledge gained in the other.

To counter this pseudo obliviousness we invite patients to join us in the audience watching their fantasies from a distance, just as Freud invited his patients to view their minds as if they were on a train watching the scenery go by (1913c, 135). In both metaphors we unabashedly suggest to patients that (1) they can do this, (2) they will be safe behind the train window or with us in the theater audience, and (3) there is something to be gained from this work. That something is, again, a new potential for joy. When we watch a good actor think her way through Helena, for example in Shakespeare's *All's Well That Ends Well,* we sometimes achieve this level of joy. We recognize that the character is in agony and turmoil yet we also know that it is a play and that this agony is for our benefit. We enjoy the intermediate space and time of the play because it offers safe exposition of questions (for example, How should a good woman wield uncanny power?) and passions that might overwhelm us or drive us to action.

Nathaniel Hawthorne (1804–64) put this well about a hundred years before Donald Winnicott uttered similar sentiments about intermediate space. In "The Haunted Mind," in *Twice Told Tales,* Hawthorne describes waking on a cold morning:

The moment of rising belongs to another period of time, and appears so distant, that the plunge out of a warm bed into the frosty air cannot yet be anticipated without dismay. Yesterday has already vanished among the shadows of the past; to-morrow has not yet emerged from the future. You have found an intermediate space, where the business of life does not intrude; where the passing moment lingers, and becomes truly the present; a spot where Father Time, when he thinks nobody is watching him, sits down by the way side to take breath. Oh, that he would fall asleep, and let mortals live on without growing older!

Hitherto you have lain perfectly still, because the slightest motion would dissipate the fragments of your slumber. Now, being irrevocably awake, you peep through the half drawn window curtain, and observe that the glass is ornamented with fanciful devices in frost work, and that each pane presents something like a frozen dream. There will be time enough to trace out the analogy, while waiting the summons to breakfast.[26]

I read this as a comment upon a certain kind of joy. This joy is available to persons able to tolerate and sustain dual registrations of past and present, of warm bed and frosty air. To know that one must leave the warm bed, that dreams will fade, that the frost patterns are not occult signs, is to know a certain kind of fullness that depends upon loss. The bed is delightful because it lets us savor the cold air against which it protects us. The frost patterns are exciting because they let us inscribe upon them scenes from our internal world. Like the good hour or the happy moment of artistic pleasure we find in them objective referents to otherwise invisible realities. Among these pleasures is the person implied in Hawthorne's reverie, the person who will soon call us to breakfast.

This kind of pleasure, this playfulness, is not available to neurotics. When Freud's patient, Rat Man, a learned lawyer named Ernst Lanser, realized he had entertained superstitious thoughts he dismissed them: "As soon as he had got the better of one of these obsessions, he used to smile in a superior way at his own credulity . . ." (1909d, 230). This disdain toward his deep wish to believe, analogous to a myriad of his other obsessional symptoms, does not count as health. Hating one part of the self is not a sign of maturation and is not a goal of analysis.

What then are the objects of analysis and what are its goals? One of our objects is that set of beliefs (fantasies, ideas, wishes, internal schemata, learned responses, etc.) that seems responsible for these moments of self-disdain. One of our goals is to help patients acquire the skill manifested in Hawthorne's account, the ability to treat oneself with empathy and not disdain. Explaining why patients cannot do this and why they often hate themselves and hate others requires a theory of causation. Explaining how we can help them overcome this habit of hatred requires a second theory of cure. Both theories, one of causes, the other of cure, depend, again, upon our assessment of the "things" with which we are concerned. We consider this question from another angle in the next chapter. There we compare the objects of a clear-cut medical discipline, diabetology, with those of psychoanalysis.

# CHAPTER 2

# Medicine and Psychoanalysis:
# Models of Psychological Disease

In the previous chapter, I suggested that neurotic suffering is the result of a deficit: a person cannot experience joy. A deficit is not a thing in itself, not a type of pain, but a type of loss, a nullity. Even though this description is useful, it does not provide a theory of what causes neurotic suffering.[1] Neither does it provide a theory as to how to cure it. Before offering theories of what causes a malady and how to cure it, we first define it. This means we must return to my original question: What are the objects of analytic inquiry? Another way to address this question is to compare the objects of analytic inquiry with the objects of an indisputable form of scientific medicine, diabetology. For diabetology, the scientific study of the disease diabetes, is a discipline with a well-defined object and with a well-defined research task.

## DIABETES AS A MODEL DISEASE AND DISEASE MODEL

Diabetes mellitus is a model disease because many of its mechanisms, once hidden, are now well known. Thanks to the work of generations of brilliant scientists, especially eighteenth-century biochemists, contemporary researchers can speak confidently of eventually mastering the disease. The term "diabetes" derives from the Greek verb *diabaino,* which means "I run through" and refers to a major symptom of diabetes, constant urination. Medical historians attribute the term to the physician Aretaeus (ca. 81–138 C.E.). Galen (129–199 C.E.) also wrote about diabetes. It was only in 1674 that a

European scientist, Thomas Willis, added the modifier "mellitus" referring to the honey-sweet quality of diabetics' urine (von Engle-hardt 1989, 3–10; Henschen 1989, 120). We know now that diabetic symptoms are nothing more than the failure of organ systems, primarily the pancreas, to produce and regulate the amount of insulin present in a given mammal. Prior to the institution of regular insulin therapy (by Banting and Best in 1921), treatment of diabetes was only palliative. To alter diabetic persons' total behaviors in the hope of prolonging their lives physicians used rigorous social constraints, restrictions upon diet, and education. Karl Menninger's father was well known for his compassionate and rigorous work with diabetics prior to insulin therapy.

Following the discovery of insulin's role in the causation of diabetes, treatment expanded dramatically to include insulin delivery. Within four months of Banting and Best's clinical trial (January 1922), a large Canadian drug company began production. Within a year, major drug firms in the Unites States, England, and Germany were producing insulin also (Schadewaldt 1989). The discovery of insulin did not solve all the problems diabetic persons face. On the contrary, while insulin preserved the lives of millions who would have died otherwise, the external use of insulin has never been perfected. Balancing the amount and types of food with the amounts and types of insulin remain daily tasks of all persons who are diabetic. Diabetes will be cured when we can implant insulin-producing cells or bio-mechanical devices that perform exactly the biological tasks of the pancreas, specifically the production of insulin and its regulation in the bloodstream. It will be prevented when we can specify the exact biological coding error that causes one part of the body (T cells) to attack another part (the insulin-producing cells of the pancreas).

Before Willis made his scientific observations non-European physicians and anatomists had noted the presence of a sugary taste in the urine of diabetic persons. By the ninth century, for example, Hindu physicians had elaborated extensive descriptions of "sweet urine" (Müller 1989). Chinese texts describe excessive urination and "diffusion thirst" by the second century. While these texts are elaborate, dense, and systematic, at least as presented by expert Western authors whom I have consulted, they do not interdigitate with scientific models of diabetes. Porkert (1989), for example, describes traditional Chinese philosophic concepts of the body and notes that the Chinese concepts are radically unlike those of Western medicine. Therefore he concludes "the utter impossibility of directly converting the statements of one system into those of the other . . ." (159). Invoking the dangers of reductionism, Porkert lambastes Western scientists who trumpet the values and methods of "Western causal analytic medicine" over the claims of China and Japan.

Agreeing with Porkert's claims are many postmodernist philosophers and psychologists. They dispute vigorously the traditional claims of European and American philosophers of science like Karl Popper (1972), who say that the growth of scientific knowledge is the hallmark of science as opposed to other human activities. Hence, a thoughtful contemporary psychologist, Kenneth Gergen, says that he would probably take his children to Western doctors should they fall ill because his culture is that of the West and *its* form of medicine (1994).

No doubt the language, culture, and philosophy of many or all Chinese thinkers differ from that of their European colleagues. Yet in principle, *their science* must be identical with that practiced in the West. Indeed, one might argue that insulin treatment became possible in the West because the systematic investigation of disease entities took place only there. By systematic, I mean the construction of better and better theories by casting out competing theories that failed one or more tests. Often this casting out was done by biochemical assay. For example, John Rollo, an English surgeon, published a book on diabetes mellitus in 1797 in which he noted that sugar was present in both the blood and urine of diabetic persons at levels that were not always detectable by taste alone (Marble 1989, 232). Rollo's reliance upon chemical assay thus permitted him to go beyond the vague boundaries of mere description and phenomenology. His findings are also essential to any valid theory of diabetic processes. Theories that *cannot* account for his findings are thus rendered invalid.

Readers familiar with American philosophy of science will recognize again the voice of Karl Popper (1972) in my emphasis upon validation and falsification. We can affirm Popper's basic claims, that science is the growth of objective knowledge, without claiming that his is a complete and irrefutable epistemology. For that is the point. It is perfectionistic to demand that the Western scientists adduce a complete theory of knowledge before they evaluate claims made by Eastern scientists. The premise of an evolutionary theory of the sciences is that over time and with sufficient critical method we (Eastern and Western) can weed out ineffective theories from effective ones.

A great deal of ordinary science consists in devising ways to test exciting ideas and melt them down to their errors. It does not matter if the exciting ideas derive from Chinese or Canadian persons.

PSYCHOANALYTIC THEORY AND SCIENTIFIC PSYCHIATRY

I have talked about diabetes to ask better the following question: Are some or all mental illnesses products of disease or malfunctioning process similar to those that cause diabetes? If so, a research program that focuses exclusively upon an eventual biological model of all major psychiatric diseases makes sense. It now appears that the discovery of the processes that lead to the endogenous creation of insulin and the hoped-for discovery of mechanisms to prevent the destruction of the T cells and rejuvenate or replace defective pancreas cells will cure diabetes. So too we should search for mechanisms within the brain (most likely) that are defective and can be altered or supplemented (see Kramer 1992).

Donald Klein (1974), a much-respected American psychiatrist, presented just such a diagram in a richly detailed theory of endogenous depression.[2] Using complex charts, Klein traces the sequences of biological causes that produce character types prone to depression only in one direction. This unidirectional flow matches precisely Klein's theory: that a biological substrate produces what we call "personality," for example, an oversensitivity to stress and interpersonal disappointment. Models of the cause of diabetes shows that the arrow of causality points only one way. Alterations at the molecular level, errors in coding by T cells, *cause* harm to the pancreas and that, in turn, causes diabetic complications. A diabetic person can delay the onset of major, eventually fatal, complications, but without an exogenous supply of insulin he or she cannot prevent them. No amount of self-control, diet, enlightenment, or insight into one's feelings about diabetes will prevent its onset, nor alter the somatic need for insulin.

If mental illnesses are diseases identical to diabetes, then we will discover eventually a causal chain that stretches from molecular levels to cellular levels to tissue and organ systems, and finally to the organism's manifest symptoms. If schizophrenia, for instance, is similar to diabetes, then we can hope eventually to cure the underlying biological malfunction, perhaps with surgery or implants, or drugs that have few side effects. These interventions would help schizophrenic persons for as long as they took their proper medications. Once the mechanisms that cause schizophrenia are discovered we can cast aside competing claims about the "meaning" of schizophrenic symptoms just as we do about the meaning of diabetes. In their stead we would cite opinions of elite science. To elicit an accurate picture of a schizophrenic patient's complaints clinical sensitivity would still be required. Once those complaints were well documented, the curative process would require manipulation of the cellular events that caused the manifest disease.

Affirming a unidirectional causal theory of psychopathology does not *prohibit* competing theories. One reads about Christian Scientists, like Sylvia Plath's father (Vaillant 1993), who reject current medical theories of diabetic disease. He refused medical care (as we construe it), opted for godly repair of what we call diabetes, and died. It is hard to imagine these competing theories will win converts among the elite.[3]

*Biological reductionism and five responses to it*

Beginning with Freud, psychoanalysts presume that mental states, termed sometimes "unconscious thought," or "fantasy," or "intrapsychic schemata," etc., are causally related to psychiatric symptoms like guilt, shame, and character pathology. The bulk of these psychoanalytic claims resides in clinical reports and detailed case histories, not traditional laboratory science (see Shapiro and Emde 1995). This neither affirms nor detracts from the basic claims of psychoanalysis: that we can isolate causal mechanisms within a patient's mind, the inner world, which *cause* maladaptation, neurotic symptoms, and other psychiatric symptoms. Freud offered, in other words, a form of psychologism.

Should we reject this form of early-twentieth-century theory just as Freud rejected vitalism in the nineteenth century? In its place we might affirm a form of biological reductionism. For example, we might affirm:

*Mental illness is ultimately the product of biological (nonmental) events. Scientific medicine should focus exclusively upon brain mechanisms and brain events that correlate with expressed psychiatric symptoms.*

I can imagine five responses to this claim which either affirm, partly affirm, or deny it:

1. Affirming it: Psychiatric symptoms and distress reported by a patient that, upon examination, reveal no ultimate physical-biological-neural chemical causes are not medical problems. They may be secondary or tertiary effects. Or they may be fictitious, or the products of deliberate or unconscious dissembling, or they might be some form of indirect protest against perceived injustices.

2. Affirming it partly: All or many traditional psychiatric symptoms are secondary complications and responses to internal brain states (conditioned by neural-chemical events). These are not fictitious diseases, merely behaviors misconstrued by both patient and some health care providers who attend to behaviors that are symptomatic, not meaningful. One might call "obsessive compulsive disorder" (OCD) a disease because patients repeat certain tasks in endless cycles, just as diabetes was named, originally, because of the excessive urination present in persons whose beta cells have ceased normal functioning. Having learned more about diabetes, we might rename it "beta cell insufficiency." When we isolate the neural events or brain states responsible for OCD we can rename that disease too.

3. Affirm it as the guiding principle of research: Beliefs about self and others and strategies of adaptation that typify character pathology, for example, are not causally related to that pathology. Rather, they are idiosyncratic or culturally provided attempts at self-diagnosis that, in light of modern science, are false. A patient's fantasies and beliefs that invariably accompany a diagnostic type will turn out to be culturally given constructs. In this sense a patient's fantasies may help us locate the particular neural-chemical process that has gone awry because we have learned to correlate particular utterances and beliefs with the presence of particular biological impairments. Compare the neurological exam and the value of examining a patient's reports about "auras." The neurologist need not also probe the religious meanings of auras to use these clinical facts to diagnose neurological diseases.

4. Affirming it pragmatically for the time being: Some beliefs about the self and the self's future may be causally related to subsequent symptoms but, as yet, we have no reliable ways to designate those beliefs. Since we can neither designate those beliefs nor isolate their mechanisms, medical science should postpone advocating any current theory. Klein (1981, 299) notes, regarding the psychoanalytic theory of anxiety as due to unconscious thought processes, that people may in fact have disavowed, unconscious impulses but we have few if any ways to *know* what these are.[4]

5. Denying it: Some beliefs about the self and the self's future are causally related to psychiatric symptoms. We have some useful ways to assess and modify those beliefs and therefore to relieve patients of their suffering.

The first response, that all real psychiatric diseases are biological-neural in origin, begs the question. It may serve as a rallying cry, as a political demarcation point beyond which we ought not to stray. However, it merely asserts a lack of interest in the problem of "ideogenic" (Wollheim 1971) causation and solves it by fiat. The second response permits mental health practitioners to value positively the patient's narrations, but grants no scientific interest to those narrations except as signs of the presence of an illness. Feverish communications signify the presence of a fever; we are not interested in the content of those communications. The third response, that some symptoms are reflections of the disease process, grants value to studying these symptoms as indicators, perhaps, of underlying processes.

Theoreticians advocating any of these first three responses assert that the causal chain proceeds from cellular systems, to organ systems, to patient behavior, and to the patient's self-understandings. Given this notion of causality, psychoanalytic theory and its many offshoots are not relevant to research into *the causes* of mental illness or mental distress. Under the fourth response one may remain agnostic about the value of psychoanalytic theory. Some belief states *may* be causally related to symptom formation but we lack reliable ways to detect them, so significant funding into the investigation of belief states is not yet justified.

Even granting the strictest claim of biological primacy, one might nevertheless justify psychoanalytic reflection, theory, and process as activities worth pursuing. For example, one could see it as helping us cope with our current ignorance. Psychoanalysis in this sense would be a palliative, like some forms of pastoral care, or a form of education to emotional realities that confront us when we do not know how to control a disease. Psychoanalysis might serve to sensitize practitioners to signs and symptoms of incipient diseases. Psychoanalytic training might enhance practitioners' ability to listen to their patients, to evoke patients' fantasies, fears, and emotional responses to their diseases. In this vein some might argue that psychoanalysis should be independent of psychiatry proper; that it is really a form of philosophy, or a Weltanschauung, a modern movement that has replaced traditional religion.[5]

In the above sense psychoanalysis offers an account of human nature made plausible to late-twentieth-century, educated Westerners. One might say that psychoanalytic treatment is a form of education: the detailed biographical and autobiographical study of the self. Through psychoanalytic treatment we hope to evoke a new ego function, an expansion of consciousness and training in self-reflection and self-monitoring. Within Freud's corpus, one can find many reasons to value psychoanalysis for these reasons and to support its place in the training of mental health practitioners who must respond to their own fantasies, pressure, and the like stemming from their work with disturbed patients (or anthropological field work among a foreign people). For example, many persons find it difficult to work with persons who have strong sexual feelings toward them. In our culture, professionals who reciprocate those feelings are considered wrong, indeed under some circumstances, guilty of a federal crime. It seems odd to suggest that a psychiatrist, say a young, heterosexual woman, whose attractive male patient makes sexual advances toward her, should ingest an anti-anxiety agent. On every occasion?

Or should psychiatrists take medications as prophylactics the way missionaries take injections against foreign diseases before they enter the rain forest? (See Kramer 1992 on "mood brighteners.") Hence, one could say that psychoanalytic training socializes practitioners to deal with sexual pressures and similar stresses and so has a significant place in the education of clinicians who deal with patients' intimate feelings. (Of course if physician-scientists merely diagnose neurochemical events, say with a super PET scan device, they will have little need to deal with emotions because they will not be dealing with patients per se.)

Taking any one of the first four positions regarding the biological foundations of psychiatric illnesses does not entail any claims about psychoanalysis or psychoanalytic education in other venues. Nor can we deduce anything from biological reductionism regarding the intricate and well-documented facts about the delivery of medical care. To understand medicine and its ritualization, implicit value structures, social construction of illness behaviors, and the ethical dimensions of care requires a social psychology of medicine. A wonderful new drug has little utility absent a highly supportive social-cultural environment that lends political prestige to its continued use. Philosophical and sociological critiques of the practice of medicine, like the definition of good service, persist in importance and persuasiveness.

Nevertheless, only the fifth response, the denial of absolute biological reductionism and the assertion that *some beliefs (or other psychological entities) cause symptoms*, makes psychoanalytic theory interesting to scientific psychiatry. For only this response justifies spending scientific effort upon the articulation of a person's self-understanding in an attempt to reverse or halt a pathological process. To affirm reasonably this fifth response we must address Klein's question. That is, to support an analytic theory of causation, we must designate the criteria reasonable persons can use to isolate the chain of events that leads from a particular set of unconscious ideas (wishes, impulses, thoughts) to a set of defenses, and from those to a set of symptoms.

Again, citing Klein (1981), we note that everyone has a notion of why they suffer psychiatric symptoms, especially if the symptoms are extreme and involve the self-system or other psychological events. These idiosyncratic theories of pathology become interesting psychiatrically only if some of them are, in fact, causally related to the genesis of the symptoms in question. Affirming a theory of "ideogenic" forces, as Wollheim (1971) puts it, that thoughts can produce symptoms, does not entail a Cartesian dualism. One need not argue that self-representations are more than a set of brain states, nor that there is a mind floating somewhere separable from the brain. However, to affirm analytic theorems as causal, one must hold that some self-representations may, for example, produce a mental set such that one misinterprets new experiences as punitive.[6]

IDEOGENIC THEORIES OF CAUSATION:
PSYCHOANALYSIS AND PSYCHOTHERAPY

Major contemporary schools of psychotherapy, from learning theory to cognitive therapy, to classical psychoanalysis, and to all other versions of psychoanalysis, affirm some version of this fifth response. For example, many contemporary psychoanalytic authors focus their attention upon hermeneutic issues, reconstruction, the conduct of analysis, nuances of communication and translation, interpretation and mutuality, and the uniqueness of psychoanalysis and the psychoanalytic experience. Yet even these authors must assert that sometimes beliefs produce symptoms.

*Current conceptualizations: Depression studies as a model*

Blatt and Maroudas (1992) conveniently summarize current work by four different groups of researchers on mental representations that ideogenic theories say *cause depression*. A virtue of using these studies is their open-mindedness and their fidelity to scientific rigor as currently defined. These studies are useful also because they support the claim that some forms of psychotherapy work better than others and that when therapy works it does so at a rate of cure higher than mere chance or placebo. I cite these studies then as a minimal justification for retaining an analytic point of view of causal factors implicated in some forms of depression.

Blatt and Maroudas note how these theories differ from one another. In contrast, I wish to note what they share. Assumptions common to all four research groups are:

1   Some beliefs about self and the self's future *cause* emotional responses.
2. Some beliefs are easily accessible and correctable; others are not.
3. Depressive beliefs center around images of abandonment or other forms of disruption of basic or primary love relationships.
4. There appear to be distinctive types of depression.
5. Psychotherapy can be extremely effective under certain conditions.

6. Psychotherapy can be effective because it permits the therapist to modify pathogenic beliefs through *some* combination of the following:

   a. learning about one's unconscious motivations

   b. recasting self-understandings

   c. acquiring the capacity for hope

   d. expressing suppressed affects

   e. problem solving

   f. resolving emotionally laden conundrums

   g. personality development and acquired reality testing

   h. interpersonal relearning and insight through transference enactment

   i. internalization of an empathic attitude toward self (cf. Luborsky 1984).

From the time of Freud's first papers on technique, psychoanalysts have focused upon the patient's self-descriptions, the patient's responses to the therapist, and the therapist's responses toward the patient. This means that ideogenic theories of psychopathology must struggle with the problems of constraints of memory and the complexity of psychoanalytic events. For these events occur in both patient and therapist and are rapid, subtle, and constantly shifting. To grasp these thought patterns and to organize them into language requires immense computational power.[7]

*What analysts study: Fantasies of self,*
*human memory as enacted*

It is not always easy to say exactly what psychoanalysts study when they study their patients. The history of the discipline, in fact, is marked by an expansion of its objects. With characteristic élan, Freud (1895d, 1900a, 1914g) extended the earlier clinical formulation "that hysterics suffer mainly from reminiscences" (Breuer and Freud 1893a, 7) into an extensive theory of memory and therefore of psychopathology. Pressing the limits of the most advanced neurology of his day, Freud elaborated a theory of memory registrations whose functioning he felt must account for human psychopathology (Freud 1891b, 1893c, 1895d; Gay 1979). Unfortunately, a hundred years later, we do not have an uncontested and rigorous theory of human memory. Lacking a rigorous theory of this fundamental human cognitive operation, our notions of psychic functioning that involve memory rest upon conceptual foundations circumscribed by metaphors, conjectures, and weak models.[8]

This gap in scientific understanding did not stop Freud from venturing forth clinical opinions about the ways in which human beings struggle with memory, especially traumatic memories. For just as an animal must recall its previous states and codified patterns to remain continuous with itself, so too the brain-psyche entity must be able to recall its previous states if it is to remain identified with itself. These previous states include not only particular contents, but also patterns of suffering and pleasure in relationship to key persons in one's life.

This fact, in turn, is one of the central pillars of the transference as Freud defined that clinical entity in "Remembering, Repeating, and Working-Through" (1914g). "Transference" names the core mystery in the analytic encounter: the processes and feelings that emerge in the patient's response to the analyst whom the patient experiences as if she or he were a person important in the patient's previous emotional life. This is easy to say and difficult to elaborate completely in an actual person's life. Transference remains the central feature of the analytic encounter and its deepest and most difficult feature (Bird 1972). Freud's bejeweled paper, worthy of monthly rereading, sets out stunning claims and insights one after the other.

For example, Freud distinguishes between remembering, a conscious psychic activity, and repeating, which is an unconscious behavior. Because of repression and other amnesias, the neurotic "does not *remember* anything of what he has forgotten and repressed, but *acts* it out" (1914g, 150). Repetition is a form of memory, but because it is active and unconscious, the patient is controlled by it. In addition, because these compulsive actions are painful and lead to even more painful consequences, they form the core of neurosis. Freud notes that while these unconscious memories are secrets from the patient and the patient's family, they are always re-experienced in the analysis: "Above all, the patient will *begin* his treatment with a repetition of this kind" (150).

This claim—which any clinician can amplify a hundredfold—may seem to be a commonplace. Yet it is commonplace only because Freud taught us how to transpose one kind of pattern onto another. Freud saw that the patient's actions were themselves transpositions of repressed memories from the medium of thought to the medium of actions. Given this brilliant insight, Freud's technique permitted him to reverse or undo, sometimes, this transposition. By assessing the pattern of a patient's actions, especially the patient's initial transference responses to the therapy, we can assess the pattern of the patient's repressed memories of significant relationships. "For instance, the patient does not say that he remembers that he used to be defiant and critical toward his parents' authority; instead, he behaves that way to the doctor" (1914g, 150).

This initial repetition is not only of angry or defiant attitudes. On the contrary, the patient repeats the patient's most disturbed and disturbing issues in response to the restraints and requirements of the psychoanalytic setting with its odd demands to say what one is thinking and to do so without acting. A patient who suffered a major loss early in life of a benign and loving nanny will arrange to repeat this loss with the analyst, citing all sorts of environmental reasons why treatment, just as it enters a stage when those repressed longings surface, must stop. In yet another form of repetition a patient whose mother treated him with a queenly superiority, disdaining his awkward efforts to succeed, will treat the analyst in precisely the same fashion. Often this occurs in a way that we cannot immediately interpret to be repetition. Expanding upon Freud, later authors noted that the patient's report of his or her earliest memory (Luborsky 1973) and the patient's total set of "characteristic patterns" (as Melanie Klein puts it) are themselves instances of memorialization. In all his major studies of the structure of the mind, what he termed his "metapsychology," Freud wrestled with the nature of memory and the "compulsion to repeat" (see Freud, 1913i, 1915e, 1917c, 1917d).

Repetition and the permanence of memory dominate Freud's comments on culture, especially his critique of religion (Gay 1983). This is not accidental. Freud's commitment to nineteenth-century notions of causality required him to locate the forces that caused a patient's symptoms in the past. So too, when he examined institutions like religion, which he argues are cultural analogues to the private neuroses, Freud searched for the actual events underlying the narratives later ensconced in myths and theologies.

Given this orientation, Freud's questions were threefold. First, he wanted to know what really happened in the archaic past. Second, he wanted to know how those events were transformed and then memorialized in a person's or a group's actions. Third, he sought ways to undo the disguises and distortions that hide the authentic past.[9] Since the analyst must typically wait to see what patterns emerge from the patient's initial presentation and especially from the transference manifestations that result, predictions about future behavior are rare. Interpretations, therefore, tend to be post facto. This, in turn, raises two problems for the psychoanalytic clinician. First, it makes psychoanalytic interpretations liable (not necessarily prone) to the errors and distortions of special pleading and bias. Because we are looking for patterns repeated sometimes in quite obscure ways we must guard against manufacturing "just so" stories that match one pattern with another. Second, because we rely upon our patient's memory of past events, and because memory is notoriously liable to error, we cannot easily assert that our reconstruction of the events that seem to have "caused" our patient's experiences is accurate.

## The Objects of Psychoanalysis, Their Size, and Their Causal Relationships

Whether or not one agrees that reconstruction of actual events is the sole or even necessary task of analysis, there are at least two related questions we must address. First, what size are the objects of analysis? What counts as the proper unit of therapeutic assessment? Second, what causal relationships obtain between these entities? Which of these units affects directly the appearance of subsequent items of interest? Both questions are theory-dependent. What we listen to, what we hear, and what counts as a good intervention all depend upon our prior commitments to our subject matter and its causal relationships.

What analysts observe when they observe their patients analytically is, it turns out, not an easy thing to say. Some of the entities that analysts have named as their objects:

- free associations (Freud 1900a)
- transference reenactment (Freud 1914g)
- the ego and its struggles with the id and superego (Freud 1923b)
- unconscious fantasy (Fenichel 1945)

- personal myths (Kris 1956a)
- core conflict relational themes (Luborsky 1984)
- microstructure of free association (Teller and Dahl 1986).
- maladaptive patterns in personality disorders (Benjamin 1993)
- self-conscious life plans (Schafer 1992)
- pathogenic beliefs (Weiss and Sampson 1986)

Even when we have chosen an entity for examination, we must observe it in some way. More importantly, we must also argue some line of causation. We assert that some process in the mind produced other things in the mind. We wish to examine these prior processes and we hope to influence them via analytic technique. Edelson (1986) presents a lucid discussion of Freud's causal reasoning that he summarizes as the claim that some psychological entities, such as unconscious wishes, *cause* other psychological entities, such as neurotic guilt. It follows from Freud's general theory of causation that sick thoughts cause (some) sick behaviors. Cure requires one to reverse this sequence, to induce the analytic relationship, to retrieve the original pathological thoughts (wishes, hopes, desires, beliefs) brought to life in transference reenactments, and then by the proper transference interpretation to sever this connection.

It may be useful to sketch Freud's causal theory as it developed from the late 1890s to the late 1930s (see table 1). This rough scheme displays two different fates of the instincts. In both, the arrow of psychic causality begins with the body (the drives), which impinges upon the mental apparatus and produces "unconscious thoughts,"

*Table 1. Freud and the fate of the instincts*

| The Drives: dualistic entities based upon biological substrates | Unconscious thoughts & fantasy structures (the id) | Wishes that conflict with reality (realities) | Successful compromises = discharge and no neuroses | Normal character type = no overt pathology |
|---|---|---|---|---|
| The Drives: dualistic entities based upon biological substrates | Unconscious thoughts & fantasy structures (the id) | Wishes that conflict with reality (realities) | Unsuccessful compromises = no discharge and thus neuroses | Abnormal character type = overt pathology |

especially unconscious wishes. Some of these wishes derive from infantile traumata, others derive from universal infantile experiences and beliefs, and others are induced by particular circumstances, parental teaching, and cultural beliefs. These unconscious thoughts (or id derivatives) impinge upon that part of the mind (the ego) which, in response to this demand for discharge, scans its environment; if discharge is safe, then discharge occurs. If discharge is not safe, then the ego must effect some form of compromise. If the compromise is successful, as in humor or other sublimations, then discharge occurs without additional suffering.

Less successful compromises are, by definition, less successful defenses. Among these less successful defenses are schizoid mechanisms, such as fantasy in which the ego fabricates stories (narrations, day dreams) in order to avoid exchange with other people. In lieu of living, the schizoid person dreams away at life. Maladaptive defenses are, again, by definition, defenses that induce subsequent conflicts with the real world, with ideals, and with social reality. For example oedipal wishes toward a parent cannot be realized in actuality without a great deal of distress. The ego defenses elucidated by classical theory are responses to this demand for work and compromise (A. Freud 1936; Brenner 1959).

Symptoms, like anxiety, depression, hyperactivity, lassitude, and neurasthenia, arise as *consequences of defensive struggles* against the upsurges in the wishes and their frustration. If, in response to these symptoms, persons develop more or less viable ways to cope with their suffering, pathological character types develop, such as what Rapaport (1960) sometimes calls "defense against defense." Fenichel (1945) summarizes this aspect of the classical theory in his textbook: "Underneath the organized periphery of the ego lies the core of a dynamic, driving chaos of forces, which strive for discharge and nothing else, but which constantly receive new stimulations from external as well as internal perceptions . . ." (16). Given these and the myriad ways a particular person has struggled and failed to avoid psychological pain, it follows that the analysis of defense, can relieve pain by showing how particular conflicts arise, where they come from, and how they derive from specific fantasies and, ultimately, specific thoughts that have remained unconscious.[10] The goal of Freudian therapy is to uncover and recover thoughts about the self that have been repressed or in some other way disavowed (split off, denied, projected) and reunite them with other parts of the self.

Freud's original formulations are well known and permitted the flowering of psychoanalysis into a worldwide movement, invigorated many branches of learning, and offered humanists ways to examine cultural artifacts with newfound psychological rigor. These and other epochal events make the classical theory worthy of the intense scrutiny it has received these past sixty years. However, problems with the classical theory are well documented.

## Problems with the Classical Theory: Back to Reductionism

From the perspective of medical sciences, evident in the disease model of diabetes, Freud's complete commitment to reductionism is not a problem. Of course, some religious persons, for example, may be distressed by Freud's single-minded reduction of their form of life to mere neurosis. Still, following the model of diabetes and other somatic entities, Freud carried out a program of reductionism with full force. For if, as Freud believed, neurotic symptoms are caused by underlying or prior psychological conditions (structures, forces, entities) then we should affirm "nothing but" claims. Diabetes is, it appears, *nothing but* the consequence of impaired insulin production. Solving the biochemical and biomechanical problems that impede insulin production will erase diabetes as a disease. So too, Freud argued in the early period, a complete analysis of a patient's fantasy life should obviate the patient's neurotic symptoms, and a complete analysis of the true history of a people's religious myths should obviate their claims to transcendental knowledge.

However, the problem with reductionism in psychoanalytic theory is, I suggest, that the objects of analysis are *not* structured like the pancreas or any other organ system. For example, it seems fair to say that the rapid advances of recent diabetology derive from both massive funding of research efforts and the organization of those efforts. The more developed the science, it appears, the more reductionistic it can be. Often philosophers designate this supreme level of development as the mathematization of a science. Verbal descriptions and weak models of entities evolve into formulae that evolve into rigorous laws expressed in mathematical shorthand. By examining the molecular structure of the pancreas's beta cells, for example, contemporary researchers can allocate the study of one aspect of beta cell function to one research group and another to a distinct group. The body is basically the same universally; it is a complex (but finite) structure of hierarchical interactions. None of its activities or systems may violate any of the numerous valid physical, chemical, and biological laws. This means, in principle, that we can isolate key subsystems and investigate them independently of other systems.

To put this another way, the body's universal and fixed organic structures and processes guarantee that some forms of research and the organization of allied sciences will be reasonable and progressive. It is reasonable to allocate one part of a problem—say, that of the biochemical structure of synthetic insulin—to a research team in Milan, and another part of the problem to a team in Calgary. The rejection of vitalism, a philosophic claim that organic systems are inherently unlike nonorganic systems, in the late nineteenth century seems crucial for advance in the biological sciences. For to retain vitalism means to retain the idea that every so often living systems can violate laws adduced in adjacent disciplines. If one retained vitalism, then biological scientists could not automatically reject competing theories that violated thermodynamic laws, for example.[11] By rejecting vitalism we make possible the rigorous study of the body. Because all biological systems must obey all biological and chemical laws, we can reject any findings, theories, or claims that appear otherwise.

Freud agreed with the rejection of vitalism and committed himself to reductionism, which he pursued vigorously. A problem arises, however, when he pursues it according to the causal schemata of classical theory. For, as I note above, he often finds that the most distant cause, the earliest memory, for example, disappears from view. In a similar way, when he pursues the causal sources of a dream, its navel, he says it seems to disappear into a nonpsychological "navel" (1900a, 111 n.1, 525). In yet another context, that of searching for the difference between accurate memory of external events and fantasy, Freud notes that the task becomes murkier and murkier.

Consequently, Freud's hopes for a psychoanalytic reductionism analogous to that achieved in the biological sciences foundered. Lacking a coherent definition of the objects of analysis and their fixed structures, we cannot easily partition our subject matter into a natural hierarchy of subunits. We cannot find its natural lines and inherent substructures. Therefore, analytic research tends to be that of expert craft persons who sometimes work together, but typically develop expertise and skill by themselves over many years of clinical work. A common analogy is to compare the senior psychoanalyst with an accomplished musician, not with a senior laboratory scientist. For example, we admire and are grateful for the brilliance of Heinz Kohut's discoveries about narcissism (1971, 1977). However, we also rue the fact that he seems to have given rise to another school of psychoanalysis (self psychology).

Another analogy might be to compare analytic expertise with that of computer software authorship. Many contemporary computer scientists are worried that software authors cannot compete with the ever growing power of computer hardware (Gibbs 1994). Disasters in software coding have so alarmed the U.S. government and other purchasers that they have instituted elaborate assessment procedures, including a five-level grade system, to measure the quality of new software products. Level one corresponds to chaos. The majority of programming teams merited this lowest of low grades (Gibbs 1994, 90). Would crack teams of psychoanalysts fare better? If one felt that each analytic school were advancing a research effort along a well-defined track then we would all feel more comfortable: Kohutions could develop new insights into the theory of narcissism, while Kernbergians could advance the front on treating sociopaths, for example. Sometimes this may happen, but typically discoveries made by one school and particularly its language are incompatible with the terms and language of another school. In conferences devoted to naming the core feature of contemporary psychoanalysis, one finds little consensus about major features of major theories.

On the contrary, a standard point of view articulated well by Hoffman (1987) is that the sophisticated analyst should always use theories like tools which one may discard or replace when necessary (213).

For nonanalysts, especially philosophers of science whose paradigmatic science is physics, this feature of psychoanalysis marks it as particularly nonscientific. Like Thomas Kuhn (1962, 1977), they view psychoanalytic theories as, at best, brilliant readings of patients' dreams, self-reports, and the like. Kuhn (1977) uses the idea of puzzles to make this point. Verging on the edge of insult he compares contemporary psychoanalysis with astrology.[12] The presence of bitter disputes between schools of astrology, for example, does not indicate the presence of scientific debate per se. Rather, these disputes indicate that different schools could not convince their opponents:

"Failures of individual predictions played very little role" (Kuhn 1977, 276–77n). Individual failures did not aid the overall project of astrology because they lacked shared criteria of what counted as a solvable puzzle.

Kuhn uses his concepts of puzzle solving and "normal science" (1962) to denote genuine science. Normal science occurs when a group agrees upon the features of a ruling, scientific paradigm, and they agree upon what counts as progress in solving puzzles formulated by its practitioners. Normal science is marked by an increase in the number of puzzles solved by those who adhere to a specific paradigm. Indeed, Kuhn criticizes Popper who focused upon revolutions in science while Kuhn focuses upon the essential, everyday experience of puzzle solving. Genuine sciences have genuine puzzles. Because astrology never had a puzzle-solving tradition it could never hope to become a science, "even if the stars had, in fact, controlled human destiny" (1977, 277).[13]

This leads us back to Freud's efforts to offer a causal theory of psychopathology. Realizing that his initial theory failed to isolate uniquely causal entities, Freud offered another paradigm. Within Freud's later texts and within the huge post-Freudian analytic literature lies a second causal paradigm that we can sketch as in table 2.

*Table 2. Freud: conflicts (sometimes) give rise to fantasy*

| Conflicts with reality realities → | Ego engendered fantasy structures → | Unconscious thoughts → | Symptomatic expressions = compromise formations → | Character types and neuroses |
|---|---|---|---|---|

The idea that the ego may engender fantasies in response to conflicts is implicit in Freud and explicit in Weiss and Sampson (1986). It has immediate utility. For if we agree that sometimes fantasy structures arise out of a person's conflicts with reality (with other people or with one's wishes), then we can examine a patient's fantasies as effects, not causes. Once ensconced as ways of life these fantasies become pathogenic and therefore, theory says, *cause* subsequent self-harmful behaviors that define psychopathology. Pursuing this paradigm has some advantages:

1. We need not claim to peer into the patient's deepest mind to deduce a specific set of unconscious impulses or drive derivatives that gave rise to unconscious thoughts.

2. We can respond to criticisms of concreteness in psychoanalytic theory made by sophisticated clinicians and analysts like Searle (1992), Donald Spence (1987, 1994), and Roy Schafer (1976, 1980, 1992). Specifically, we can address Schafer's critique of substantives in analytic theory and the error of misplaced concreteness. For example, if a patient complains about having "two selves" we need not deduce from this evidence that there really are "two selves" present inside this person.

3. We need not claim that on all occasions an original and specific trauma and its associated sexual or aggressive instincts caused later neurotic functioning. This does not rule out discovering traumatic and causal events nor the tasks of reconstruction and reexamination. However, we need not designate a nonpsychological event or substance, such as "an upsurge in drive derivatives," as *the cause* of each neurotic condition.

4. If we do not claim that there are always original impulses that have remained unconscious and of which the manifest contents are derivatives, we can avoid some conundrums of interpretation theories. The existence of multiple, persuasive but incompatible readings of the same themes in a patient hour presents a major problem. According to Freud's initial, unidirectional model of causation, we wish to find the hidden forces which precede the appearance of manifest contents. If two well-trained and equally skillful analysts examine the same materials and yet arrive at distinctly incompatible readings then something is wrong. Either both are wrong and we have not yet reached bedrock, or one is right and the other wrong, or neither is right. I am suggesting that many times the latter is the correct assessment: neither is correct because there is *no original unconscious, unitary intentionality* to be discovered. *Sometimes* patient materials yield well-defined and easily located unconscious meanings, for example the classic parapraxes (Freud 1901b). *At other times* parapraxes are merely consequences of

depressed affect, for example, and, when examined, do not reveal singular, unconscious wishes.

5. We can attend to a central aspect of the analytic experience: that a major portion of the patient's behavior (thoughts, dreams, feelings) is shaped by the analyst's expectations (mindset, training, biases). In the unidirectional model of causation these undeniable aspects of analytic work are embarrassing and unprofessional for they seem to show that we have erred and contaminated the laboratory of observation. If we admit that often a patient's reports, dreams, and symptoms are shaped by the patient's current struggles to deal with adaptive failures we can also admit that our obvious values and our obvious biases will shape those contemporary reports. It is not surprising, then, that sometimes Jungian patients have Jungian dreams and Freudian patients have Freudian dreams.

6. If conflicts sometimes produce fantasy we can explain the fact that sometimes analysts act a lot like witch doctors and other symbolic healers without impugning the scientific status of analysts (or witch doctors). For psychic conflicts, by definition, are failures to solve adaptive tasks. These failures leave the stage open for anyone to enter and impose upon the messy situation found there a semblance of order.

7. If we consider the patient as an active agent constantly inventing new responses to old conundrums, we can account, in part, for the nagging problem of multiple readings that plagues psychoanalytic discourse. Is there always a single best interpretation of a dream? Are all neurotic symptoms structured like puzzles or cryptograms or rebuses? To rephrase this, if neurotic presentations result from the disassembly of a once coherent structure then there should be one best way to reassemble them. We know, for example, that there is one best way to reassemble a jigsaw puzzle because we know that once upon a time it was a complete and coherent whole. It might take a long time, but in principle one can solve any such puzzle because one knows that each piece must fit somewhere and that the best solution will yield no leftovers. If neurosis and character pathology occur when a pristine whole shatters, we could, with sufficient time and effort, reassemble that original unity, just as the Iranians reassembled American documents that had been shredded by U.S. embassy staff in 1979.

However, if some neurotic self-understandings are the result of an initial *failure* to comprehend accurately why one suffers, for example, then there is no original unity we can reconstruct via interpretation. In these cases the tasks of reconstruction and interpretation will be endless. We will find no single key, no single code, and no single fixed meaning to neurotic presentations. This conclusion will be ruinous to the psychoanalytic enterprise only if one believes as a matter of faith that scientific reasoning must be, ultimately, reasoning about the causal connections that obtain between material entities. A competing metaphysics, which Freud advanced in the nineteenth century, as do many psychologists and philosophers in this century, is that reasons and motives and wishes may function precisely as causes. To comprehend a person's reasons, wishes, intentions, etc., is to comprehend the structure of a causal chain that begins in the person and eventuates in an action or attempted action.

I have suggested that this common experience, the failure of rationality, has a common consequence: the spontaneous elaboration of solutions based on primary process formulas. I am suggesting that unconscious ideas we see daily with our patients and their illogical and binary structures derive not from an origin in binary forces (the two great classes of instincts, the drives), but because they are the breakdown products of failed rationality. This failed rationality typically occurred very early in the patient's life. Around that core are wound the patient's self-understandings, or, in Roy Schafer's language, the patient's narratives about who the patient really is and why the patient suffers.

It may be helpful to distinguish two different sources to this failure of rationality. The first we might label generic human struggle to comprehend what mind is. The second source is a specific child's struggle to comprehend the child's mind and that of the child's dominant objects.

GENERIC HUMAN STRUGGLES: WHAT IS MIND?

What is mind? Can we map it? Can we explain the mind by claiming that it functions like a particular machine, say a supercomputer? In psychoanalytic parlance, what is the ego? Can we map it completely and without remainder? If the mind is a mental structure known through phenomenological features, can we map those, one for one, onto a real or physical substrate? This common question rests upon a couple of errors. It presumes that we can treat the mind or ego as if it were a reducible object analogous to the objects with which ordinary science and ordinary medicine are concerned. I have suggested that this is not so and that this error accounts, in part, for the piecemeal advance in psychoanalysis and its related fields.

Mapping can be exhaustive only when the object mapped permits complete reduction. The human genome project is a particularly good example. This project is a multiyear, multibillion dollar effort to delineate fully the human genome by mapping its chromosomes, and denoting the complete sequence of the deoxyribonucleic acid (DNA). This project is justified by the immense potential it offers to understand genetically transmitted disease. It is made plausible by the fact that the genome is ultimately a collection of immensely detailed instructions, encoded in biological data, for creating other biological entities. Given that the human genome is a relatively fixed, highly redundant set of codes, it can be decoded, given sufficient time and resources. The size of the project and its potential have spurred on brilliant strategies such as "Shotgun sequencing of the human genome." However, each depends upon the basic insight that this object, the genome, is knowable fully and indeed, can be attacked through automated procedures. Mapping the human genome will give us a Rosetta stone for human biology.[14] Invoking the Rosetta stone is particularly apt since it refers to a device with which earlier scientists decoded encrypted information. A parallel instance is the decipherment of Linear B, an odd script that puzzled classical philologists until Michael Ventris developed a brilliant strategy for finding the missing key (Chadwick 1958).

*What is mind?*

Mapping a multidimensional entity onto an entity with fewer dimensions is always a form of reductionism and distortion. Map makers must decide which features they wish to preserve and which features they can sacrifice. So too, when psychologists wish to map the limits of "Mind" they must chose which features of the natural world entity, "mind," they wish to preserve and which to sacrifice. Among hundreds of current texts on cognitive psychology, neurology, and philosophy of mind that address this question, John Searle's book *The Rediscovery of Mind* (1992) suits our purposes best because he is clear and evenhanded.

Searle provides a lucid critique of some popular theories of mind offered by contemporary experts, especially those who seek to show that folk psychology is intrinsically wrong about the mind. While I find Searle's argument forceful, we need not claim that his is the last word on the philosophy of mind. Rather, my scope is much more limited. I wish only to point out how difficult the whole topic is and therefore how every competing theory of mind must contend with formidable obstacles. Searle is particularly effective in demolishing the most popular contender, materialism, as a theory of mind or, as he says, "The Recent History of Materialism: The Same Mistake Over and Over" (1992, 27).

Contemporary materialism, which holds that mental events are really material processes and that consciousness is but an illusion, repeats a form of dualism inherited from Descartes, according to Searle. He makes a psychological point (one might say a Freudian point) about materialist theories of mind. These he notes are "obviously false" (3), deriving from the terror felt by philosophers who feel they must choose either materialism or some form of spiritualism, and the latter is fraught with religiosity and obscurantism. Consequently, most elite philosophers and others who dominate discourse in theories of mind feel compelled to use vocabularies like "monism" and "materialism," which are tied to ideological commitments to the Unity of Science and the Progress of Reason.

Searle's general approach is to lay out the basic claims of materialism and then note how its peculiar claims, such as "terms like intention do not refer to mental life," depend upon this forced choice. This choice seems constrained by Descartes's famous efforts at reductionism in which all things are to be categorized either as "mental" (spiritual) or "physical."[15] The peculiarity of this demand emerges when one considers the way these terms might be used, the heavy-handed way Descartes uses them, and the multitude of things in our world that do *not* fit either category: "[T]he world contains points scored in football games, interest rates, governments, and pains. All of these have their own way of existing—athletic, economic, political, mental, etc." (26). To deny this obvious fact, for example that my pains and my inner life and my worries are mine alone and "intrinsically subjective," philosophers and psychologists pledge allegiance to a metaphysical claim: the only "real" things are "physical objects" or some such pronouncement. (As usual when one presses just what these are we run into countless problems of definition and usage, etc.) As Searle notes, "[A]fter all, do we not know from the discoveries of science that there is really nothing in the universe but physical particles and fields of forces acting on physical particles?" (30).

To uncover the unconscious sources of the adamancy with which these theories are held, Searle offers a kind of anthropological study of the "exotic behavior of a distant tribe" (31). I like this model of inquiry since it fits well my use of Searle's critique: that when people are pressed into offering up theories of mind, especially when driven by anxiety, they typically fall into metaphysical claims which verge on incoherence. Searle spends 254 pages making this point. This suggests there are numerous traps, puzzles, conundrums, and the like into which sophisticated persons must fall. While I happen to share Searle's distrust of materialism and enjoy his critique, we need not agree with any offered replacements. Central to Searle's critique is the Wittgensteinian point that the very language and demands of metaphysical theories of mind make them prone to outlandish errors. Indeed, Searle uses psychiatric language again: "If we were to think of the philosophy of mind over the past fifty years as a single individual, we would say of that person that he is a compulsive neurotic, and his neurosis takes the form of repeating the same pattern of behavior over and over" (31). He asks a bit later: Why should materialists fear ascribing reality to consciousness? "The deepest reason for the fear of consciousness is that consciousness has essentially the terrifying feature of subjectivity. Materialists are reluctant to accept that feature because they believe that to accept the existence of subjective consciousness would be inconsistent with their conception of what the world must be like" (55).

While he is being sarcastic, I take Searle's point seriously: well-educated, modern persons have trouble making sense of metaphysical claims about the mind, dispositional states, subjectivity, and so forth. Searle takes on each of the materialist theories one by one. For example, radical behaviorists deny any relevance to terms like "inner world," indeed to any mental state that they redescribe as either behaviors or disposition to behavior. In rebuttal, Searle cites Putnam's (1963) argument about the superactor and superspartan: "One can easily imagine an actor of superior abilities who could give a perfect imitation of the behavior of someone in pain even though the actor in question had no pain, and one can also imagine a superspartan who was able to endure pain without giving any sign of being in pain" (35). The even stronger commonsense rebuttal is that to be a person is to have mental states, like desires, wishes, and beliefs, and we find ludicrous any metaphysics that denies them. Those metaphysics include artificial intelligence theories that extend the computer metaphor to the mind that asserts that the Mental is the software, the brain is the hardware or wetware, etc.

When confronted with these commonsense rebuttals, some philosophers take the "heroic age of science" maneuver in which behaviorists (or other materialists) are, like Copernicus, ahead of their times and see beyond mere folk psychology into the real. Aside from the philosophic merit of this claim—which seems small, since it merely asserts a similarity of being ridiculed—is the emotional edge it presumes: it takes heroic behavior to affirm behaviorism. Those who are brave affirm materialism; those who are not brave remain stuck in the Middle Ages.

Given that we have no single, coherent theory of the normal mind, it is not surprising that we have no single, coherent theory of the mind in distress, of psychopathology. The illogical features of many theories of psychopathology are well documented. Thomas Szasz (1961) built his reputation upon the corpses of many theories of mental illness that he pilloried unmercifully. Without sharing his hostility one must agree that politics, fashion, and other nonlogical and nonscientific forces often change the language and conception of what counts as psychopathology. Particularly glaring instances surround sexuality. What counts as normal and what counts as psychopathological forms of sexuality seem shaped by political agendas and political compromises. The vociferous debates with American psychiatry about forms of homosexuality, for example, denote the presence of something other than mere scientific discourse.

> All persons must struggle with two basic limitations: we do not have a rigorous or complete or non-contradictory theory of mind and we cannot avoid living lives entrenched in uncertainty. Who we are, where we are going, where are our children going, and what is the meaning of our existence are not questions we can answer in any decisive way. For instance, an adult sense of life requires us to accept uncertainty. (Ekeland 1993, 66–67)

This is an adult insight because it could not be said by a child or a person burdened by severe character pathology. Ekeland writes charmingly about myths and mathematics and the universal demand to see meaning in nature evident in folk religion and myth. In contrast, the evidence from developmental psychology and child psychiatry adduced above, for example, suggests that children *cannot* comprehend the concepts of uncertainty. This means that no child can match what we call adult or rational beliefs about causality, for example, much less topics like the nature of money or war or death, or sexuality. We recall reconstructions and interventions Freud made to his famous patients, the venerable Rat Man and Wolf Man. For example, to the former Freud announced that the boy's terror at a bird that seemed to come to life evoked both terror that his masturbating caused his sister's death (erection = bird rising up = uncanny power) and his later convictions about his father's resurrection (bird dead then living = resurrection of the dead = his father's "rising") (Freud 1909d, 309). One doubts any child could possibly articulate these thoughts or comprehend their unity.

A corollary to our general failure to know fully what the term "mind" designates is that benign responses to children's questions do not emerge from the latest pronouncements of science academies. I recall a nice scene in *Lies My Father Told Me* (Kadár 1975). A young boy asks his beloved Jewish grandfather why the leaves turn color in autumn. Grandfather answers, "Because God paints them." The adult man transmits to the child his conviction that there are patterns in nature and his own life and that this pattern is a good thing which he names God. Naming this pattern "God" means that he feels we should honor it and ourselves as creatures of infinite, personal value. Art, painting, and an ancient religious tradition are fundamentally linked to one another. They—the boy and his beloved grandfather—are parts of this whole. The boy's question is meaningful and the Jewish grandfather gives it a meaningful response. An equally good response might be afforded by an atheist mother who talks to her daughter about the hidden colors beneath the summer green. She might explain that autumn is a great cycle of transformation, how little girls and mothers and the leaves all share a common ancestry and destiny. Or as the poet put it, "The leaves are beautiful when they fall/ to whom are we beautiful as we fall?" These kinds of responses reflect the child's question, and respect the child's struggles with becoming a person with a mind, conveying a shared existence in a shared world.

Harmful responses would be silence, arrogance, and other responses that attack the child's need to discover in one's parents avenues to the world of actualities that lie outside the self. Extensive evidence from child psychiatry and the analysis of severe character pathology in adults suggests that children cannot remain uncommitted and disconnected from their caretakers. We do not wish the infant or child to take a statistical point of view regarding the likelihood that mother will remain loving and dad will remain supportive. Folk psychology and common sense typically subsume these needs under the rubric of security. In the more exacting language of child analysis and child psychiatry are distinctive terms like the "Background Object of Primary Identification" (Grotstein 1981), the "Transitional Object" (Winnicott 1953), and "Representations of Interactions that have been Generalized" (Stern 1985). Equally relevant is Kohut's basic concept of the loving and invested Self-Object that transmits to the child illusions of perfection and permanency that gradually decrease over time.[16]

Both sets of terms, naive and scientific, designate the child's demand to find *permanency and certainty* in other persons. Both sets illustrate also the child's paradoxical ability to find permanency and stability in the external world by virtue of having projected them from within the internal world. We can affirm this basically Freudian insight without straying from the narrower confines of academic psychology. Stern noted this in his rigorous study of infants' acquisition of trust (1985, 111ff.). All versions of learning theory require us to explain how infants *fabricate* from the flow of sensations and differences semblances of unity and order.

Winnicott's famous description of the child's feelings toward the transitional object illustrate well the issue at hand. Winnicott (1953) advanced a set of paradoxical claims about the infant's response to objects he named transitional. These are special objects, like blankets or cuddly toys, with which children soothe themselves in numerous instances of stress, like going to sleep. Such objects, Winnicott says, must appear to be both alive *and* not-alive, loved *and* hated, external *and* internal, unchanging yet over time changing with the infant's changes: "It comes from without from our point of view, but not so from the point of view of the baby. Neither does it come from within; it is not a hallucination" (1953, 5). The qualities ascribed to the transitional object are qualities that derive from the child's mind and they are, therefore, indirect portraits of

the child's notion of mind, of what mind really is. That Winnicott
has to use paradoxical language to name this quality of mind suggests that we cannot yet designate it any other way. A child who
demands of herself a reasonable, noncontradictory, portrait of mind
is obeying a commonsense demand made upon all scientists. Not
having read Searle and Winnicott, she cannot know that this is a
doomed enterprise. Hence, when she discovers that she cannot comprehend "rationally" why she suffers emotional distress, she deduces
that once again she is at fault.

## Specific Human Struggles: What Is Mind?

John Searle and Ludwig Wittgenstein, who are philosophers and
not child psychiatrists, argue vociferously against ascribing theories
to folk psychology. How do theories differ from what I have just
called notions of mind? Does the difference lie in the degree to which
an infant or child is called upon to create a novel explanation for its
suffering at the hands of the child's caretakers? It might seem that if
clever people, like philosophers, have trouble making sense of mental terms like "wish" and "belief" and "disposition," and their theories are, as Searle says, often incoherent, then surely the same problems occur in folk psychology? This issue weighs heavily upon philosophers, but also upon psychoanalysts and child psychiatrists who
must deal with naive notions of mind which seem to dominate some
patients and some children.

Searle helps us again when he notes (1992, 58–63) that to ascribe theories to ordinary usage of English terms like "wish" and
"mind" is peculiar. First, as Wittgenstein (1953) argued, ascribing
theories to folk usage is an odd form of philosophizing not justified
by ordinary speakers. Second, using terms like "mind" and "wish" is
part of know-how, a way of coping in complex exchanges between
sophisticated members of a culture. Third, ordinary speakers do not
postulate theories about their beliefs, they just have beliefs, or wishes,
or impulses, or desires: "Conscious desires are experienced. They
are no more postulated than conscious pains" (Searle 1992, 59).

Do "beliefs" and "desires" function in folk psychology the way
that "phlogiston" functioned in eighteenth-century physics? When
scientists know more about the real entities underlying theoretical
ones, like phlogiston, they jettison the name and concept because

they are theory relative and the theory is now proved less useful (60). Searle notes this is quite nakedly false for commonsense terms like belief. While the term "phlogiston" was offered precisely as a theory to explain observed behaviors, terms like "beliefs" and "wishes" name parts of real, human experience just like the terms "ranch houses, cocktail parties, football games, interest rates, or tables and chairs" (60).

When ordinary people want to refer to a part of their world that deals with themselves as agents they use words like "mind," "wish," and "belief". When philosophers press them to say what these terms "really mean," to indicate the theory of mind implicit in using these terms, most people blanch. Those trained in academic argument may retort and join the battle with their opponents. When they do so they enter into the quicksand with which Wittgenstein and others have made us familiar. To put this another way, Searle lets us see with more clarity that few (if any) people can proclaim a coherent theory of mind when they are pressured to do so. More importantly, most people can avoid the issue altogether.

But this is not true of children who later become neurotic. In contrast to those people who can avoid the conundrums and worries of the philosophers, children raised in abusive or neglectful environments must struggle with a "theory" of mind.[17] Just like children with acute kidney disease, these children learn too early about the fragility of their parents' minds and therefore about their own exquisite dependencies. Traumatized or neglected children forced to concoct instantaneously theories of mind fare no better than the philosophers when this burden is thrust upon them. They find no help from popular culture. For example, the truisms and wisdom of folk psychology do not, when added together, make a coherent theory of behavior. For every adage like "Look before you leap," are equally venerated counterclaims like "He who hesitates is lost." For every "Absence makes the heart grow fonder" is a counterpart, "Out of sight out of mind." When we recall that children assume the task of understanding mind under dangerous and frightening circumstances it is not surprising that the theories that result are disjointed. Are they also pathogenic?

Some important consequences flow from these generic limitations and struggles with the problem of mind. The principle consequence is that no single answer and no single theory can claim transhistorical value. Unlike Western theories of diabetic disease, which are incontrovertible, Western theories of mind can claim no special status compared to non-Western theories of mind. There is, as yet, no single right way or best way to know what mind is. There is, therefore, no incontrovertible basis for claiming to understand fully human being and our destiny. We may marvel at the oddity of other people's beliefs about the mind (as we avoid examining our own). So too when we survey the history of religious beliefs and religious wars we marvel at an immense number of absurdities proclaimed by each side. Yet when we examine our own wars and the rhetoric that surrounds them we find similar claims that the issue at hand is cataclysmic and requires immediate action and the death of tens of thousands.

Infants and children sometimes find themselves immersed in conflicts between what they want and need to be (for example, individuated) and what they feel an important person requires of them (for example, bonded to a depressed father). If a child is assailed by doubts (for instance, about an angry mother's intentions) it is reasonable to worry over every little thing she says, her tone of voice, her bearing, etc., to the limit of one's ability. This common feature of childhood obsessions reveals the consequences of a kind of unending iterative process. Children raise questions like, Why is mother alcoholic? which no one can answer. Lenore Terr (1990) notes that children who have been victimized by adults ask (reasonably enough): Why did these people hurt me?

The child's attempt to answer this question stumbles against major limitations. First, the child's cognitive status may be such that the child cannot comprehend ideas and relationships that are beyond concrete operational status. Piaget's findings and those of his followers suggest that much. Granting validity to the idea of "concrete operational" stage means that the child cannot grasp some things, like the concept of emotional ambivalence or the passage of time, that require more advanced reasoning (see Wellman 1990).

Second, when pursued with obsessive intensity, the child's game of "why" quickly exhausts the banks of human knowledge. A parent may explain to an anxious child why they have no money ("Because the stock market crashed") and why the stock market crashed ("The president overinflated the money supply") and even what inflation is ("A condition in which too much money chases too few goods") but will falter at some point, for example, "What *is* money, really?"

Third, the child does not know very much. Mom and dad define the world. The child identifies with the parents' language, thought, and modes of defense because they are the world. If mother and father manifest irrational and confusing ego functions it is those ego functions that the child internalizes in some fashion (see Schafer 1968 for an articulate description of the range of responses). Since children wish to comprehend their world and find in it reasonable and predictable patterns, and yet they also internalize their parents' (irrational) ego functioning, their "theory" of mind cannot be coherent. For to gain a coherent understanding of mind they would have to reject fully their parents as exemplars and gain coherence. This children cannot do until they gain the freedom offered by adulthood and some form of intensive confrontation with their idiosyncratic notions of mind.

Fourth, the child must struggle with fundamental and often indescribable needs, realties, and tension states. Very few adults can find the words and images adequate to these states. Lucky children and adults do not have to find the words because they can rely upon the empathic response of another person who comprehends their needs. In contrast, children raised in incoherent households and by emotionally damaged adults cannot rely upon those adults to intuit their needs. When they cannot manufacture exact and persuasive speech to signal their distress and gain relief, they evoke a repertoire of defenses, especially denial and dissociative modes, to ward off painful experiences. The quality and variety of boredom, for example, visited upon children is worthy of Darwinian efforts at differentiation.

Fifth, in families where empathy is rare or nonexistent, no one comprehends the child's private understandings. Hence no one can detoxify the child's malignant thought patterns and internal representations. As Freud said, they grow in the dark and take on monstrous proportions.

Sixth, the method of iterative reflection, the obsessional style, the worrying over, that typifies childhood anxiety does *not* match well the range and quality of emotional suffering that cascades through normal and abnormal childhoods. It fits objects whose inherent structures are reducible to well-defined parts or that can be counted, categorized, and mastered by obsessional devices. If emotions are not hierarchical entities that permit this kind of dissection, these common obsessional efforts to reduce anxiety will not succeed. We return to this topic below in chapter 5, when we consider contemporary theories of emotions.

If we hope to understand mental suffering we must isolate what we take to be its components. One way to do this is to consider certain beliefs as themselves pathogenic and to explain neurotic life, especially its self-defeating and joyless character, as the product of these beliefs. Looking at a child's experience of "mind" may help us understand why neurotic suffering often stems from efforts to understand the mind of one's caretakers.

## PATHOGENIC BELIEFS AND PREDICTING PARENTS' BEHAVIOR

The difficulty of defining what is mind is universal. Neurotic suffering (and all psychopathology that is ideogenic) is particular. Why are some people neurotic and others, who have equally deprived childhoods, not? Why should traumatized children and others who develop adult neurotic character pathology bother themselves with the theory of mind under any circumstances? To address these questions I return to Freud's third paradigm, "conflicts give rise to defense," and a contemporary research effort led by Joseph Weiss. Suggesting that neurotic suffering derives sometimes from failed rationality is a version of what Joseph Weiss terms "unconscious control theory." Weiss has stressed the utility of recovering Freud's "second hypothesis," that the ego not only suffers passively the upsurge of drive demands; it also exerts control over the person's unconscious mental life. In a narrow sense, Weiss claims that the ego can regulate the appearance of unconscious materials, including fantasy. Weiss and his colleagues claim that this "higher mental functioning hypothesis" (Weiss and Sampson 1986) permits us to see how patients will bring forth formerly repressed materials when they judge it is safe to do so. This common clinical occurrence and others like it, such as transference tests in which patients unconsciously reproduce prior object relationships with their analysts and judge the analyst's ability to respond in novel and facilitating ways, suggest that human beings can judge, think, and evaluate unconsciously. In a larger sense, Weiss says, we can account better for upsurge in neurotic actions by viewing them as tests of beliefs he labels "pathogenic."

I focus briefly upon his explication of unconscious guilt and pathogenic beliefs. Weiss is at pains to show Freudian roots for his ideas ("The theory is both Freudian and new" [323]). He contrasts his notion of unconscious guilt and other affects with Freud's earlier automatic functioning hypothesis. Weiss contends that the automatic functioning theory was Freud's effort to explain psychopathology as unfolding "without reference to experience, belief, or guilt" (45). Reviewing Freud's later pronouncements and contemporary analytic theory, especially work by Arnold Modell (1965, 1971, 1988), Weiss argues that often patients' psychopathological actions are driven by beliefs. These he labels pathogenic beliefs (PB). I summarize a few parts of his extensive discussion.

Children and adults, if the latter are traumatized severely, infer consequences about their behavior and the responses of important others. For example, a boy, pursuing normal developmental goals, like autonomy and separation, may learn that his mother feels wounded by his maturation. Modell (1965, 1971) gives vivid accounts of this condition, which he names separation guilt. Expanding upon this concept, Weiss stresses "the part played by real experiences in the acquisition of separation guilt; a child whose mother appears to be deeply upset by his attempts to become more independent of her is, all else being equal, more likely to develop separation guilt than a child whose mother is unhurt by his attempts to become more independent of her . . ." (1986, 50).

We can summarize the typical PB features in Modell's cases. A standard patient story has the following unconscious beliefs about his or her place in the world:

1. If I get good things (fame, fortune, love, happiness) I am taking them from someone else. (The limited good theory.)
2. These other people, like mom, dad, or siblings, will be hurt by my success. They have made this clear many times to me.
3. They will punish me by withdrawing love or support or protection or they will hurt me directly (rape, torture).
4. I will be harmed or die if they withdraw their protection or they will kill me if I leave them. I cannot live without mother, or father, or my sibling.
5. I do not want to die: hence, I'll compromise and seek only *partial* pleasures and *partial* happiness.[18] I won't marry the person I really love or enjoy fully my achievements. As one of Kurt Eissler's patients put it, when she died she would beat "Death" because he would only find a husk empty of life, not a robust person who had lived intensely.[19]

According to PB theory, from these pathogenic premises ensues a vast array of neurotic compromises, symptoms, and self-destructive actions. These compromises are actions like self-denigration in which the patient oscillates between two poles. One pole is the patient's genuine, libidinal, urges toward joy and expansiveness of self. The other pole is a set of beliefs and commitments to which the patient feels profound obligation. As Freud reported a century ago, an abused child typically becomes an adult whose sexual life recapitulates the violence done against the child. Sometimes the adult takes both roles at once. Weiss describes Mrs. A, for example, a patient who "allowed herself to be influenced by other people's wishes, feelings, opinions, and expectations to such an extreme degree that she feared she would lose her sense of self in any close relationship . . ." (1986, 59). These beliefs had devastating consequences: Mrs. A would oscillate between paranoid suspiciousness of others, retreat, grow lonely and desperate, and then at the height of one form of misery plunge into another. Other persons might use drugs, masochistic sex, or other behaviors to alter their extreme unhappiness. Then, in a typical neurotic counterpoint, they might retreat into shame and, to soothe that pain, seek occult or spiritual relief.

Weiss almost understates the importance of his theory. For by seeing Mrs. A's extensive range of symptoms as the consequences of failed rationality he deprives them of an existential status as "things in themselves." That is, rather than see Mrs. A's behaviors as the product of "paranoid ideation driven by neurological deficits" or an upsurge in "destructive impulses," he evaluates them as products of a certain kind of thinking. Neurotic symptoms of this type, in other words, are neither primary nor definitive of the patient's pathology: they are secondary to the patient's secret, unconscious belief system. When we can isolate those beliefs we can explain the symptoms as the desperate actions of an anxious person. For example, we learn that Mrs. A gave up her boyfriend at age eighteen because she felt that as she got happier her mother got sicker and sicker. To protect her mother's health she sacrificed the happiness she might have gained with a man who loved her.

So too, Mrs. A exhibited classic neurotic behavior when she found ways to deprive herself of happiness, joy, success, and pride: "After being elected president of the college debating club, she lost interest in the position, felt fraudulent, became alienated from the group, and resigned" (62). Neurotic push-pull, ambivalence, conflict, etc., are all terms employed since Freud's original discoveries to describe these kinds of behaviors. Weiss offers an explanation for these common occurrences. That explanation is that Mrs. A wished to succeed but not if it meant harming people she loved. Her mother taught her that Mrs. A's maturation, individuation, and success were all actions that meant she would abandon the mother who needed her desperately. Hence, when Mrs. A accomplished anything that resembled progress or sensed that she might be approaching joy she found a way to ruin her happiness. So too, because her mother attacked Mrs. A's younger sister, who was less attractive than she, Mrs. A "believed that if she had not been bright, well behaved, and attractive her sister would not have seemed defective to her parents and would not have been mistreated by them" (63).

Mrs. A and her analyst reconstructed the origins of this profound fear. It "stemmed from her repressed pathogenic belief that if she were independent of others or demonstrated superiority to them, she would damage or torment them" (60). Regarding the patient's father, Weiss adds "The patient unconsciously believed that her father desperately needed to feel intellectually superior to everyone, including his wife and children" (64). These beliefs are pathogenic because they had painful consequences for Mrs. A. She involved herself with a very sick man and attempted to cure him through her love (67). As Lorna Benjamin (1993) puts it, Mrs. A's pathology is a form of love; she will find a man whose needs are immense and cure him just as she should have cured her father (and mother and sister). Of course, these attempts at cure rarely work, a fact that satisfied Mrs. A's unconscious demand for compromise. Sooner or later, patients like Mrs. A will be labeled masochistic for choosing such hurtful relationships.

A LINE OF INQUIRY

The theory of pathogenic beliefs (PB) offers an exciting possibility for our examination of the objects of analysis. It gives us a way to talk about idiosyncratic elements, the child's mind and its wonderful complexities and subtleties, without reducing them to generalizations or unprovable metaphors. PB theory explains why we must hear in detail the *exact* contents of patients' fantasy lives, their major relationships, especially self-object relationships, and how they navigated

their developmental crises. We wish to comprehend the unique response to suffering that distinguishes each human life. We can add
another feature from Weiss's generalization about the *origins* of PB:
pathogenic beliefs tell children how to act in ways that will preserve
their relationship to their parents.[20]

I find striking a feature of these cases that Weiss does not emphasize. In many, if not all, of these encounters children derive pathogenic beliefs from their understanding of their parents' minds. For
example, Weiss describes the "most profound and powerful feelings
of guilt" (1986, 47) pertain to children who feel they have hurt
their parent. They harm them not physically but emotionally, that
is, mentally. For example, by maturing and leaving home the child
feels she or he is abandoning mom or dad to loneliness or some
other wretched emotional state. The child can prevent this suffering
simply by contorting the child's deepest needs to individuate and to
separate from the child's parents. Weiss describes Modell's (1971)
patient, a successful man who felt he had won his achievements at
his sister's expense. To punish himself for this unconscious guilt he
"deadened himself by drinking so as to be no better off than his
sister" (1986, 53). Another of Weiss's patients, Mr. M, obsessed
about a girlfriend whom he provoked into dumping him. Thus, he
identified with his mother whom he felt he had harmed by "rejecting" her (55). Yet another patient, Miss W, "believed herself more
attractive than her petulant mother. She had competed with her
mother for her father's love and, as she had experienced it, defeated
her. She felt responsible for her mother's unhappiness . . ." (57).

In another case, Weiss notes that a male patient observed that
his mother seemed to enjoy punishing him for keeping a messy room.
His mother was depressed. As a young boy, the patient inferred that
while she complained about his messy room and asked him to "improve," the mother secretly felt better when she yelled. Hence, he
continued to be messy and so make her happy. That the boy became
miserable as a result of her attacks was an early lesson that love is
suffering. This does not bode well for his future attempts at marriage.

If we can stand on Weiss's shoulders, as he stands on those of
others, we might extend his notion of pathogenic belief to include
another rule: Pathogenic beliefs are theories of mind that aim to
predict another person's behavior. This is not an arbitrary task. The
effort to understand and predict another person's behavior is not

driven by intellectual efforts to solve interesting puzzles. As Weiss and his colleagues note, in each case a child had to figure out a way to survive in dangerous circumstances. Children have no other way out. Children raised by disturbed parents are like Fletcher Christian on HMS *Bounty;* they are caught on a ship with a brutal captain. Other children are like the crew of the USS *Cain* confined to a ship run by a demented leader. Like these adult crewmen children raised in abusive and incoherent households must *do* something. Their first act is to attempt to comprehend the rules of the game as laid down by autocratic and frightening powers, mom and dad. Their second act is to obey these rules, or attempt to obey them. Because these rules derive from a parent's troubled and divided mind they are inevitably contradictory. Hence their third action is to do and undo, move toward and them move away from people they love and opportunities they might enjoy.

# CHAPTER 3

# Pathogenic Beliefs,
# Personal and Public Specimens

## PATHOGENIC BELIEFS AS THE OBJECTS OF PSYCHOANALYSIS

In the previous chapter, I discussed Joseph Weiss's theory of pathogenic beliefs. I summarized what I take to be essential features of this theory in eleven claims. We can reduce these to the assertion that patients are neurotic because they maintain a set of unconscious beliefs that require them to choose a life of suffering and self-harm over a life of joy and self-acceptance. To Weiss's theory, I added a corollary: pathogenic beliefs derive from a child's theory of mind that aims to predict another person's behavior. This idiosyncratic theory contributes to the creation of neuroses because it saddles the child with an impossible task: assess and predict the other person's mood. Because the child cannot fulfill this continuous assignment, the child eventually fails. These inevitable failures prove to both the child and the child's parent (or other persons) that the child should do better next time. As I note below, we find precise parallels to this demand in other relationships where a powerful person or group exerts control over less powerful people and blames them for errors that emerge from systemic failure. To illustrate this parallel I discuss three similar public occurrences, the Creationism debate, the "Quality" movement in American industry, and Soviet-U.S. confrontations during the Cold War. I suggest that childhood neuroses and these three public events share manifest similarities because they share a common latent origin. I suggest that all four instances derive from fallacious beliefs about human nature. These beliefs give rise to rules of conduct and management that, in turn, give rise to perfectionism.

Perfectionism, I will suggest, is an essential component in the creation of personal and public pathologies.

In contrast to the ordinary harm that befalls us all, neurotic suffering always includes a dimly perceived sense that we have been part of its genesis. That I may get cancer is perhaps my fate, but not my fault. That I marry four abusive persons in a row suggests that I may have had some part in these catastrophes. This accurate, but incomplete, bit of self-analysis naturally adds to my sense of failure and is summoned up whenever I touch upon those wishes and thoughts in my current life.

In the previous chapters I explored five questions:

1. Do pathogenic beliefs (PB) stem only from the child's "mind," or are there additional sources?
2. Among these additional sources, do we find nonintellectual learning?
3. Do PB evolve into a larger, more comprehensive "theory" of psychopathology?
4. If PB evolve, can we understand these evolved artifacts using rudimentary evolutionary theory?
5. Are these evolved artifacts instances of what Ernst Kris (1956b) and other analysts have termed "the personal myth"? (See also Lacan [1953] 1979.)

In this chapter I suggest that the answer to all these questions is yes. PB are pathogenic, not merely personal or idiosyncratic. No doubt we all have idiosyncratic beliefs about our bodies, the geographic location of Paris versus Rome, the best kind of vacation, and all those thoughts Freud labeled as superstitions and surmounted beliefs (Freud 1919h). None of these is pathogenic because none of these requires us to affirm suffering over pleasure.

Neurosis means living with the absence of joy. To be neurotic is to feel that one has constantly failed to accomplish something essential. A nightmare common to this state is the examination dream in which one must take a test in an obscure subject that one has never studied. (An exact instance is the examination dream in Ingmar Bergman's film, *Wild Strawberries* [1957]). To be neurotic is to be constrained, afraid of novelty, and liable to fall into dread. Wild sex, drinking, drugs, manic moments, rage attacks, and so forth can dull the pain or make it disappear for an evening. However, the cacophony of dread and doubt always return and with them cycles of anxiety and defense and joylessness.

Contemporary analytic theory of the neuroses is a developmental theory. It says that neurotic suffering is the product of the patient's earlier response to suffering, especially suffering that occurred in childhood. Like any reasonable mammal, the child articulates a plan of how to decrease pain and how to increase pleasure. If the source of the child's suffering is the action of emotionally disturbed parents this means the child has to concoct a "theory" of the parent's mind, of the parent's psychopathology, in order to predict the parent's behavior and, if possible, control the parent's actions. In the last chapter, I suggested that this meant the child could not rely upon the child's folkways of using terms like "mind, "belief," and "wish." Lucky kids, raised in good-enough homes do not create "theories" of mind, because they do not have to. Unlucky kids raised in traumatic or neglectful households cannot escape this task. Because this task is endless, so too is their suffering.

From these infantile "theories" of mind flow additional pathogenic beliefs. For example, a young girl learns that her mother is distressed when the little girl is "too silly." In this story, mother is distressed because she fears the girl is drawing attention to herself and thus committing the sin of selfishness. From these training episodes the little girl learns this general rule, "When I feel silly [or playful] mother will be angry and withdraw from me." Given this valid insight the child discovers defensive maneuvers that reduce her immediate suffering but increase subsequent burdens. For example, she may deduce additional "rules" such as (1) "When I begin to feel this way keep mom occupied," or (2) "When I begin to feel silly, pretend that I don't," or (3) "When I feel silly, exaggerate my silliness so mom will yell at me quickly and get it over with."

These maneuvers work because they let the child avoid immediate pain. Yet, by using them in various combinations the child conforms to the Other's psychopathology. The child gains momentary control over how and when she suffers but also learns to be on guard constantly and acquire the conviction that her destiny is to engage forever in similar relationships. These maneuvers and the rules derived from them are the seeds of neurosis. For each rule requires the child to suppress a natural, unrehearsed part of herself. Instead of spontaneity, she institutes rigorous self-examinations. Questions like "What am I feeling at this instance?" and "What are they thinking about me?" and "How can another person use my feelings against me?" dominate important relationships. These questions center upon understanding and predicting the other person's unspoken assessments of the child. Instead of learning how to *discover* another person's mind, through talk or play or some other form of expression, the child strives to *predict* the other person's feelings and therefore their actions. While this goal is reasonable and understandable, it is also unattainable.

### CASE ILLUSTRATION: DANNY AND THE CHURCH

In a famous passage in *Totem and Taboo* (1912–13), his essay on primitive religion, Freud comments upon the "asocial" nature of neurotic life. By this he means that neurotic fantasies and pathogenic beliefs tend to arise within the secrecy of the child's mind. Freud says that adherence to social institutions can help prevent the occurrence of neurosis because it may help decrease the power of these secrets.[1] Although Freud always denied religion a dignity equal to that of other social institutions, especially art, we need not agree with this exclusion. Indeed, given the wealth of spiritual wisdom available in many religions, like other social institutions it ought to prevent or at least inhibit neurotic conditions. Yet, every clinician knows that religious faith does not inoculate persons against doubt and neurotic depression. A common case is that of a child whose beloved parent dies and to whom religious rituals, which promise comfort, bring no relief. The rituals seem hollow to the child and at best mock the child's wish to believe exactly as the child's religion requires. Why do these ancient rituals, developed over centuries, sometimes fail to comfort their practitioners? What has not occurred?

Consider the story of Danny. When he was six, Danny's beloved mother died suddenly. His family was devout and tried to use the ritual resources of the family's religion to account for her death and to help the family grieve this terrible loss. In order to get on with life and raise his family as best he could, Danny's father remarried soon after burying his first wife. Alongside the devastation of losing his mother, this new marriage presented Danny another task. His stepmother was a woman who had also lost her spouse recently. In their effort to heal the two damaged families the adults failed to see that Danny's new mother was severely depressed. Desperate for mothering, Danny perceived that his stepmother would not be available fully to him unless she were happier.

To make her happier the little boy acquired complex ways to manage his feelings. First, he learned to stifle overt signs of grief for his biological mother and any other feelings that might distress his stepmother. For to grieve his beloved mother would mean, he thought, that he favored his first mother over his stepmother. Second, Danny felt that this would harm his new mother and increase her suffering. Then he feared that she would retaliate against him and perhaps abandon him. This idea he could not bear, since his first mother's death proved that such things can occur. Third, he sought refuge in moments of secret, hallucinatory revival of his dead mother. These dreamy states were comforting until he woke from them. Then he felt "crazy" for he realized she was not there in the room as he had imagined. In contrast to mourning, with its semipublic features and expressiveness, these hallucinatory moments shamed him. On waking from them he felt as if he were hearing for the first time the news of her death. Because he told no one about these moments, he deduced that he was deviant and odd. These bits of self-scrutiny deepened his conviction that he must avoid exposure at any cost.

In turn, these convictions made genuine, *public* mourning for his first mother impossible. Because they were not public, the boy's idiosyncratic "theories" of her death and his need to control his grief became permanent and pathogenic secrets. Believing that both his father and his stepmother were already overburdened with their losses, he reasoned that telling them about his hallucinations would lead to more problems. Therefore, while his family's religion offered numerous public avenues to celebrate his mother's life and to mourn her, the boy knew secretly that he dare not take part. These public rituals were too exposing and too dangerous. He might miss her too much, hallucinate her presence and then bring unmanageable shame to himself and to his family. Looking for guidance, he studied his grieving father and grieving stepmother. Since neither of them revealed unseemly emotions about their tragic losses, and both of them soldiered on, he deduced that he should follow suit.

By obeying what he took to be the family's commandment, Danny sealed away thousands of memories of his first mother's love. In this way her death made growing up wearisome, for at each juncture he felt vulnerable to his old terrors. During normal grade-school crises, for example, he went through agonizing periods of yearning for his lost mother. However, yearning evoked memories of his hallucinatory experiences and these evoked the original pain of her death and the profound shame that followed. These unending painful moments evoked, in turn, his childhood theory that if he held onto his first mother he would harm his new mother. To avoid that catastrophe Danny tried to control his yearnings and wishes using his boyhood devices: secrecy, obsessive self-examination, intense guilt, and the like. At ordinary developmental stages, like leaving grade school, the ups and downs of adolescence, his discovery of sexuality, and leaving for college, sustaining memories of his mother's love were not available to him. This real, although invisible, loss made each turning point into a crisis. In defense against the anxiety each loss aroused, he discovered cocaine, aggressive sexuality, and crazy driving at high speed. These latter behaviors and devices became the core of his adult neurosis. Each device decreased his anxiety but each made genuine discovery of his actual feelings impossible.

Like other skillful people Danny could finesse many parts of his adult relationships, especially if he were "in charge." For example, by giving to others he gained their respect and thus controlled their responses to him. Yet, inevitably, his immaturity and his pathogenic beliefs caused him to fail. While narcissistic people might gladly take everything he offered them, less self-centered friends tired of his controlling generosity. This inevitable friction led Danny to add to his "theory" new, devastatingly wrong conclusions such as: "I failed to transform my feelings sufficiently" and "Next time, anticipate and plan for spontaneity." These contradictory rules, in turn, gave rise to another feature typical of neuroses and character pathology: an endless effort to control other people. Indeed, a constant refrain heard from those who live with persons like Danny is that they seek to dominate others constantly. Naturally, they do the same in therapeutic relationships. They eventually fail there, too, and this visible failure confirms pathological deductions that life is miserable and they are worthless.

Variations on patients' assignments to transform their damaged parents include savior fantasies, a feature of many future therapists and ministers. They also prefigure a spectrum of responses ranging from narcissistic entitlement to sociopathic rage, the latter expressed as "I was hungry and was not given what I need and deserve: hence

I'll take now what was promised me in the beginning." When these patients face new situations that evoke their old terrors, they naturally regress to their original defensive strategies. Their shields go up and all incoming information from this new and novel relationship is blocked at the boundary. Lacking access to new information that might signal a safe and novel form of relationship, the negative transference dominates. A state of crisis ensues, ambassadors are withdrawn, and the war comes.

## THAT UNCANNY UNION: THE COEVOLUTION OF PREDATOR AND PREY

It might seem that I am blaming parents for the willing creation of childhood neuroses. I am not. We rarely meet a patient whose parents showed malice aforethought and willed themselves to harm their offspring. On the contrary, most cases of childhood neuroses and their adult variants derive from complex interactions that evolve over many years. Indeed, the interactions that take place between mother and child in the first seven years of life, for example, number in the tens of thousands. Unhappy moments, like those between Danny and his new mother, do not represent her conscious effort to attack her stepchild. The subheading to this section, the coevolution of predator and prey, may seem extreme if we extend it to cover ordinary relationships between child and the child's caretakers. It is unfair if it means that parents wish to be predatory toward their children.

I use it to emphasize the child's perspective and to link that perspective to ecological parallels in natural environments. For predators and prey do not "hate" each other and do not evolve their complex interactions out of moral judgments about each other. I stress the evolutionary aspect of these interactions to highlight another pathogenic belief typical of childhood neurosis, namely, that the complex interactions and "mind reading" that seem to occur between parent and child or between two sibs is the product of an uncanny power. In this way children misunderstand the developmental processes that give rise to complexity.

> It is almost as if the human brain were specifically designed to misunderstand Darwinism, and to find it hard to believe. (Dawkins 1986, xv)

I cite this passage to suggest how hard it is for *anyone* to understand how simple, evolved processes can produce intricate outcomes. Dawkins is not talking about children and their pathogenic beliefs about their parents' minds. He is talking about present-day adults who do not accept Darwin's account of the origin of species. Their refusal irritates Dawkins, a well-known defender of Darwinism in this and a more recent book, *Climbing Mount Improbable* (1996). Dawkins's remark about the human brain's struggle with Darwinism leads him to consider the difficulty mortals have with comprehending the time scale relevant to Darwinian processes: "Our well-tuned apparatus of skepticism and subjective probability-theory misfires by huge margins, because it is tuned—ironically, by evolution itself—to work within a lifetime of a few decades" (xv–xvi).

I add another bit of evolutionary speculation. This is to guess that even scientists were once upon a time infants and then children. Children enter a vastly complex world not only of species but also of human personalities and human culture. Human personalities and human institutions are, in some sense, human products. They are also presented as complete and finished to infants who find themselves immersed in a cultural world preformed by their ancestors. Relying upon Freud without naming him, Dawkins notes that humans project this interpersonal experience back onto Nature through religious affirmations that a supernatural Deity designed everything at one fell swoop. From within the infant's and child's experience this is exactly how personal and cultural life appears.

We are born into language and we are born into families where each thought and feeling is conditioned by the thoughts and feelings of our *immediate* emotional environment. The intellectual objections Darwin raises against Creationist reasoning are incidental to these convictional and emotional experiences. Contemporary psychoanalytic clinical evidence and studies of infant development reveal some of the origins of these beliefs (see Gay 1992 and 1997). Darwin's replacement for this common worldview is that of the sophisticated, *adult* naturalist. He came to this adult view by drawing upon centuries of accumulated scientific knowledge. Thanks to this long tradition, Darwin enjoyed the abstract intellectual ability to envision an immensely long period of time:

> Thus, from the war of nature, from famine and death, the most exalted object which we are capable of conceiving, namely, the produc-

tion of the higher animals, directly follows. There is grandeur in this view of life, with its several powers, having been originally breathed by the Creator into a few forms or into one; and that, whilst this planet has gone cycling on according to the fixed law of gravity, from so simple a beginning endless forms most beautiful and most wonderful have been, and are being evolved. (Darwin 1859)[2]

Children and infants cannot share this sentiment since (1) they do not know about "gravity" and its marvelous universality, and (2) they live moment to moment. So too, when analytic patients misperceive our therapeutic intentions, just as when they misperceive their boss's criticism, they do so in a regression induced by panic and anxiety. In those regressive moments time stands still. The past is now present. They cannot stand outside their immediate and intensely real sense of "danger." They cannot assume a lofty view of their past and they cannot see themselves as the grand outcome of their developmental stories. We need a theory to explain their errors (and perhaps, too, Darwin's sangfroid). We presume that patients in the midst of traumatic encounters, including transference encounters, perceive something and then interpret it (erroneously) according to innate or acquired schemata.

Where along the line of information flow do these errors occur? Was it in us, their objects of perception, or in the transmission from us to them, or in their "minds"? Contemporary analytic theory, of which PB are one small part, assumes with Freud that patients perceive something within the ebb and flow of emotional waves that recalls an earlier but similar relationship. This something may be a minor resemblance between me, the therapist, and another person in the patient's emotional life, or it may be a vague parallel. For example, a patient, raised by an alcoholic and distant mother, experienced me as "crazy" and "scary" because I happened to be a professor and she recalled girlhood terrors about Professor Frankenstein. Given Freud's fundamental insight about transference, we know now to recognize and welcome these moments.

Outside the analytic or therapeutic frame, transference repetitions like this often lead to disasters. A common cycle begins when a boss, for example, acts in ways that happen to evoke memories of previous, conflicted object relations. This accurate bit of data evokes instantaneously a web of past suffering that is reexperienced in the here and now, and this suffering evokes defenses. As Freud first discovered, in this form of negative transference a rapid cycling occurs between initial perception, recognition, recollection of painful object relationships and defenses against them. The patient's characteristic style of coping with these earlier conflicts, what others see as the patient's unfortunate tendencies, begins with an accurate perception that the boss's tone of voice is like his dad's. This evokes unconscious automatisms, what Freud termed unconscious fantasies, and these, in turn, evoke a sense that that past is now present. The past is not symbolically present, it is present actually and the patient's worst fears are realized. The patient's errors turn on these momentary errors: time has not moved forward, I will suffer again as I always have.

Theoreticians have offered many different ways to explain this feature of neurotic life. Indeed, neurotic persons also offer homegrown theories as to why they continuously repeat mistakes. I have suggested that the theory of "pathogenic beliefs" (PB) is useful because it offers a psychological theory about neurotic choices. Its focus on beliefs fits the broad outlines of psychoanalysis, the study of unconscious psychological processes. PB are mental contents which we can, sometimes, comprehend through empathic listening (Kohut 1971). Unlike biological differences, which are incommunicable, one person's beliefs about the self, about guilt and responsibility, for example, are commensurable and communicable to other persons. Or so it seems. We take it as a matter of heuristic faith that we can, usually, comprehend our patients' experience if we and they can find the right language, and attend to the transference reenactments and to the transference-countertransference dramas as they unfold.

For example, we can often learn that our patients felt as children that they had to cure one or both of their parents. "Curing" mom or dad means bringing them back to a state where the parent can take care of the child. These attempts to cure the parent derive from the moment by moment reality of psychic pain and the questions it provokes: What is this pain? Where does it come from? How can I decrease it? The child's first resource will be the personality and beliefs of the child's parents as models of self-understanding. I note six features of the encounters that generate these tasks.

First, adults—parents or other caretakers—are dominating and powerful. The young child is perhaps two feet tall, while the adult is usually two to three times that height. (We recall numerous fairy tales about giants and recognize in them the child's experience of adults.) These gigantic, all-powerful beings must know complex things beyond the child's ken. What middle-class child has not marveled at the capacity of adults to drive cars, get money from machines, and make big decisions, not to mention seeing adults naked?

The immense gap in children's knowledge of the external world of adult life extends to their understanding of their internal worlds, their minds, and their bodies. Attempting to articulate her father's tripartite theory of the mind, Anna Freud (1936) once noted that healthy children do not exhibit boundaries between the superego, ego, and id. Only when there is significant psychological distress can we locate boundaries between the ego and the superego, say, when a person feels condemned by the person's self. The same is true of the body's internal organs when they are healthy and functioning correctly. For example, healthy people (who are not trained in anatomy) cannot locate their kidneys. Healthy kidneys function automatically and silently. Healthy children might learn to use the word 'kidney' correctly to answer questions on a biology test, but that knowledge will remain dominant only within the confines of book learning. It will not enter any other "module" (quoting Fodor 1983). Healthy children learn about the kidney in high school and assign it a place in their encyclopedia. It will *not* enter their deeper, earlier sense of physical self that is constituted by concrete operational thought. In contrast, consider a young boy whose kidneys malfunction and who experiences abdominal pain. This child *must* both conceptualize the kidney and learn ways to decrease the suffering of which it is the source. On analogy, we note how adults who have bad teeth can learn to drink hot and cold liquids without suffering. By delicate adjustments of tongue and breath I keep hot coffee away from the afflicted tooth. I do this in response to hundreds of pain indicators shooting from my tooth to some part of my brain. Luckily, no one asks me to verbalize *how* I do this. That is, no one asks me to explain which muscles I use or how much breath I send wafting over my tongue. These maneuvers require me to assess incoming pain sensations, record them, adjust my facial muscles, compare how this posture feels to how another felt, and to allocate my breath in hundredths of a second. I do this instantaneously and learn to enjoy my coffee in comfort.

Compare this trivial example to infants and children who endure repeated emotional pain hundreds of times. Would they not also apply the exquisite perceptual, conceptual, and behavioral schemata available to them to find pleasure and decrease their suffering, even if momentarily? They do so by examining the textures of their immediate surroundings. For example, consider how many complex and subtle events must occur for an infant to acquire language. More than we can currently say. Does it make sense to suppose that infants would not apply similar computational energy upon assessing the moods and dispositions of their caretakers? They would have to locate, record, and respond to what I have called "emotional affordances" (Gay 1992). They would do so automatically and with dedication. For example, today mother's voice has an edge that suggests she'll be angry if the child seems too happy or silly. So the child suppresses that affect and creates an internal barrier between one part of the self and another. Another child might learn father will be angry if I don't attend to him, so suppress any impulse to display myself and, instead, focus on dad. At each iteration the child adjusts to likely expectations and does so in reactive and preconscious ways, just as I learned to round my tongue and blow on my hot coffee.

Second, in interactions between an enraged, excited, or frightening adult and child the adult typically tells the child *why* the child deserves this attack (or criticism, or sexual abuse, or rejection, or another form of punishment). If a rare child, a budding young Freud, initially doubted she caused her father's depression, her father would soon lose his temper and pronounce, "If you were a better child I would not be upset!" Typically, adults who inflict pain do so with vehement explanations: "I'm doing this to punish you, to control your bad behavior, to make you safe, to cleanse you, to train you." Extremely common is the refrain: "Your badness makes me do this to you." Since the parent is often at rope's end and the child's failure to respond instantly to the parent's mood is the last straw, the parent is not wrong. On that occasion it *was* the child's "bad attitude" that precipitated the parent's attack. On these occasions the child must affirm what the child and parent have just witnessed, not imagined. Something about the child *was* the very thing that set the parent off on her or his tirade and attack.

Third, in complex family relationships, say between an older sibling and a younger sibling, each partner has hundreds, if not thousands, of opportunities to adapt modes of attack, defense, and projective explanations as to why it is the other person's fault. In this way patterns of attack and abuse become exquisitely adjusted techniques for inflicting pain upon the other and avoiding, momentarily, pain inflicted by the other. In a long-term psychoanalysis of patients with this kind of history, the analyst learns how the older sibling, for example, scouted the younger sibling's vulnerabilities. The sibling who is on attack examines with exquisite care the face of the other sibling, looking there for signs of shared suffering. From this shared pain emerge a primitive bonding and indicators of how to control that sibling later.

Fourth, the victim helps the attacker by accepting the latter's abuse. In these interactions a common inversion takes place. The parent or older sibling who suffers psychic pain typically manipulates the child or younger sibling into helping them soothe that pain. Ideally, we expect the parent to be the primary care taker and self-object for the child in Heinz Kohut's sense (1971, 1977). In psychopathological encounters the child becomes the parent's self-object and this becomes a way of life. This self-object inversion has seductive aspects. A little girl, for example, who is sometimes smacked around by an alcoholic father, learns that when she absorbs father's rage father seems to feel better: he rewards her for her good will and thus makes it more likely she will tolerate his rage the next time.

A simple moralizing approach to these children's lives, or to adult patients from whom we hear similar stories, tends to cast the abuser into a single role, the bad person, and the child into another, the passive victim. The ethics of these situations is not obscure: using persons against their will is wrong. However, if we remain within the world of ethical judgment, we project this dichotomy onto the child's complex experience, including the child's fantasies about those scenes. Moralizing about abuse can obscure the child's accurate recollection that the child's suffering *did* alter the other person's emotional state.

We want to empathize with every aspect of the child's and the patient's experience, including their accurate perceptions that inverted self-object relationships offer seductive pleasures. If we moralize about the misuse of our patients we cannot help them undo this powerful and often invisible bondage to their suffering. The common refrain heard from an abused wife, for example, that her husband needs her and he is "really a good man when he's not angry" are not invalid. The husband needs his wife in the sense that he and his wife have discovered that by hitting her he feels better. Later he needs her to forgive him and to remove his lingering feelings of remorse. In each act of the drama the wife is correct: her suffering is not in vain. She can see the effect she has upon her husband's moods and this validates, on each occasion, her *special power* to heal him.

This conviction that they possess special powers is central to neurotic persons' pathogenic beliefs about their "destiny." It has at least two themes. The first is: I am lovable when I am helpful; my suffering and pain help the other; thus, suffering is a good thing because it heals the other and keeps us united. (A variation on this theme is: Since my suffering is a good thing, the more I suffer the more I demonstrate my love.) The second theme is: I must guard against acting in ways that "cause" the other to harm me, so I must attend even more carefully to the other person's inner states and feelings: "Children in an abusive environment develop extraordinary abilities to scan for warning signs of attack. They become minutely attuned to their abusers' inner states. They learn to recognize subtle changes in facial expression, voice, and body language as signals of anger, sexual arousal, intoxication, or dissociation" (Herman 1992, 99).

Fifth, because children become attuned to the inner states of significant others they often become skilled at "reading" the moods of persons beyond the family. From their early training at home they branch out and use the same devices and methods to examine others at school and later in their work environments. When they are successful at guessing the other person's moods or intentions their methods are rewarded. This naturally entrenches these maneuvers and devices further and they accrue even greater value. Failures evoke increased neurotic scrutiny and thus reinforce the neurotic solution; no learning can take place. For example, Houdini pointed out, gently, the numerous occasions upon which mediums known to Sir Arthur Conan Doyle were caught cheating. Doyle merely shrugged and said that yes, on those occasions they had to cheat because their astral powers, etc., failed them, but not when they had channeled spirits for him. When children caught up in inverted self-object relationships are wrong about another person's mood, when they are incorrect in their assessments, they cannot coolly examine the source of their errors. On the contrary, their anxiety skyrockets. Because they are driven by anxious anticipation, grounded on lived experience, errors of judgment signify imminent disaster.

These new disasters do *not* cause neurotic persons to abandon the methods that characterize their forms of relationship and attention. Since these disasters evoke their original suffering and validate their original fears, neurotic children and neurotic adults summon forth their best line of defense, which is *increased* scrutiny and *increased* vigilance. For example, given a childhood terror of female sexuality and relentless sermonizing against sexual temptation, many a Christian boy has reasoned from premise (1) "My [good] mother never has sex" and premise (2) "Only bad women have sex" to the conclusion (3) "Only a bad woman will have sex with me." This standard mythology of female sexuality, the virgin-whore complex (Freud 1912d), cannot be invalidated by meeting a nice woman who is also sexual. That merely proves that one has misjudged her. A public person who dramatized the virgin-whore split is the English-American director Alfred Hitchcock. His many movies depict two kinds of women: "Virgin Bitches" who have sex with no one, including the movie's main character, and "Prostitute Bitches" who have sex with everyone except the hero. We note that in both cases the woman is despised: the virgin tempts you but never gives in, while the whore gives in all the time thus ruining the illusion of distinctiveness and fidelity. Each woman evokes sexual hunger, but offers no relief from the neurotic man's demand that his sexual partner be a virginal woman. According to this pathogenic belief, therefore, both virgins and prostitute bitches deserve punishment.

While there are many sources to the virgin-whore split, one of them is relevant to PB theory. This is the common Christian teaching about sexuality and especially about the female body. As Freud notes, quoting Augustine's famous misogynist denunciation of human origins, many a theologian has believed that we are born from women "inter urinas et faeces" (Freud 1912d, 189; also Freud 1930a, 106 n. 3). This peculiar condensation, denying that women have a third aperture, the vagina, assimilates birth to defecation and urinating: the baby is just another waste product from the interior of a woman's body. This is another illustration of premise two: only bad women have sex. This premise cannot be invalidated by a demonstration that some women are both good and sexual since we can show that those women are *imperfect* in some way or other. Even the most refined, exquisite, empathic, and devoted woman defecates. This fact makes her disgusting and proves that being sexual, having genitals that both attract and repel, is a source of pollution and danger. Images of women as spiders, monsters, gigantic beasts, and endlessly harmful sirens all turn on this profound fear.[3]

Sixth, in cases of overt misuse, as distinct from neglect or some other disaster, the Other, the person who misuses the child, assumes an awesome stature. For not only is the Other usually older than the child, the Other often *can* read the child's feelings and *can* manipulate the child's need to be loved. This perverted use of empathic skills negates the boundaries that separate the child from the Other. Because the Other focuses his or her intense needs upon the child, the Other studies the child just as predators study their prey. Whether consciously or unconsciously, the Other learns what scares the child and which particular feelings, like guilt and shame, can be used to persuade the child to bend to the Other's wishes. Because the child relies upon preconscious intuitions of the other's emotional states the child cannot name and cannot comprehend upon what grounds she or he has these intuitions: "This nonverbal communication becomes highly automatic and occurs for the most part outside of conscious awareness" (Herman 1992, 99).

The brilliance of those who perpetuate inverted self-object relationships derives from their acquired ability to relieve their suffering by targeting these intuitive and more vulnerable persons. The predator becomes adept at gauging the terror and limits of the targeted other. Because targeted children cannot name and cannot locate the source of dread in ordinary space and time they locate it in uncanny domains, in magic, and thus their mental landscape is dominated by the occult (Freud 1919h; Gay 1989). Because the Other also operates unconsciously, genuine remorse has little effect upon the next episode of abuse. The real tears of the alcoholic mother, for example, do not wash away her deficits and do not teach her how to enjoy adult relationships. As long as those interpersonal resources remain unavailable to her and as long as her character remains in deficit, the need to drink will persist and so too her need to use her children as self-objects. Naturally, we find these issues entangled in the child's developmental history. The interpersonal crises and developmental failures that typify the neurotic child's story need not take place amid overt violence and overt neglect. As any parent can attest, even with the best intentions and using the best resources, we easily fail to comprehend our godlike status in the eyes of our children.

While the child's internal world, sexual pressures, naive misunderstandings, and the like play a role in the genesis of neurosis I have focused upon six features of parent-child interaction and the commonality of inverted self-object relationships. I run the risk of exaggerating the influence of "external" factors upon the production of psychopathology. However, I am willing to risk that error because I wish to underscore the commonality of pathogenic beliefs. In the next section, I describe three public instances of pathogenic beliefs separated entirely from clinical settings.

### PATHOGENIC BELIEFS IN PUBLIC DISCOURSE: CREATIONISM AND AUTHORITARIANISM vs. TQM

*Creationism and the demand for perfection*

As I noted above, children are thrown into families and cultures of immense complexity and scope. If these institutions and practices were the product of conscious, deliberate planning their architects would be godlike in their powers. Only godlike wisdom and godlike perfection could produce these wonderful things in a single instance. Both Jewish and Christian religions affirm this portrait of divine power in their creation stories. Freud noted a common incident from his boyhood when his mother, endeavoring to validate the Bible's account of creation, rubbed her hands together producing "dirt" (dried skin) thus proving that humans are formed from soil as we learn in Genesis 2:7.

In reasoning that godlike powers produce their world children recapitulate the thinking of adult theologians and philosophers who deduced that only a god of infinite powers could create immensely complex structures, like the amazing variety of species. I stress this odd alliance between children's beliefs and some forms of theology because it reinforces my general point about neurotic suffering: it stems from the child's "reasonable" approach to the child's distress. It is as reasonable as the thinking manifested in many public institutions. Before the Darwinian revolution elite European thinkers held that mere mortals could not comprehend the variety of species. They argued that only an omniscient Designer blessed with infinite wisdom, could create wonders like the exquisite balance between predators and prey and like the unimaginable complexity of the mammalian eye. This Great Designer, God, was known by God's handiwork. We creatures can only admire, not explain, and never duplicate these marvelously complex entities.

Charles Darwin rejected this argument and said that these amazing objects, like the human eye, are not products of an infinite Mind that created them immediately and from nothing. On the contrary, Darwin says these complex products are the result of a simple set of recursive rules operating over immense spans of time. We see parallel events occur in the pathological worlds of abusive or neglectful adults and abused children. For even when older siblings or hurtful parents wish to make amends they do so within the thought world, the pathogenic beliefs, of their psychopathology. They swing, for example, between alcoholic bingeing and perfectionist moralizing about themselves. The latter often winds around an archaic religious belief: since they have done terrible things the only permissible alternative is perfect renunciation and reparation. This fails, naturally, and the most obvious avenue left to them is drinking. In this way the self-attacking style of many persons, which one might label "character pathological," resembles the perfectionism evident in so-called Creation Science attacks upon Darwinism. In their speeches and publications Creationists attack Darwin and evolutionary theory for not explaining *all* aspects of the living world. Darwinians have not uncovered a complete fossil record that replicates exactly missing links between species.

Creationists typically reason in the following way. First, Darwinian theory has not solved all problems related to evolution. Second, there are major gaps in the fossil record. Third, Darwinian theory thus has no value as science. This form of reasoning presumes that science is an activity like that of fundamentalist theology: it should yield a complete account instantly and without remainder. In other words, science ought to operate like biblical literalism. It should be written once and for all and address all possible questions. Just as certain forms of fundamentalism demand that persons affirm "inerrancy," that the Christian Bible is completely and wholly valid, so too its competitors must make similar claims.

Fourth, since Darwinian theory has no value as an absolute answer we might as well accept the mythology of Christian fundamentalism. For example, on one web page we read:

> The big issues! Two of the biggest weaknesses of evolutionary theory are: 1) There is no adequate explanation for the origin of life from dead chemicals. Even the simplest life form is tremendously complex. 2) The fossil record, our only documentation of whether evolution

actually occurred in the past, lacks any transitional forms, and all types appear fully-formed when first present. The evidence that "pre-men" (ape-men) existed is dubious at best. So called pre-man fossils turn out to be those of apes, extinct apes, fully man, or historical frauds. [A bit later we learn from "Dr. David N. Menton, Ph.D."] "There is no reason not to believe that God created our universe, earth, plants, animals, and people just as described in the book of Genesis![4]

The maddening tone of this debate lies in part in the authors' deceptions. Having lost the nineteenth-century scientific debates, twentieth-century Creationists mask their religious intentions under the guise of disinterested critiques of Darwinism. Thus, they attack standard scientific claims about the age of the earth, arguing for example that it may be only ten thousand years since the mantle of the earth formed. When faced with thousands of bits of contrary evidence, amassed in discrete sciences, Creationists avoid that part of the record and instead focus upon marginal speculations. When that fails to impress most science teachers they often try to alter public school teaching. Sidestepping the scientific debate, many Creationists use legislative and court systems to force school systems to recognize their version of religious fundamentalism as science.

The cognitive and emotional burdens falling upon children raised in environments of inverted self-object relationships are more debilitating than one might at first believe. For while an outsider may marvel at the apparent irrationality of the child's subsequent beliefs, we should not. The child's task, at age six, for example, is identical to that of the analyst who struggles to comprehend these horrors from the safety of a sophisticated, adult posture. Even from this vantage point the analyst cannot claim to know why a parent, for example, became enraged and attacked the child. We try our best, but we cannot reconstruct exactly why a parent failed to protect our patient's happiness. I am suggesting we view long-term, psychopathological encounters as the products of complex ecological exchanges between family members. They are not solely the products of conscious or unconscious motivations. They will not yield fully to the child's effort or ours to understand "Why?"

While this question is eminently plausible, it is not answerable. To ask "Why does my mother hate me?" is identical to asking "Why did the United States fight a war with Mexico in 1846?" or "How many people will buy personal computers next year?" or "How long is the coastline of Maine?" or "What is love?" or "Why is God letting me suffer this way?" There are no single, definitive answers to these questions. These questions are logically identical to those Claude Lévi-Strauss finds at the core of public myths, for example, "Why did a Loving God bring death into the world?" These questions are overtly reasonable. Because they are logically unanswerable, a benign response is to tell a story, a myth that at least respects our wishes even if it cannot satisfy them.

However, misused and neglected children cannot usually understand this abstract point of differentiation. For they face two immediate demands: produce a working theory of mental illness and figure out ways to prevent its reoccurrence. These demands they cannot satisfy. They cannot concoct an adequate "theory" of their parent's illness, for example, and they cannot control their parent's psychopathology except, often, by succumbing to some form of misuse or seduction. These are actions, not understanding. The only plausible answers to these profound and unanswerable questions will be mythological.

### Authoritarian Management versus "Quality" and W. E. Deming

Before we label persons with character pathology as deviant and unusual we might note how common their problems are in any interpersonal system where fear dominates. For example, in his many studies of management the late W. Edwards Deming helped lay the foundation for the "Quality" movement in the modern business world. Postwar Japanese business people and government officials lionized Deming for teaching them how to improve products and services continuously. From his extensive work on errors of management I take three apparently simple claims: (1) systems, not workers are the usual source of failure; (2) fear decreases performance at every level; and (3) "people can face almost any problem except the problems of people" (1982, 85).

To say that systems of interaction are responsible for failure in a manufacturing plant is to say that only poor managers lambaste their workers for poor quality output. Deming says that managers who make this common error fail to note that workers cannot alter the systems in which they find themselves: they can only respond to them as best they can. So too a child raised in an alcoholic home must adapt to an inherently unstable and irrational system of reward and punishment, of shame and hopelessness. We cannot locate the child's subsequent pathology merely within the child's mind. Rather, we must locate the child's behavior in a complex network of reward and punishment, private fantasies, and, often, intergenerational training in pathogenic beliefs. Each of these elements interacts with the child's immediate suffering and anticipated future suffering.

Fear decreases workers' performance because it means that they cannot take chances with new ideas, including those that arise from thousands of interactions they have in their everyday work with actual products and processes. Deming gives hundreds of examples of typical error and oversight in manufacturing where the same problems are reproduced because managers did not bother to ask their employees how to perform their jobs better. On the contrary, just like abusive parents, many old-fashioned bosses and managers use either silly carrots, like "Employee of the Month" awards, or big sticks, like financial threats and demotion, to control their workers. The first device quickly loses its luster since people see through it; the second increases anxiety and this decreases productivity. A drop in productivity, in turn, increases the managers' anxieties that drive them to use even sterner measures and devices.[5]

Deming's third claim is that the problem of managing people and their emotional responses challenges managers more than any other. Faced with these challenges, "people . . . go into a state of paralysis . . ." (85). This drives managers to concoct numerous forms of review and blaming, but since fear often dominates these debates nothing important happens. In sharp contrast, the basic features of Deming's system are to create an environment in which fear does not dominate and in which continuous learning can take place. These two factors make possible an upward cycle of review, assessment, and improvement of the process. Having learned to be on guard as a child, like a soldier on sentry duty, the neurotic patient's first question is not "How are you?" but "Who goes there, friend or foe?" Failure to answer convincingly in the affirmative leads to one deduction: foe. Foes require minimally surveillance and suspicion, and sometimes active hostility.

Further, because pathogenic beliefs operate (unconsciously) like a ruling and timeless ideology, every counter instance in which, say, a person in authority does *not* harm one counts merely as propaganda or false consciousness. No future state of affairs, whether a seemingly benign person, nor utter invalidation of their predictions,

counts against the timelessness of these original truths. Patients under the spell of pathogenic beliefs have no truck with those who
wish to challenge their transcendental insights.

Thus, when they contemplate the collapse of Soviet commu-
nism, some Marxist theoreticians claim that this disaster was merely
the result of *moral* failure. This kind of personalism demarcates pathogenic beliefs typical of children who cannot understand the reasons
for their suffering, except on the grounds of moral fault. Because
their suffering is often designated as punishment, and only "bad"
children deserve punishment, suffering indicates that they are bad.
A similar kind of reasoning appears in religious fundamentalism:
human suffering is a form of punishment from God. Since God would
not do anything unjust, we must deserve the pain we receive.[6] If we
cannot locate sufficient reason for our punishment in our deeds,
then we can locate it in our ancestors' deeds. If that fails, then we
can locate the reason for our suffering in our original parents, Adam
and Eve, whose sins caused God to cast human beings out of Paradise.
Scripture tells us that Eve was more guilty than Adam, for she per-
suaded him to disobey God. From this mythological story fundamentalist theologians have no difficulty deducing that all women (who are
like Eve in that they are female) are less trustworthy than all men.[7]

Assessing the reasonableness of either public or private readings
of an other's intentions requires us to assess the prior issue: what is
the total structure of these external entities, the Soviet Union or,
say, an alcoholic father? Again, as Freud discovered, the psychological calculations that issue in a state of war communiqué occur automatically and unconsciously in a fraction of a second. This means
that the patient *cannot* access the full range of thoughts and feelings
that drive the patient's response. The patient's family and friends
cannot comprehend the instantaneous quality of these subtle and
far-reaching computations. On the contrary, when provoked by the
patient's hostility the patient's family evoke *their* pathogenic beliefs.
Then the old battles begin again.

PUBLIC AND PRIVATE FORMS OF PSYCHOPATHOLOGY:
THE PURSUIT OF PERFECTION

I have discussed Creationism and authoritarian management versus
"Quality" management to indicate how similar they are to an

individual's pathogenic beliefs. We could as well have discussed witchcraft allegations in primitive tribes, the Red Scare in the United States, and other public instances of hysterical allegation. For these events share a common thread: they occur when their participants feel overwhelming anxiety and forsake due process. Due process means that we place our faith in a process of open discernment, critique, and evaluation done in public venues according to public rules. In the ideals of scientific process, of just government, of the open market, and of psychoanalytic discovery we find a shared value: no person stands above the process. In a general sense, this amounts to affirming the Western ideal of the humility of science as prophylaxis against totalitarianism and charismatic excess.

This standard piece of Western thought, hard won through centuries of religious wars and persecutions, means that zeal, conviction, and "faith" have no weight as evidence for or against a particular claim. For example, by citing Darwin and Freud as heroic scientists, it does not follow that they were always correct or that their opinions ought to be sacrosanct. I have noted some of the ways we Freudians can go wrong. Even Darwinians, who identify themselves with the ideal of disinterested, scientific process, can be driven by their anxiety to avoid Creationist political pressures, and minimize problems and anomalies of contemporary Darwinian theory.[8]

The anxiety that drives authoritarian leaders is not induced by shifts in their brain chemistry; it is induced by shifts in their sense of the future. (If a cardiologist tells an elderly patient that he has massive cardiac damage, the patient's resulting depression is not caused by changes in brain chemistry. Rather, the changes in brain chemistry, which correlate with depressive affect, are caused by the change in the patient's beliefs about his future.) The managers whom Deming studied had diverse brains but the same mind: they "knew" that only authoritarian management would work with their employees. Like Creationists and Soviet ideologues, these managers staked everything on their grasp of an unchangeable and permanent truth.

Members of all three groups despise novelty in any form. Each group affirms that there has been one revelation (to Henry Ford, to St. Paul, to Karl Marx) and the contents of that revelation (the law of all against all, Jesus as the Christ, and the labor theory of value) are fundamentally and eternally true. Given this conviction, no new information, say from customers or the marketplace, can alter the content of one's fundamental truths. A traditional joke among predatory males about their dates who reject sexual advances is that "'No' means more beer." In a similar way according to authoritarian management, workers who resist having their pay cut and their hours lengthened need additional education. So too if a "known" witch denies she is a witch this only means that Satan has taught her how to lie as well as cast spells upon her neighbors. When tortured sufficiently to admit her sin she can then be destroyed.

Novelty is dangerous because it always entails the possibility of someone not affirming the Truth of scripture. To guard against this constant danger one must maintain constant vigilance. From the Soviet KGB to the American FBI, police forces are inherently hierarchical and oriented toward dutiful obedience to superior officers. In direct contrast, markets flourish with competition, free trade, and the flow of information from "below" upward. Police forces do not. They depend upon centralized power and they carry out its execution "downward." Police deal perpetually with secrets and they seek perpetually information about dissidents and others who entertain revolutionary ideas.

Thus, police gather data on persons who enact those novel ideas, as the FBI did in its multiyear probe of Martin Luther King, Jr. Police are especially interested in novel ideas that might inspire political groups to reorganize the power base of the police. King deserved to be investigated precisely on these grounds. By claiming civil rights due Blacks under the U.S. Constitution but denied them in practice, King threatened to undo the cozy power relationships that undergirded Jim Crow laws in the South and racist institutions in the North.[9] King became revolutionary and dangerous by claiming rights to due process guaranteed in the transcendental American documents, the Constitution and the Declaration.


## PATHOGENIC BELIEFS, CONVICTIONS, FALLACIOUS RULES, AND PERFECTIONISM

In chapter 1 I noted twelve or thirteen features of the neurotic life. In chapter 2 I suggested that these stem from pathogenic beliefs that result from an impossible assignment: comprehend the mind of others who fail to maintain a good enough emotional environment. In this chapter I have extended this idea to examine parallel public instances of pathogenic beliefs. These public instances illuminate the neurotic life because we see in them modes of thought and convictional experiences that occur in private transactions between children and their caretakers.

Both public and private pathogenic beliefs evolve into fallacious rules. In calling these "rules," I am contrasting them with pathogenic "beliefs" because rules are generally articulated, while beliefs need not be. I described Danny, a boy whose mother died suddenly and whose effort to comprehend his stepmother's suffering engendered five pathogenic beliefs about his role in her life. This number is relatively arbitrary since one might find operative in another patient's story beliefs not evident in Danny's story. When pathogenic beliefs are generalized they become rules of conduct that children like Danny use to guide their interactions.

The first four rules are errors of folk psychology; the fifth is an error of folk information theory:

Rule 1. Everything that happens and that people do is caused by some form of intentionality.

Rule 2. There must be ways to control these intentional, causal agents.

Rule 3. Affects can be controlled by "willpower."

Rule 4. Perfection is a worthy goal and entails controlling affects in self and others.

Rule 5. Novelty is (always) bad.

Each rule shaped Danny's private "theory" of human being and appeared in each of his pathogenic beliefs. In turn, these pathogenic beliefs became "natural" to Danny: they defined the way things are and they appeared to him as unshakable and obvious. What I am calling rules, pathogenic beliefs, and convictional experiences are cognitive aspects of persons' responses to the destruction of what once were "natural" truths and permanent realities:

> Man tends to regard the order he lives in as *natural*. The houses he passes on his way to work seem more like rocks rising out of the earth that like products of human hands. (Milosz [1953] 1990, 25)

Czeslaw Milosz, a renowned Polish poet who won the Nobel Prize in 1980, recorded these reflections of life in Nazi-occupied

Warsaw and then postwar life under Soviet domination. Although he was treated well by USSR standards, Milosz broke with his masters and left Poland in 1951. While his vision of the USSR is similar to that offered by Western commentators, Milosz writes from within the system and offers, therefore, a point of view far more empathic than those afforded outsiders. I cite Milosz's comments about people's conviction that their world is "natural" because, from an analytic point of view, this is exactly what one wishes most people to believe, for "natural" means solid, predictable, and well ordered.

When these beliefs, which are aspects of basic trust, are shattered by war and other atrocities, internal and external catastrophes ensue. Milosz describes a man walking down a street after a bombing raid: "[H]e stops before a house split in half by a bomb, the privacy of the people's homes—the family smells, the warmth of the beehive life, the furniture preserving the memory of loves and hatreds—cut open to public view. The house itself, no longer a rock, but a scaffolding of plaster, concrete, and brick; and on the third floor, a solitary white bathtub, rain-rinsed of all recollection of those who once bathed in it" (26). Matching this external destruction of intimacy and privacy is an internal destruction of old habits, even those about life and death: "Once, had he stumbled upon a corpse on the street, he would have called the police. . . . Now he knows he must avoid the dark body lying in the gutter, and refrain from asking unnecessary questions" (27).

This destruction of a sense of "natural" coherence and stability is complete when, after the military battles stop, the omnipresent state assumes complete control over every aspect of its citizens' lives. With this control comes the seduction of intellectuals who can avoid the anxiety of competing in market economies, which do not allocate public funds for authorized artists: "Since it is not a planned economy, the Western state cannot come to the aid of people working in the various arts" (38).[10] Artists, writers, even critics and other literary workers receive state funds and, in return, are asked only not to challenge the truth of official, scientific, socialism. Since its teachings are, allegedly, logical truths and empirical facts, to challenge them is tantamount to insanity and political suicide. At the very least, one's subsidies would dry up immediately.

While some Eastern artists and intellectuals were no doubt craven, this hardly accounts for the general esteem that so many afforded the official truths of socialism. Milosz illuminates this latter fact when he describes the traumatic origins of Eastern intellectuals' demands for a new form of aesthetics: "The work of human thought should withstand the test of brutal, naked reality. If it cannot, it is worthless. Probably only those things are worth while which can preserve their validity in the eyes of a man threatened with instant death" (41). This dictum, which Milosz carefully circumscribes by adding "probably," captures well a common feature of traumatized individuals: only a method of ego defense that speaks to one's deepest horror merits attention and belief.

With a painterly eye, Milosz recounts what seems an autobiographical moment: "A man is lying under machine-gun fire on a street in an embattled city. He looks at the pavement and sees a very amusing sight: the cobblestones are standing up right like quills on a porcupine. The bullets hitting against their edges displace and tilt them. Such moments in the consciousness of a man *judge* all poets and philosophers" (41, his emphasis). From within horrifying moments these insights emerge as truths that merit constant reiteration. Those who were not lying on streets with bullets flying overhead or stumbling upon corpses or watching their neighbors disappear have no right to challenge the truth of these revelations. This seems almost tautological for, surely, we should not challenge patients' beliefs that their suffering merits our sustained interest?

In Eastern Europe, Milosz says, intellectuals who lived through catastrophes of war and its aftermath, reject what he terms "emotional luxuries" (41) such as psychoanalytic novels, the Western focus upon erotic problems, and religion. In concentration camps and in burned-out cities they saw learned philosophers fight over scraps of bread and elegant bourgeois families hunt for potatoes scavenge amidst corpses. Another intellectual, "Beta," whom the U.S. Seventh Army had liberated from Dachau-Allach, knew, "Since the world is brutal, one must reduce everything to the simplest and most brutal factors" (131). The only rejoinders to utter brutality are to seek utter transformation, and, Beta held, to reject the softheaded nonsense of Jewish-Christian values. Because the Soviet planners made precisely these promises and seemed able to fulfill them, Beta wedded himself to the party's propaganda machine.

While Milosz renders Beta's story and those of others with much skill, we perceive in these accounts errors made by children raised under traumatic conditions and whom we later see in analysis. One error is to argue that people reveal their "true" colors as individuals and groups when under extreme duress. For adult Polish intellectuals, that so many refined and otherwise elite persons perished in the midst of war, and that their values evaporated in the death camps, proves that their prewar values are worthless. In a similar way, abused children discover certain truths about themselves, for example, while cowering in a bedroom closet, hiding from an alcoholic parent. These "truths" become revelatory markers of their true selves, indelible brands of what they really are. From their deepest suffering emerges their innermost being. Thus, many times in *Mein Kampf* (1925) Hitler says that his transformation from petty bourgeoisie into revolutionary thinker occurred through especially "brutal" suffering. Indeed, "brutal" is a word that courses through *Mein Kampf.* In chapter 2, for example, he says, "In this respect Fate was kind to me. By forcing me to return to this world of poverty and insecurity, from which my father had risen in the course of his life, it removed the blinders of a narrow petty-bourgeois upbringing from my eyes. Only now did I learn to know humanity, learning to distinguish between empty appearances or *brutal* externals and the inner being" (Hitler [1925] 1971, 23).

Chief among these blinders are sentiments, self-doubt, and values that depend upon a sense of guilt: "Only when an epoch ceases to be haunted by the shadow of its own consciousness of guilt will it achieve the inner calm and outward strength *brutally* and ruthlessly to prune off the wild shoots and tear out the weeds" (30). This resolve, born in suffering and rage, produces the strength that guarantees survival. Nature, and thus history, herself demands it. As Hitler says, "By thus *brutally* proceeding against the individual and immediately calling him back to herself as soon as he shows himself unequal to the storm of life, [Nature] keeps the race and species strong, in fact, raises them to the highest accomplishments" (131, emphasis mine).

Because truths that originate in suffering and terror are indelible and universal, no new experience can alter them. Indeed, anything, any idea or any person, that threatens to dissuade one from these truths must be denied, or, if required, eradicated. Rule four, "Novelty is bad," thus receives constant support in all totalitarian systems: "Science for science's sake, art for art's sake, are equally abhorrent to the Nazis, our socialist intellectuals, and the communists.

Every activity must derive its justification from a conscious social purpose. There must be no spontaneous, unguided activity, because it might produce results which cannot be foreseen and for which the plan does not provide" (Hayek 1944, 178).

A second error is to agree with the poet lying in the street, watching bullets ricochet off cobblestones, that only artists or politicians who can speak *from* these experiences merit our respect. Mao Tse-tung typically refers to his revolutionary experience and the feelings that war evokes as criteria by which to judge the value of new doctrines. The dread of "revisionism"—an invariable term of totalitarian thinkers—is that the old ways of thought and social intercourse, destroyed in the revolution, might reappear. Since Marx had shown "scientifically" that the rise of the proletariat was inevitable, one might think that revisionism would *recede* as a danger, certainly as the revolution took hold and its benefits became clear to the masses. However, this form of optimism is not typical of communist thinkers. On the contrary, as the horrors of the ancien régime fade away, the original feelings, especially rage, of the revolutionary period also fade. Thus, as the revolution and its fervor fade away the dangers of revisionism increase. Explaining the necessity for ceaseless revolution, Mao said to André Malraux (in 1965):

> What is expressed in that common place term "revisionism" is the death of revolution. What we have just done in the army must be done everywhere. I have told you that the revolution is also everywhere. I have told you that the revolution is also a *feeling*. If we decide to make of it what the Russians are now doing—a feeling of the past—everything will fall apart. Our revolution cannot be simply a stabilization of the past. I am alone with the masses. Waiting.[11]

Mao aligned himself with the fervor of radical youth for it alone gives him hope of perpetual revolution against complacency and other evils of institutional life, especially stabilization. These evils stem from softheartedness and other moral failures. Indeed, throughout communist writings are constant citations of horrors, injustice, and suffering—of the working classes—which must be remembered else current party members fall into complacency and forgetfulness. Thus, when Khrushchev and other Soviet communists of the 1960s sought peaceful coexistence with the West they were correctly (according to Marxist scriptures) accused of revisionism and forgetfulness. Mao and other Chinese communists denounced them for forgetting that class war is violent war.

Comrade Mao Tse-tung said:

> [R]evolutions and revolutionary wars are inevitable in class society and . . . in their absence no leap in social development can be accomplished, the reactionary ruling classes cannot be overthrown and the people cannot win political power. (322)

He stated:

> The seizure of power by armed force, the settlement of the issue by war, is the central task and the highest form of revolution. This Marxist-Leninist principle of revolution holds good universally, for China and for all other countries. (1963, 267)

He stated further:

> Experience in the class struggle in the era of imperialism teaches us that it is only by the power of the gun that the working class and the labouring masses can defeat the armed bourgeoisie and landlords; in this sense we may say that only with guns can the whole world be transformed. (273)[12]

These dicta, which permeate Stalinist and Maoist discourse, grant to trauma and horror an ontological status *superior* to joy and love. They wind the core of person's or a group's identity around its worst suffering, its nightmarish realities. While we do not doubt the reality of intense suffering, we may doubt its ontological standing as a "thing" around which persons can weave a substantial identity. To the deep question—"Who am I?"—there must be *more* than a long narration of suffering. In saying this I may seem callous. I hope I am not callous and can be clear.

To return to the issue of individuals, when patients who come from brutal homes affirm this belief—that they are defined by their suffering—they make themselves despise the core of their own being, a core that is *not* one of hatred and "brutality." Hence, Milosz says that his friend, Beta, was an especially gifted writer but chose to debase himself by writing hack propaganda pieces for the regime: "His mind, like that of so many Eastern intellectuals, was impelled toward self-annihilation" (1953, 131). A few years later he asphyxiated himself.

## PERFECTIONISM AND "RULES" OF ANALYSIS

In ordinary psychoanalytic practice the patient's accidents, errors, and slips become interesting when they seem motivated by nonconscious factors. As part of his general heuristic method Freud insisted upon examining parapraxes, for example, as clues to his patients' hidden wishes (Freud 1901b). This technical requirement means that when a patient overpays us, for example, we wonder why. If we happen to forget a patient's name, psychoanalytic technique requires us to free associate and try to discover what *might* have motivated our forgetting. This requirement seems identical to Rule 1: Everything that happens or that people do is meaningful and "caused" by some form of intentionality.

But we do not also assert that *every* variation in a patient's behavior is motivated and demands analytic scrutiny. This would produce quickly an obsessional stalemate. If a patient arrives for a 9:00 A.M. appointment at 8:58 one morning and 9:01 the next should we demand to know why this discrepancy? Obviously not, since to arrive at exactly 9:00 A.M. each morning would require exact obedience on the patient's part and this slavish obedience would be another form of resistance.

As usual, the standard analytic value is balance and openness to novelty, not a robotic obedience to "rules." For example, Ralph Greenson in a much-cited article, describes a patient who had had six years of analysis with another therapist:

> When I requested information, he often answered by free association so that the result was bizarre. For example, when I asked him what his middle name was he answered: "Raskolnikov," the first name that occurred to him. When I recovered my composure and questioned this he defended himself by saying that he thought he was supposed to free associate. I soon gained the impression that this man had never really established a working relation with his first analyst. (1965, 160)[13]

Analytic values, like "free association" and Greenson's notion of the working alliance, cannot be realized through obsessive attention to exactitude that ignores the ebb and flow of ordinary variations. Hence, for every technical admonition that affirms one rule, such as "Attend to the patient's feelings first," is another that affirms a counter rule, such as "Have no hard and fixed rules" about the process of analysis itself. Implicit in these apparently contradictory teachings is an analytic value, enunciated by Freud and subsequently by all major theoreticians, namely, that psychoanalysis is a process of discovery. Over a long time and through multiple errors and corrections we try to comprehend the patient's experience of the patient's worlds: body, self, others, and the "real world." This mission rests upon a profound Freudian value that is essentially religious: the conviction that human beings, by definition, are of infinite worth and that spending hundreds of hours listening to them, welcoming negative and positive transferences, is a valid use of intellectual resources.

To establish and endorse a process of discovery as preeminent means that its participants, patient and analyst, or scientist and colleagues, or voters and prime minister, abide by a set of rules that govern the process, not the *outcome* of any particular exchange.[14] Thus, not knowing the outcome or which side will win means that democratic elections, as when the British booted out Winston Churchill following his great victory over the Nazis, are not necessarily "rational" or moral in a perfectionistic sense. In contrast, communist "elections" are always rational in the sense that we know precisely who will win before the votes are counted. Those who adhere to the unshakable moral truths of the dispossessed and the victimized, that is, those who remember the horrors of the past and retain its emotional intensity, merit permanent reelection.

Those who forget or, worse, forgive past wrongs are backsliders and revisionists: they merit excoriation and perhaps prison. A middle ground, that is, a genuine sense of past horrors and the capacity to forgive denotes another Freudian value: mourning. For mourning is another process of recollection, experience, and sorrow. To mourn is to locate suffering in a specific time, the "past," and to recognize it as separate from the present. For those who have not yet mourned, this seems impossible, a betrayal of those who suffered.

Czeslaw Milosz addressed this task in two recent poems. One celebrates human pleasures the way John Keats or William Wordsworth might, the second attacks those who merely celebrate joy and forget the horrors undergone by so many: "The two poems placed here together contradict each other. *The first* renounces any dealing with problems which for centuries have been tormenting the minds of theologians and philosophers; it chooses a moment and the beauty of the earth as observed on one of the Caribbean islands. *The second*, just the opposite, voices anger because people do not want to remember, and live as if nothing happened, as if horror were not hiding just beneath the surface of their social arrangements." Through the act of writing Milosz makes public our limitations as human beings. We want to know the "laws of history," including our individual stories, and we want to believe that someone, whether Danny's parents or Chairman Mao, knows these essential truths, indeed, knows how to transcend these contradictory features of human experience.

The cost of this transcendence, a demonic reversion to hero worship and the cult of personality, is inevitable because by claiming to have mastered the Laws of History, totalitarian thought organizes all individuals toward a single pole, the lodestar, the Center. Against this inexorable conclusion, traditional Jewish and Christian teachings about God affirm our irreducible strangeness from one another and ourselves: "Transcendence is the relation that relieves men of having to be everything for each other. . . . They no longer have to fight so anxiously for their identity, because they are now allowed to believe that God truly knows them."[15]

# CHAPTER 4

# Pathogenic Beliefs, Perfectionism, and the Production of Psychopathology

## PATHOGENIC BELIEFS, PRIMARY EMOTIONS, AND PERFECTIONISM

The objects of psychoanalysis, I have suggested, are beliefs and feelings that interact in such ways that patients cannot learn from numerous painful encounters. Typical of the mental suffering that psychoanalysts confront is that patients feel doomed to repeat actions, especially emotional relationships with others, that they recognize will produce suffering. In the previous chapter I narrowed my discussion to focus upon pathogenic beliefs since this gave us a useful way to integrate some parts of contemporary analytic theory with contemporary cognitive theory. I now expand the discussion to include contemporary analytic theories of emotions (or affects). Clinicians of every stripe have long known that psychopathology entails both faulty cognition (including beliefs) and misaligned feelings (or affects or emotions).

Therapist-generated insights, when they are correct descriptions of a patient's beliefs, by themselves are not sufficient to change a patient's pathology. Similarly, reliving painful affects without insight merely repeats the patient's everyday suffering. In the language of classical analysis, the goal of an intensive and reconstructive therapy experience is to establish, then cure the transference neurosis. This designates a reenactment in which infantile (pathogenic) beliefs coincide with intense emotional experience. As Freud says, we cannot cure neurosis in effigy; we must permit patients to enact fully their deepest emotional convictions that we (as therapists) are distressing persons from their past with whom they must struggle.

129

In agreement I have stressed the interpersonal dimension of the genesis of pathogenic beliefs. Regarding my patient, Danny, I suggested that some pathogenic beliefs derive from intense interactions between parents and children in which children attempt to comprehend and to control their parents' moods to the degree those moods frighten and disorganize them. They do so not out of intellectual curiosity but to prevent further suffering by themselves and by their parents. Describing typical beliefs that evolve from such encounters, I named five fallacious rules. These were:

Rule 1. Everything that happens and that people do is caused by some form of intentionality.

Rule 2. There must be ways to control these intentional, causal agents.

Rule 3. Affects can be controlled by "willpower."

Rule 4. Perfection is a worthy goal and entails controlling affects in self and others.

Rule 5. Novelty is (always) bad.

There are numerous transformations of these rules. For example, parents may cite their version of the New Testament and decide that children should act in a "godly" fashion, here defined as acting like Jesus is said to have acted (Rule 4). Another set of parents may declare, "What was good enough for Jesus is good enough for them," meaning that to learn something new about oneself or other people is an affront to God and general human decency (Rule 5). Another transformation is contradiction. To select a nonreligious example, some parents idealize current psychological theories and affirm the contrary of Rule 5, asserting that novelty is *always* good. Below I cite other transformations in beliefs typical of dissociative patients who manifest so-called multiple personality disorder (MPD).

This brings us back to my earlier questions about the objects of psychoanalysis: what are they? To put this into concrete terms, what size are our objects? What are their boundaries and their limits? Where are they located? A neurosurgeon operates upon a human being seeking in the patient's body the tumor that presses upon the patient's spinal cord. The tumor has a certain mass and reality. When the tumor is removed, we hope that the patient is cured. In this standard medical account, cause, effect, and cure are aligned temporally and we feel comfortable with the claim that this is a moment of scientific medicine. What is the mass and reality of psychic tumors?

I suggest an answer in this chapter. In brief, I will suggest that the objects of analysis are pathogenic beliefs (PB), which arise in response to errors by both parents and children in the regulation of children's intense, primary affects. Primary affects are complex bio-logical-psychological events that occur within a person and which have a typical shape or activation contour (Stern 1985). A typical affect event has a shape, a curve of intensity that builds up slowly, then rises faster and faster, is satiated, and subsides. The good enough parent (or therapist) perceives this activation contour arise in the child (or patient), permits it to unfold, and then permits the child (or patient) to resolve it slowly. Because the curve of primary affects is a real thing, a tangible series of bodily experiences, it cannot be digitized. That is, like other real things and real experiences, affect curves are not merely ideas or concepts or verbal entities that can be named and replaced with their logical equivalents or by quantifiable measures. On the contrary, affect curves are best communicated through *analogue* devices like those available in poetic metaphor or dramatic action.[1] (And for this reason poetry and religious discourse are always metaphorical, a topic we take up in the next chapter.)

Analogue communications are direct, structurally determined evocations of the shape of the original affective experience. In a famous poem, Sylvia Plath says about her deceased father, "At twenty I tried to die / And get back, back, back to you."[2] These lines communicate complex affects of anger, unrequited love, identification with the dead father, and loss through the analogue devices of slant rhyme, rhythm, and beat. A reductive, verbal interpretation of the poem's lines might be "She has mixed feelings about her father's death." This is a digital, abstracting rendition and does not evoke emotional intensity. We can translate verbal artifacts like this abstract interpretation from English into a foreign language with no loss of semantic values. The meaning of this particular interpretation is reducible fully and therefore might be translated into another language because the interpretation has no poetic or artistic merit. It has no value as an analogue to the poem's artistic force. (To say I want "one half" of an apple pie is exactly equivalent to saying I want "50 percent" of the said pie: the two expressions are logically identical and therefore fully exchangeable with one another.)

Pathogenic beliefs, I will suggest, are like these abstract interpretations of the meaning of Plath's poetry. They are the child's reductive attempts to digitize the activation contours of the child's strongest emotions. Because *no one* can effectively digitize affects, these maneuvers fail: the child's sense of danger and disorganization increases. When these failures occur many times over, as they always do in a child's life marked by empathic failures and inverted self-object relationships, they inculcate a dread of affective life. Hence, the poverty of neurotic life typically includes instinctual anxiety as defined in Freud's later theory of signal anxiety: any upsurge of a particular, internal sensation associated with disorganizing affects evokes anticipation of suffering and realistic fear *(Realangst)*.[3] Joy is a strong, affect-laden experience. It cannot occur in the presence of intense anxiety. Freud challenges one of his own theorems, his dearly held theory that repression causes anxiety and then rejects it: "It was anxiety which produced repression and not, as I formerly believed, repression which produced anxiety" (1926d, 109).

With pathogenic beliefs firmly in place, children in these circumstances assign themselves the impossible task of controlling their parents' moods. Of course, every so often it appears that by being especially good, for example, a little girl can cause her father to stop drinking. These intermittent successes naturally affirm the child's sense of her mission and its plausibility: "I really can make daddy better." When he begins drinking the next day or the next week the little girl plunges back into her task and reaffirms her destiny: "I am one who serves, when dad is cured (again) I can go on with my life." For example, the little girl in this story may find a way to leave her drunken father by becoming a drug-addicted prostitute whom he boots out of the house. Or she may fulfill her parents' expectations like the heroine in the film *Looking for Mister Goodbar* (1977) whose sexual recklessness made her death likely. Or she might marry a man who is even sicker than her father, attempt to transform him, and under the guise of this new ministry leave home. Alternatively, she might find a profession that pays her little money, is dangerous, and requires her to rescue alcoholic men. It is this sense of her destiny, of her life's mission, that generates despair. To lessen her despair she may chance upon a dozen modes of defense that temporarily ameliorate her pain. These behavioral styles unite with her despair to form a way of life that psychiatrists label a disease, for example, a masochistic character structure, which may drive her to seek therapy.

## PATHOGENIC BELIEFS AND AFFECTS:
## PB AS COGNITIVE MAPS

In his account of multiple personality disorders (MPD), Colin Ross (1989)[4] cites cognitive behavioral theories of the genesis of psychopathology. Relying primarily upon psychoanalytic texts, especially the work of Weiss and Sampson (1986), I have made similar comments about pathogenic beliefs. Common to both literatures is the concept that patients' beliefs about their primary relationships are causally related to their psychopathology. I have followed this line of reasoning and suggested that these beliefs shape the objects of analysis. Ross, who is sharply critical of psychoanalysis in general, summarizes his extensive work with MPD patients' beliefs in a section he labels "The Cognitive Map of Multiple Personality Disorder" (125). He uses the term "map" in at least two ways. The first denotes the charting he does to keep track of a patient's different selves (the patient's alters) and their stories. The second denotes the organization of what he terms eight core assumptions typical of MPD patients.

Strictly speaking, neither of these is a map. On the one hand, the chart of a patient's stories is not a map if we mean by that an iconic (analogue) and rule-bound representation of one entity by another. Rather Ross's charts sum up his patients' lengthy narratives and plotlines. Given that his form of therapy of persons labeled MPD requires hundreds of hours, summaries of patient narratives are necessarily briefer than complete transcriptions. As plot summaries, we might assess these maps as representative of those stories. But we have no independent evidence that they map the actual history of a patient's life. Indeed, to call these summaries maps prejudges the veracity of these stories. Like the term "memory," which appears constantly in Ross's text and similar accounts of MPD,[5] the term "map" presumes these accounts of various parts of the self, the alleged alters, are accurate renditions of the patient's actual experiences. The evidence for MPD is decidedly mixed.[6] Given the vagaries of memory, the fantastic elements of many of these stories, and notorious problems of validating the historical accuracy of these accounts, we cannot agree that plot summaries map anything other than patients' fantasies.

On the other hand, Ross's summary of typical beliefs, which parallels the five rules I name above, is valuable to any clinician working with persons prone to describe themselves as divided or multiple. Ross says these eight items name the "guiding beliefs that appear to underlie and drive the disorder" (125). This is a very strong claim that he modifies correctly with the verb "appear." It is strong because it entails a theory of causality and hence cure: patients diagnosed as MPD manifest symptoms caused by beliefs generated out of intense suffering and abuse. These beliefs drive them to create alter personalities. To undo this, consequence therapy requires therapist and patient to investigate the alleged life history of each alter.

| *Ross's Patients* | *Ordinary Psychological Terms* |
|---|---|
| 1. Different parts of the self are separate selves. | Divisions of the mind |
| 2. The victim is responsible for the abuse. | Theory of personal causality |
| 3. It is wrong to show anger (or frustration). | Theory of personal causality |
| 4. The past is present. | Theory of temporality |
| 5. The primary person can't handle the memories. | Theory of ego strength |
| 6. I love my parents but she hates them. | Theory of unity of the self |
| 7. The primary personality must be punished. | Theory of moral life and causality |
| 8. I can't trust myself or others (126–27). | Theory of future ego capacity |

Each of these beliefs is a prototheory of cause and effect relationships that hold between the patient's emotions and their effects upon others. For example, beliefs three, seven, and eight are generalizations about the trustworthiness of other people based upon the patient's prior experiences. Of these prototheories, perhaps the most surprising is the sixth. For on the surface, patients labeled MPD seem to demonstrate that the self can be fragmented so that one part has one set of feelings, like love, and another part has another set, like hate. However, as Richard Gottlieb (1997) notes about a patient many might label "MPD," one can conceive of MPD pathology not as the product of subpersonalities inhabiting one body, but as a prior fantasy of unity: "*It is possible* for me to be more than one person, to stand apart from myself, to be at once 'Me' and 'him'" (914, emphasis in original). This sense of self is deeper and more primary than those proffered in the manifest claims of MPD. For each of the alters, etc., with its own history, depends upon the executive, creative functioning of a directorial ego rather as the alters who populate Shakespeare's plays depend upon his genius. Standard texts on dissociation, hypnoid states, double consciousness, and the like are pre-Freudian (or non-Freudian) because they refuse to follow Freud's road, to triangulate the nature of the unconscious ego by assessing its manifestations.[7]

In this chapter I revert back to contemporary child psychiatry and to child psychoanalysis to understand better person to person interactions, between parent and infant and patient and therapist, from which pathogenic beliefs *derive*. We can agree that pathogenic beliefs are related to psychopathology, but, again, these beliefs are not maps in a strict sense. That is, pathogenic beliefs are not formally related to fixed causes nor to some original objects or experiences from which they derive. Consistent with my previous discussion, I find it useful to consider to what degree pathogenic beliefs are *intermediate* causes of psychopathology.

First, as I suggested above, most people have an assortment of beliefs about the mind and causation that, when examined by rigorous logicians, yields a tangled web of error, folk psychology, inconsistency, and the like. Yet, for all these logical and cognitive errors, normal people do not manifest psychopathology. Second, we find that depressed people say depressive things about themselves, and that a good deal of therapy consists in examining those self-representations—as Freud noted some eighty years ago in "Mourning and melancholia" (1917e). Yet, the presence of negative self-representations in depressed persons does not prove that these negative self-representations cause depression.

Persons with manic-depressive illness, for example, report, often with exquisite nuance, how puzzling it is to feel their mood lifted by their medications and then discover that their self-images have also improved. Negative self-representations coincide with depression and their absence seems a good sign that the patient is getting better, but they may be no more than concomitant signs of another process that issues in depressive affects. I know certainly that I shall die someday but this unhappy goal of life does not render me depressed. At an extreme, we note that some Christian saints may describe themselves with extremely negative language yet also speak of their joy in leading a Christian life. So too, religious doctrines, like the Christian notion of original sin, affirm utterly negative evaluations of a person's self yet do not necessarily produce depressive affect.

Why not? What is the difference between a flood of negative self-representations that occur in a depressed patient and those that course through the lives of a saint or, indeed, anyone who puts aside infantile narcissism? One way to answer this question is to review case histories of analytic patients and attempt to draw some useful conclusions. In the next section I consider two patients, one contemporaneous and unknown, the other from ninety years ago and famous, enshrined as Freud's patient whom he named Rat Man.

## Mr. N. and Rat Man; Pathogenic Beliefs as Intermediate Causes

In a recently published case history, Judith M. Chertoff (1989) describes a male patient who formed an intense, negative father transference to her. Chertoff emphasizes her patient's negative oedipal responses to her as competitor and thus father, which proves that at least some male patients can develop a full-scale, paternal transference neurosis toward their female analysts. I find this persuasive. Her language, classical Freudian, and her use of its concepts, especially the notion of transference neurosis, clarify the case history. I note two key elements in this transference neurosis. First is her patient's fundamental impression (belief) that his father could not abide his competitive feelings toward him. Second was the boy's belief that the intensity of his feelings would harm his father and anyone else who occupied a similar role (Chertoff 1989, 692–93).

Like others ruined by success (Freud 1916d), Mr. N had paradoxical responses to any semblance of increased happiness and nearing a goal: "[H]is excitement and happiness often precipitated anxiety and a sense of impending doom. His difficulty with competitive feelings toward me, as the father who he felt had been excessively threatened by his capacity, was often disguised by his more conscious rivalry with his sisters" (Chertoff 1989, 693).

Mr. N perceived that his father was uneasy about the boy's intense emotional states, especially when they revealed the boy's narcissistic yearnings for recognition and status. In response to these accurate perceptions, I think, Chertoff's patient experienced his narcissistic feelings as dangerously "out of control." For the lesson inflicted by his father's uneasiness (or downright hostility) was that at the first hint of such feelings (narcissistic tensions) from within himself the boy must guard against their public emergence: "For example, when we examined his anxious reaction to expressing any awareness of his increased effectiveness, his associations led first to concerns about overpowering his little sisters. . . . He described his need to be "ever so careful," because criticisms of analysis "could blow you away. That's my father," he said; "it seems like death" (693).

Like many patients, Mr. N became especially cautious at the end of the analytic hour because he feared being caught in the middle of a strong feeling, especially love for the analyst, which might not resolve within the hour. This repeats his and other patients' common experience of being caught in the midst of strong feelings that they or their parents aborted, often because the parent became alarmed at the intensity of the child's affects. Chertoff's patient "described his fear of feeling 'cut off,' and remembered the times, in childhood, when he had been hurried out of the bathtub (now associated with masturbation) to make room for a younger sister. In addition, he recalled that, after father's stroke, he had had to stoop down to help father in and out of his chair. We soon clarified the temporal connection between this event and the onset of his obsessional symptoms" (693–94). Naturally, a phrase like "being cut off" has a host of psychosexual associations, including castration, and other attacks upon the boy's sexual life. These concerns are present, I think, but do not exclude the typical feature of these stories: that the boy and his father cannot tolerate his expressing or having *any* intense feeling, including sexual excitement, that escapes control.

These intense encounters with his extremely needy father naturally found expression in a somatic idiom, in this case the boy's hernia (which has, again, a somatic echo to the boy's worry about his genitals and their vulnerability [694]). Normal, unavoidable erections frightened the boy. Erections occur in boys and men as unbidden awakenings of emotional interest. For many adolescent boys erections are potentially embarrassing for they reveal that the boy is out of control and they broadcast his most private thoughts. To have strong feelings is like your guts falling out. This idea derives from what were probably hundreds of interactions with his father (and other adults) who actively trained the boy in this mode of anxiety and hyper-alertness.

That the boy's father, like Rat Man's father, indulged in rage attacks does not prove that Chertoff's patient wished to mimic these. On the contrary, these every-so-often rage attacks by the boy's father became another form of emotional education: "See, even I, your father, cannot be passionate without falling into frightening and chaotic behaviors." In a standard all-or-nothing response to strong feelings, the lesson is that one either restricts fully an emotional state or it overwhelms one. It is not surprising that Chertoff's patient abhorred the idea of having children since he understood, again correctly, that he did not know how to treat children except as his father treated him.

A parallel anxiety about the power of his erotic emotions and their destructiveness centered upon the boy's heterosexual yearnings:

> For example, a dream in which he stole the Torah from a Temple and pursued an adventurous course was followed by one in which he was fighting to keep the devil from getting out of the television set, and a session in which he experienced himself as a "blob of jelly." When I interpreted his need to make himself a blob to avoid seeming "dangerously attractive" (his words) to me, thereby keeping the devil in check, he responded by revealing his recent fantasies about what it would be like to be married to a psychiatrist. (696)

I like this passage because it denotes the gravity of this man's suffering: to pursue his life's goals is tantamount to attacking the holiest item in his father's religion, the Law, the essence of Judaism. His associations to the devil also depict an utterly uncanny power that contends with God (the father). His wish to be big and strong is, he believes, equivalent to the wish to overthrow righteousness with Evil. To reveal another common wish, to marry the analyst or at least be sexual with the analyst, is so dangerous that he must reduce himself to mere jelly, a harmless, phallus-less stuff.

## RAT MAN AND "THE FEAR OF VIOLENCE OF HIS OWN RAGE"

In a similar way, we might add a note to Freud's discussion of the "omnipotence of thought" evidenced in his famous patient whom he nicknamed "Rat Man" (Freud 1909d). Rat Man exhibited perfectionistic demands when he described events in which he tried to assess the influence of his wishes upon the lives of other people. Freud recounts two occurrences in which his patient's wishes seemed to be validated. In the first, he believed that by hating an old man who had thwarted his sexual wishes he had caused his death. In the second, he believed that by withholding love (and sexual response) from a woman he had caused her suicide. Freud ascribes these instances of the omnipotence of thought to the "megalomania of infancy." I suggest that a part of the omnipotence derives from his encounters with his father and father's mind.[8]

Freud says the precipitating *cause* of Rat Man's adult neurosis was his conflict "as to whether he should remain faithful to the lady he loved in spite of her poverty, or whether he should follow in his father's footsteps and marry the lovely, rich, and well-connected girl who had been assigned to him" (1909d, 198). Freud concludes that Rat Man resolved this dilemma by falling ill and that this "flight into illness was made possible by identifying himself with his father" (199 n. 1). The conflict was, we are told, between love for one woman and "the persisting influence of his father's wishes" (199). By adopting obsessional habits Rat Man could postpone his education, postpone entering adult life, and thus postpone the task of choosing one of the two women. At first glance, it is puzzling that following in his father's footsteps, a common enough event, would precipitate Rat Man's obsessional neurosis.

Freud's solution to this puzzle was to trace back this adult incident to the patient's oedipal past, to an ancient struggle between his "amatory" wishes and his father who, we learn, once beat Rat Man for something naughty the boy had done. In response to this beating follows a famous exchange: the furious little boy calls his father names of common objects, since he knew no adult swear words, and the father "shaken by such an outburst of elemental fury, had stopped beating him, and had declared: 'The child will be either a great man or a great criminal!'" (205). This scene, Freud tells us, made a permanent impression upon both the boy and his father who never beat him again. Yet from that time on the boy "was a coward—out of fear of the violence of his own rage" (206).

I take this complex sentence to mean that Freud believes the little boy experienced this episode as a turning point since it seemed to show that if he felt hostile and angry he could erupt into a tirade.

This tirade, the expression of the full range of his anger, was dangerous because it was powerful enough to control his father. For his earlier tirade had troubled his large, soldierly father sufficiently to make him stop beating the boy and to utter his oracular prediction. This (omnipotent) prediction of the little boy's future marks him, again, as uncannily dangerous.[9] Proclaimed by his beloved and idealized father this speech looks into the future when the boy shall choose either good (and become a great man) or evil (and become a great criminal). Seeing his large, manly, idealized father blanch at the intensity of the boy's anger proved to the boy that *no one* could tolerate the full expression of his feelings. Freud records that the boy henceforth acted like a coward, since any other response might call forth his rage and his rage would precipitate disaster.

Like Chertoff's patient, Rat Man became obsessively careful about the expression of any affects that threatened to get out of hand. Since many of these linked sexuality and ambition to his feelings about his father and his overestimation of his wishes, he became scrupulous, especially about achievements and intense feelings tied to sexuality. That Freud had to put up with numerous negative transference encounters supports his general claim that his patient was deathly afraid of expressing any feelings tainted with competition and ambition. The "painful road of transference" (209) revealed Rat Man's continuous anxiety about his capacity for aggression and his belief that given sufficient provocation he could and would harm Freud: "He recalled that his father had had a passionate temper, and sometimes in his violence had *not known* where to stop" (209, emphasis mine). I emphasize this last phrase because it denotes the boy's intense, and accurate, perception that his father could not always contain his own anger. Because, as Freud says, the boy identified with his father, he also identified with this deficit. The boy concluded, reasonably enough, that both he and his father were dangerous persons whose temper and other passionate outbursts could lead to unforgivable actions.[10]

Even given my narrow reading of these cases, we do not yet know why these efforts to control the expression of intense affects, like anger, pride, or hatred, should cause neurotic conflicts. For surely all children have to learn self-control? Many or most children have strong feelings yet few become as obsessional as the Rat Man or as disturbed as Chertoff's patient. Freud reflected upon this question and offered a partial answer. His patient, like other obsessional patients, overestimated the power of his hostile feelings "because a large part of their internal mental effects escaped his conscious knowledge. His love—or rather his hatred—was in truth overpowering; it was precisely they that created the obsessional thoughts . . ." (238–39).

In brief, Freud offers a metapsychological explanation, drawing upon libido theory (238–39): intense love and intense hatred coexist in an unconscious state where they are "split apart and one of them, usually the hatred, have [*sic*] been repressed" (239). Owing perhaps to a biological propensity, the child's innate sadistic components are especially strong. These impel such children and adults to develop reaction formations and to repress (or displace or split off) sadistic impulses that derive from these original components. When intense love and intense hatred coincide, as in Rat Man's story, the result is stasis, a paralysis of the will that typifies obsessional neurotics.

Problems with this metapsychology derive from general criticisms of libido theory and from specific aspects of this case. If the sadistic impulses are "innate" and fixed at the level of character, how can mere talking change anything? Why would "working through" have any effects upon drives that Freud says are inherent and unchanging? If the Rat Man's propensity to obsessive actions is primarily a product of extra strong sadistic components, why would psychoanalysis help cure him? Compare curing him of his fascination with attacks upon the father's anus with his innate need to drink liquids: the first yielded to analysis, the latter, we would guess, could not.

That psychoanalysis is the deconstruction of false and pathogenic beliefs does not mean that we supply patients with replacements, with valid beliefs that are scientifically rigorous and philosophically pristine. For there are none of those available, thus far. Hence, cure cannot mean merely that we replace our patients' faulty beliefs about the mind with scientific theory: rather, we replace a systematic error with a more open-ended, rough and ready orientation toward their emotional lives. We attempt to deconstruct their wishes and claims to have fabricated a paranoid completeness. We try to find ways for them and us to tolerate their strongest feelings. The "school of suffering" designates this essential part of transferences as reenactment and repair. Like the hero or heroine caught in the evil count's castle, at midnight when evil has its fullest power, we summon up ghosts and live through the full range, the full expression of their (and our) terrors.

## PRIMARY AFFECTS, ACTIVATION CONTOURS, PERFECTIONISM

A common, if not universal, neurotic belief is that there must be ways to control fully strong affects in oneself and other people. This belief in a perfect response is a central target of therapy not because it is conceptually false, but because it becomes a way of life that is painful and makes joy impossible.

To outsiders, neurotic beliefs are obviously wrong, yet neurotic persons find their beliefs validated constantly. For example, to outsiders Rat Man appeared to be an intelligent and happy man destined to lead a fine life. However, to Freud he revealed a life lived in torment. How might we understand this difference? Rather than ascribe a wholly different mentality to neurotic persons it seems useful to see how these beliefs arose and how they are validated in their adult, everyday worlds. This requires us to imagine ourselves living from within their moment to moment and day by day experiences. More specifically, we try to imagine how they respond to their strongest emotions and why they seem to fear them so much.

To pursue this idea I assume that there are primary emotions similar to those named in Charles Darwin's famous study, *The Expression of the Emotions in Man and Animals* (1872).[11] Following Darwin, psychologists and developmentalists have claimed that human beings share a species-wide repertoire of emotional expressions, and, we assume, emotional experiences. Darwin named fear, surprise, anger, disgust, sadness/grief, and happiness or joy. Contemporary biologists and developmental psychologists, like Ekman, Sorenson, and Friesen (1969) have supported Darwin's claim about these basic categories by examining non-Western, preliterate cultures.

Quite fascinating are findings by Paul Ekman and his collaborators,[12] who compared the emotional responses of Japanese and Americans to watching stress-inducing films. When observed secretly the two groups manifested similar emotional responses to the films. When asked, face to face, about their feelings the Japanese group appeared to mask feelings they felt were inappropriate: "The Japanese appeared to have masked their negative feelings by politely smiling. Slow motion video tape analysis showed the micromomentary occurrence of characteristic negative emotional expressions, and then showed them being replaced with a polite smile" (Griffiths 1997, 53). I appreciate Griffiths's emphasis upon the rapidity of this shift, which he says occurs in a micro moment. For this suggests that (1) Japanese like all other human beings share an ancestral set of affects, (2) they have learned to perceive their expression of these affects in a tiny fraction of a second, and (3) they adjust their expression of negative affects depending upon their social environments. When they believed no one observed them they felt and showed negative affects. When the Japanese subjects knew the interviewers were observing their facial expressions they evoked a part of their conceptual repertoire of secondary affective expression, the polite smile, to mask that primary emotion.

To put this more broadly, Ekman's data suggests that human beings are inherently structured to experience these six primary emotions. Their secondary responses to these primary emotions are conditioned by social and interpersonal learning. This fits precisely my earlier comments about Rat Man and the other patients discussed above. For there we saw that we can account for much of Rat Man's anxiety about competing with other men, for example, with his father and with Freud, by noting how profoundly he "learned his lesson" about expressing anger, a primary emotion. In similar encounters, where a titanic, much loved and much feared, parent inscribes a lesson about inappropriate affect upon a child the result is a deeply embedded anxiety response to any expression of the same affect later.

Agreeing that there are *primary* emotions does not rule out another *secondary* class of emotions as wholly dependent upon cultural learning, as constructed, in this sense. Primary emotions can be hypercognized or hypocognized (Griffiths 1997, 160–67): "Roughly this means that people talk about them more, or talk about them less" (160). For example, if we say that Japanese are typically trained to feel shame about expressing fear in public encounters then shame counts as a secondary emotion. Saying this does not mean that shame has less importance than fear. On the contrary, shame and guilt, to name two standard secondary emotions, may motivate all kinds of actions, ranging from altruism to suicide. To the degree they signify one's obedience to a cultural norm, manifesting secondary emotions also signifies one's primary social identity, for example, as "Japanese."

I assume that children must confront their own primary emotions and those of people near them the same way all humans must confront gravity and eventually, perhaps when they grow up, death. That is, these primary affects are real things in the way that the need to breathe, eat, and confront sexuality are real things. They occur universally and automatically. They cannot be imagined away and they are not culture specific. Primary affects derive from a common biological and evolutionary heritage.

## ACTIVATION CONTOURS, VITALITY AFFECTS, FEELINGS

Activation contour is an idea I import from Daniel Stern's major studies of infancy (1977, 1985) and the development of self. An activation contour is the general pattern of a rise in emotional intensity, a series of vitality affects, which issues in satisfaction and relief. It is an observable series of behaviors, with associated internal experiences, in which an infant (or child or adult) carries out a more or less fixed routine. For example, an infant learns to suck its thumb:

> The infant initially moves his hand toward the mouth in a poorly coordinated, loosely directed, jerky manner. The entire pattern—thumb-to-mouth—is an intrinsically motivated, species-specific behavioral pattern that tends to completion and smooth functioning as the goals. During the initial part of a successful trial, while the thumb is getting closer but is not yet in the mouth, the pattern is incomplete and there is increased arousal. When the thumb finally finds its way into the mouth, there is a falloff in arousal, because the pattern is consummated and "smooth functioning" of sucking (an already consolidated schema) takes over. (1985, 59)

Stern describes six features of the baby's emotional behavior that the mother could "match" or "attune" to. He emphasizes the *mother's response* to these six dimensions. I wish to emphasize how each of these dimensions reflects an internal event for the baby and so constitutes an "emotional" scaler for that baby. These six dimensions are:

1. Absolute intensity of behavior, e.g., loudness
2. Intensity contour: changes in intensity over time

3. Temporal beat: a regular pulse is matched
4. Rhythm: set of unequal pulsations is matched
5. Duration: the time span is matched
6. Shape: spatial qualities of the action are matched

(1985, 146–47)

Each of these categories uses an abstract name to designate an intensely felt experience evident in both baby and mother (and often shared by the observers as well). Attunement occurs when the mother plays with her baby, when she matches the shape of her baby's emotional state. It does not occur when she mimics her baby's actions. Matching between baby and mother is often cross modal. For example, a parent's voice rises and falls as the baby's level of exertion rises and falls. Stern notes that attunement is not mimicry, nor matching "the other person's behavior *per se*, but rather some aspect of the behavior that reflects the person's feeling state. The ultimate reference for the match appears to be the feeling state (inferred or directly apprehended), not the external behavioral event" (1985, 142).

Stern supports this claim, as do other baby watchers, when he notes that infants whose mothers are "attuned" to them respond differently than infants whose mothers are not attuned. In the well-attuned couple the baby plays easily; only when the attunement is consciously broken does the baby respond, "as if to say, 'What's going on?'" (150). A simple learning theorem, that mother reinforces one behavior, cannot explain the importance of matching the infant's rhythms with mother's rhythms. Babies perceive when their mothers alter their usual pacing: "Many more such individualized perturbations have been performed, all indicating that the infant does indeed have some sense of the extent of matching" (151; 153–54).

*Body zones as sources of qualitative richness*

The six dimensions Stern describes are observable features of a mother's response to her infant's interior experience. Stern says that infants perceive shifts in their mothers' responses. Then infants must be able to locate and assess these dimensions of their internal experience.

Another source of stimulation for the infant is the workings of its own body, especially those parts of its body associated with pleasure and pain. Infants assess these tensions and qualities with an accuracy similar to that displayed when they assess the external world. This invokes Freud's insights into the sexual zones and their importance to all ego development (Freud 1905d). These six dimensions of observable behavior must apply also to these sensations associated with *unobserved behaviors* as well. These hidden, internal experiences and sensations are as real as any other type of sensation. In addition, each of the sense modalities, like taste, is specific to an internal experience. It has its own qualitative richness that yields to the infant a distinctive pattern of tension, pleasure, and pain.[13]

Following the work of S. Tomkins (1962, 1963, 1980), who spoke of patterns of neural firing that issued in Darwinian affects, Stern describes patterns of affective experiences that share a rush of feeling. These moments are experienced as the same because they share the same pattern of tension, rhythm, and other sensed qualities that make up a fixed pattern. In this way when a mother hushes a baby by singing or by rocking or by cradling she may evoke the same pattern of experience and thus the same rush of feelings. Many of the arts evoke similar feelings in the viewer or participant through intermodal expression.

Recognizing the sameness of an experience of one's affect amounts to recognizing "a temporal pattern of changes in density of neural firing. No matter whether an object was encountered with the eye or touch, and perhaps even the ear, it would produce the *same overall pattern* or activation contour" (Stern 1985, 59, emphasis mine). Activation contours, thus, may derive from the alleged six primary emotions, but they can evolve into complex and relatively autonomous forms. Later in adult life, artists, for instance dancers, can evoke the same pattern of feeling, the activation contour, that is an elaboration of the Darwinian affects: "Dance reveals to the viewer-listener multiple vitality affects and their variations, without resorting to plot or categorical [Darwinian] affect signals from which the vitality affects can be derived" (56).

How many activation contours are there? Sterns says this is an empirical question (59 n. 10). However many there are, they share a common form, namely a temporal sequence that shows a rise and fall in sensations that can be reproduced in different sensory modes. Stern employs a psychoanalytic point of view when he stresses, continuously, that these contours are real things that occur within a person's experience of self. Since these contours are not visible from objective, exterior points of view, only a psychoanalytic, or other rigorously phenomenological point of view, can name them. Because these are contours, that is, fixed shapes, they can be evoked through different senses; the rush of cold air on one's face is identical, as contour, to the rush of falling.

In Stern's language, "These contours of activation give rise to vitality affect at the level of feeling" (57 n. 8). For W. B. Yeats the beautiful motion of a bird "pernning in the gyre" (from "Demon and Beast," 1918) signifies aimless joy, the antithesis of the horror of World War I and the bloodshed of the Irish rebellion of 1916. We note that the original experience, the vitality effect of sailing on currents of air, is an evoked affect. More so, it depends entirely upon the poet's empathic imagination of himself like that bird. This makes the image powerful and effective. Most of us will not sail on air like the falcon but we can imagine ourselves in the bird's place, thanks in part to Yeats and other poets who focus our attention upon this wonderful part of nature. We have been buffeted by swirling water, or swung around, or wafted up and down and these patterns of the rise and fall of sensation are sympathetic analogues to "the gyre." Yeats and his commentators add to this poetic insight a host of secondary, theological and philosophical explications.[14] However, these are readings of the poem, not equivalents to it.

## VIRGINIA DEMOS AND THE INTERRUPTION OF AFFECTIVE EXPRESSION

Given Stern's notion of affect contours, what happens if they are disturbed or prevented from reaching a resolution? Like Stern, Virginia Demos also depends upon the work and theorizing of Tomkins. She expands the notion of empathic communication by distinguishing six types of infant-parent interaction.[15] Relying upon a psychoanalytic theory of affect (from Demos 1984a), we can isolate a three-part sequence in the development of an infant's response to its own strong affects:

1) A triggering event or stimulus evokes an affect in the infant.

2) The primary affect, negative like fear, or positive like joy, occurs automatically.

3) The infant responds to his or her affect by defense and
   planning a future response.

If we assert that infants always manifest some version of the six primary affects, we presume that the affects triggered in these circumstances are primary. Hence, we assume that like the Japanese subjects described above, infants manifest one or more innate, primary
affects. In turn, significant adults, typically the mother, respond to
this initial manifestation with some form of acceptance, control, or
punishment. To become Japanese, for example, is to learn through
hundreds, then thousands of such encounters the proper way to
evaluate one's primary affects. We might name these secondary emotions using general terms like guilt or shame, or rely upon terms
specific to a particular culture. For example some scholars refer to a
specifically Japanese emotion *amae,* "a highly rewarding sense of
being dependent on another person or organization" (Griffiths 1997,
101). If this is plausible, the term *amae* will not yield to an exact
English translation since it names a complex form of internalization
and learning specific to Japanese child rearing and Japanese culture.

In her studies of American children and their mothers Demos
describes how a well-functioning parent, say the mother, may recognize the triggering event, identify correctly the infant's affect state,
and recognize the infant's struggle to deal with its affect. In addition, "she can decide to respond to none, some, or all three components [of the infant's experience]; and her response can take a variety of forms" (18). From this theorem and an associated claim about
empathy (that empathy is inference about the inner state of another
person) Demos generates a six-part typology. Each type describes
how a parent interacts with the infant at *specific* moments. (These
are *not* types of parenting, but types of interaction.) Her discussion
might be summarized in table 3.

In this table the "yes" denotes correct recognition; the "sometimes" denotes partial failure to recognize the infant's or child's internal experience. In type I mode, the parent recognizes the trigger,
recognizes the particular affect it arouses, and recognizes how the
child attempts to cope with that affect. By acting appropriately, that
is by recognizing, naming, and containing the child's fears, the parent can decrease or end the child's negative affect, and increase the
child's positive affect. To recognize this sequence of experiences,
"inside" the baby, is to permit the child to have a full and completed

*Table 3. Six Types of Interaction and*
*Effect on Affective Response*

| Parent Interaction Type | Recognize trigger | Recognize affect | Recognize child's plan | Negative affect | Positive affect |
|---|---|---|---|---|---|
| I | yes | yes | yes | ends | increases |
| II | yes | yes | yes | persists | persists |
| III | yes | yes | yes | persists | decreases |
| IV | yes | yes | yes | persists | increases |
| V | sometimes | sometimes | sometimes | increases | decreases |
| VI | no | no | no | increases | decreases |

cycle of both the primary emotion and response to it. This makes learning and adaptation more likely.

While type I is the purest moment of empathic understanding between parent and child, it may not always be ideal or possible. Type II, in which the parent cannot reduce immediately negative affect, but can prolong positive affect, is a feature of much parenting, for example, a visit to the dentist. Like other analytic theorists, Demos suggests that parents who are less attuned[16] to their child's inner world and who either misinterpret or ignore the process that produces negative affect in their children, produce the sickest children. Type V and type VI modes of interaction generate the most severe deprivations in the child's life. Margaret Mahler's classic studies (1968, 1975) on parent-child interactions and separation traumata pertain here. Children of alcoholic parents or parents prone to psychotic states or severe altered states of consciousness have numerous experiences of type V and type VI parenting.

Self-object failures occur along this spectrum of parental oversight, hostility, and, in the extreme cases, rage. Naturally, if because of organic or physical limitations, an infant cannot perceive the good enough parent, its actual experience of parenting will be of type V or VI. Conversely, some children can extract from type V or type VI parenting semblances of emotional supplies sufficient to make ego maturation possible.

Demos's study of child-parent interactions yields valuable clues to the interpersonal mechanisms by which specific ego functions, or ego capacities, are deformed by parental response. In brief, since types IV, V, and VI increase the child's negative affect and decrease the child's positive affects associated with a particular challenge, these types of parenting squelch adaptive forms of problem solving. This squelching may be specific to particular kinds of behavior (such as sexuality) or intensity levels ("too much noise!") or references to others ("act this way in these circumstances") and other parameters; in all cases, though, the child's developing sense of mastery in specific areas is hampered.

For example, Demos discusses a particular fifteen-month-old girl throwing a ball back to an older child. Because the girl's throw was not good enough the mother refused to acknowledge the little girl's efforts and her enthusiasm. "By the third and fourth repetitions of this sequence, the child's expression had become sober; she was no longer clapping" (28). One can imagine, using Wallerstein's charts (1988) like his "Scales of Psychological Capacities," that a steady diet of such instruction would create a woman whose "self-esteem," "zest for life," and "effectance-mastery" were compromised.

Further, as a consequence of these compromises and failures, all tied to negative, secondary affects like shame and guilt, we would tend to find that behavioral extremes, such as perfectionism and grandiosity, mark the adult woman's efforts to control herself and people close to her. For from within the little girl's experience at the first trembling of strong feeling, especially those that might reveal her inner, narcissistic tensions, her mother tended to intervene with some form of anxiety-driven effort to control the child's emotional experience. This common error means that the child could not learn that a strong feeling has a natural rise and fall and that one need not abort it.

Stern notes that while a modern, educated father may say that he believes masturbation is normal and expectable, his disdainful, emotional responses emerge simultaneously with these pronouncements. What the child hears on one channel, the official, auditory one, is contradicted on another, the unofficial but more powerful one of emotional signaling (1985, 209–10). The child thus acquires a dual evaluation of masturbation: it ought to be O.K., but really it is a loathsome and harmful habit. A good child would not engage in it, especially since it displeases father. Because this latter insight is nonverbal and contradicted by the father's official pronouncements, a reasonable child deduces that the child's conflicts about masturbation are yet another sign of badness *within* the child.

Masturbation is a complex, overt action that both child and adult can designate just as they both can record and remember that father officially announced his noncondemnation of it. The father's subtle, nonverbal, affect-laden responses, the catch in his voice, the way his eyes shift and so on, cannot be designated easily. While the boy may recall vaguely that his father seemed different when he spoke about this topic, the boy cannot name the difference. Given that most adults cannot name even a few complex, feeling states, even though there are probably hundreds, it is not surprising that children fail to use language with sufficient exactitude to name their accurate perception that something is wrong between them and their parents. And because they cannot name the difference they cannot locate the source of their distress, except to note that, once again, something is wrong inside of them.

CHAPTER 5

# Affects: Darwinian, Cultural, and Blitzkrieg

I suggested we follow Daniel Stern and others who distinguish the so-called Darwinian affects from secondary, cultural elaborations of them. Darwinian affects, like fear, anger, sadness, and joy, constitute our mammalian heritage and are therefore primary.[1] Culture-specific elaborations of them are secondary, and therefore are shaped by both group and individual experiences. If we accept this attractive distinction, we may designate emotions like guilt and shame as secondary affects. Both primary and secondary affects may be so painful that they merit clinical attention. Certainly, we know that guilt and shame can evoke suicidal wishes. Beyond Darwinian and cultural affects, though, is a third class. This third class I call "blitzkrieg affects," using a term suggested by André Green (1977). Like the "lightning war" of the German armies, blitzkrieg affects evoke disorganizing terror: they are beyond the capacity of art and religion to name and to comprehend fully. In this profound sense they lie beyond the work of culture for neither language nor other expressive forms seem capable of containing them. Only psychoanalysis or similar *procedures* that permit a person to relive blitzkrieg affects in safety are able to evoke and contain them.

If there are three types of affect how can we distinguish them from one another? In this chapter I suggest that both ancient and modern authors have always known the difference between primary and secondary affects, or what I will term "cultural affects." However, with the advent of the psychoanalytic process modern Western intellectuals saw more clearly that beyond these two types of affect lies a third: blitzkrieg affects. Through his creation of psychoanalysis

Freud provided three things: a new observational technique (grounded on free association); a ritually protected place (the analytic setup); and a way to wake sleeping demons safely (through the drama of transference reenactment). When these devices are in place blitzkrieg affects make themselves visible to both patient and analyst.

Other methods used to evoke and constrain blitzkrieg affects derive primarily from religious or cultic groups. Perhaps within groups whose mental life is delineated by a mythic system blitzkrieg affects are "contained" by the group's shared metaphysical maps. When Dante descends into hell in *The Inferno* (begun around 1307), he takes us into the most degraded and chaotic circumstances he can imagine. Yet even those terrible things, the summation of all that is evil, are constrained within a vigorous rhyme scheme and a theological mapping that locates hell as a knowable and therefore limited dimension of human being.[2]

## FROM PRIMARY AFFECTS TO SECONDARY AFFECTS: THE WORK OF CULTURE

### Aristotle, Kant, and Hawthorne

To the list of secondary affects like guilt and shame, we could add "positive" emotions like pride, righteousness, courage, and numerous other ethical and aesthetic capacities that have an affective core. For example, in *Nicomachean Ethics*, his majestic treatise on Greek values, Aristotle traces the genealogy of his culture's highest virtues, like courage, back to their origins in primary affects, like fear, pleasure, and joy: "Though courage is concerned with feelings of confidence and of fear, it is not concerned with both alike, but more with the things that inspire fear; for he who is undisturbed in face of these and bears himself as he should towards these is more truly brave than the man who does so towards the things that inspire confidence. It is for facing what is painful, then, as has been said, that men are called brave. Hence also courage involves pain, and is justly praised; for it is harder to face what is painful than to abstain from what is pleasant" (book 3, chapter 9).[3]

Aristotle says the moral category "friendship" also arises out of primary affects: "This being granted, it necessarily follows that he is

a friend who shares our joy in good fortune and our sorrow in affliction, for our own sake and not for any other reason. For all men
rejoice when what they desire comes to pass and are pained when
the contrary happens, so that pain and pleasure are indications of
their wish. And those are friends who have the same ideas of good
and bad, and love and hate the same persons, since they necessarily
wish the same things; wherefore one who wishes for another what
he wishes for himself seems to be the other's friend."[4]

In *Critique of Practical Reason* (1788), Immanuel Kant mounted
an effort similar to Aristotle's. Like Aristotle, Kant wished to define
the characteristics of the highest value, love of the moral law, by
reference to its origins and organization of lower values: "There is
something so singular in the unbounded esteem for the pure moral
law . . . the voice of which makes even the boldest sinner tremble
and compels him to hide himself from it, that we cannot wonder if
we find this influence of a mere intellectual idea on the *feelings quite
incomprehensible to speculative reason* . . ." ([1788] 1991–94, emphasis mine). One doubts that everyone, everywhere, would tremble
at the "voice" of practical wisdom announcing the pure moral law.
To "tremble" upon hearing the voice of the pure moral law requires
one to have acquired a complex repertoire of basic affects, like fear
and love, organized into higher emotions like respect and admiration. Of course, noting that the feelings Kant attributes to those
who hear the voice of practical reason are culturally founded, does
not demonstrate that Kant is wrong. Rather, to evaluate Kant's reasoning we must evaluate his subtle comments about self-consciousness. For example, he says, "The consciousness of a free submission
of the will to the law, yet combined with an inevitable constraint put
upon all inclinations, though only by our own reason, is respect for
the law." This amounts to a theory of what the term "respect" means,
and it merits our respectful consideration.

In a similar way, when a novelist evokes a culture foreign to our
own, we glimpse that culture's secondary affects. Because secondary
affects evolve in complex and subtle ways, perhaps through many
generations of ego and superego elaboration, few if any actors within
that culture can comprehend them fully. On the contrary, we count
as geniuses those artists and psychologists who can bring them to
light. For example in *The Scarlet Letter* (1850), Nathaniel Hawthorne
(1804–64) looked back two hundred years to his Puritan ancestors.
Through artistic imagination and empathic reconstruction he retrieved

the Puritan distinction between religious despair and private, personal "fretting." This is most evident when Hawthorne describes Reverend Arthur Dimmesdale's reflections upon his sexual sin:

> The minister, on the other hand, had never gone through an experience calculated to lead him beyond the scope of generally received laws; although, in a single instance, he had so fearfully transgressed one of the most sacred of them. But this had been a sin of passion, not of principle, nor even purpose.[5]

As a minister, Dimmesdale knows and preaches his culture's moral rules and the control of the passions, especially sexuality. Having broken one of them, Dimmesdale nevertheless remains safely embedded within that moral system. In this sense his guilt counts as a secondary affect, of immense pain but not incalculable. On the contrary, having had an illicit sexual encounter, Dimmesdale names it using the vocabulary of Puritan theology and psychology. Indeed, now that he "knows" sin and has tasted its pleasures and pain he comprehends even more fully the "reality" of sexual sin. He is thus "safer within the line of virtue" than he was prior to meeting his lover, Hester Prynne. While he frets and suffers the authentic pain of guilt and remorse, these are not (yet) catastrophic affects: Dimmesdale's place in the world and in an eternal world order is disturbed, not destroyed.

Indeed, even at the novel's climactic scene, when Dimmesdale confronts his abandonment of Hester and their child, he escapes the ultimate horror, according to Puritan theology, of dying without full confession. By broadcasting his horrible sin Dimmesdale regains his place in a moral and absolute kingdom: even his nemesis, Roger Chillingworth, cannot touch him: "'Hadst thou sought the whole earth over,' said he, looking darkly at the clergyman, 'there was no one place so secret—no high place nor lowly place, where thou couldst have escaped me—save on this very scaffold!' 'Thanks be to Him who hath led me hither,' answered the minister."[6]

Dimmesdale salvages his place in the honored rolls of his culture by his tearful and heartfelt confession that is blessed even by the sun: "[He] turned to the dignified and venerable rulers; to the holy ministers, who were his brethren; to the people, whose great heart was thoroughly appalled, yet overflowing with tearful sympathy, as knowing that some deep life-matter—which, if full of sin, was full of anguish and repentance likewise—was now to be laid open to them. The sun, but little past its meridian, shone down upon the clergy-man, and gave a distinctness to his figure, as he stood out from all the earth, to put in his plea of guilty at the bar of Eternal Justice."[7]

Like novelists and anthropologists, psychoanalysts become ac-culturated to their patients' private worlds, their folk cultures, and their idiosyncratic modes of affective expression.[8] I am agreeing with Charles Brenner (1974) when he says: "[E]ach affect is unique for each individual. Each person's affective life is his own and is never identical with that of another, since each person's wishes, memories, perceptions, fears, and expectations are never identical with those of another. More than this, an understanding of the connection be-tween affects and ego development and functioning illuminates, at least in part, the question of variations in the manifestations or ways of expressing affects from one person to another" (545).

BLITZKRIEG AFFECTS: "ADVANCING IN FORCE
TOWARDS THE HEART OF THE EGO"

In his lucid history of the concept "affect" André Green (1977) employs a linguistic metapsychology to distinguish two broad classes of affect. His first class encompasses the two types I have named Darwinian and cultural: each is "integrated as solid material into the other significant material in the unconscious (and preconscious) chain—in this case affect is subordinated to the organization of the chain and its meaning lies in the sequence which it belongs to. Here affect takes on the function of signifier *(signifiant)* like the represen-tation or any other material coming into unconscious formations" (148–49). To define the second class he uses linguistic terms and classical Freudian metaphors:

> By its intensity and its meaning (signification) [this second type of] affect overflows from the unconscious chain, like a river which leaves its bed and disorganizes communications, destroying the sense-mak-ing structures. In this second case, we are dealing not with a signal affect in the ego, but perhaps *with real instinctual impulses from the id which have broken the ego's barriers and are advancing in force to-wards the heart of the ego in the manner of a Blitzkrieg.* The disorgani-zation of the chain is responsible for the traumatic affect which may

paralyse or have a tendency towards compulsive action, if they do not bring in their wake a reaction of stupefied immobility. (149, emphasis mine)

Like Brenner (1974), Green is suspicious of theorists who rely upon a developmental model of affects. In place of their (and my) distinction between primary affects and secondary affects he adduces a strong distinction between affects located within a chain of signification *(chaîne significant)* and those that overflow and break links in the chain (150). The second class are those that "advance towards the heart of the ego." Indeed, a blitzkrieg is a lightning war, perfected by the Germans in World War II; we recognize that Green wishes us to savor the terror that these kinds of affect can induce. Green lumps together what I have called Darwinian affects and cultural affects since both may be designated and linked through linguistic significations. Keats did this through language, Mozart through music, and contemporary geniuses do this through film. These linkages, in other words, need not be verbal; but they must permit expression and communication.

Green seems to me accurate as phenomenologist and respectful of the Freudian heritage. Somehow in a successful psychoanalysis, affects of the blitzkrieg type are tamed through the frame of therapy, the analyst's and patient's bravery, and enter eventually into speech. A good enough analyst asks his or her patients to bring into the analytic setting precisely affects of this type, their worst feelings and deepest fears, and to revive them in the transference. Like Freud, Green stresses that these affects are not merely ideas, nor are they products of primary process thinking, "for if such were the case, the analyst involved in deciphering them would not share the patient's tension. The invasion, the impotence, the distress, all give rise to an internal panic which drives the subject to exceed the limits of psychic space by various mechanisms: confusion—which is in fact a dissemination and dilution of conflictual tensions; cathartic action operating like a massive affective storm; somatization; perverse excitation; or the overcathexis of external perception which monopolizes all psychic attention" (151).

How might we understand these standard features of the analytic adventure? Green acknowledges many contributions made by Melanie Klein and her followers, especially the notion of projective identification and the ubiquity of archaic fantasies. Yet even when one feels certain that this dream or that transference element matches an archaic paranoid fantasy, for example, there remains the lengthy work of patient and analyst struggling slowly through numerous iterations in the "here and now." We agree that our job as analysts is to supply meaningful connections, usually through speech, where before there were none. In Freud's language, our goal is to make what was not "me" part of "me." We realize that we always do this in a creative fashion, especially if the "not me" began in terror and disorganization. We might understand Winnicott's definition of the good-enough parent as an adult who defends the child against overwhelming anxiety which, if unstopped, destroys the intermediate place of play. For when dominant this kind of anxiety (a blitzkrieg affect) overwhelms other affective expression and therefore affective resolution. The good-enough analyst is one who recognizes the toxicity of such anxiety and other blitzkrieg affects and defends the patient against their resurgence. Freud investigated the boundary region between nonverbal affects, especially blitzkrieg affects, and verbal and other symbolic representations. Yet his was a verbal therapy and verbal theories always press toward but never fully reach the nonverbal side.

*Blitzkrieg affects as the unimaginable*

While Green's passionate words are provocative, their poetic force may obscure the epistemological problem: how do we verify analytic claims to bridge the gap between these two types of affective experience? Indeed, Green says that a "classical" analysis cannot usually contain blitzkrieg affects. This brings us back to the chronic issue of the scientific merits of psychoanalytic theory and practice based upon it. Using the terms of this book, theorists who take a "constructivist" view, like Roy Schafer (1980), nominate as the objects of analysis the patient's interior narratives. While the psychoanalytic process depends upon narratives, blitzkrieg affects possess such force that patients easily imagine death to be a better choice than proceeding through them. Why? If we agree with Green that blitzkrieg affects are among the central objects of analytic reflection then we wish to know more about them and their ontological status. Are they (1) memories, (2) verbal constructs, (3) "mythic" narratives, or (4) something else? I consider briefly the first three options and then suggest reasons to accept the fourth.

If blitzkrieg affects were merely memories, that is, accessible and locatable recollections of previous experience, they would not be terrifying. When they reappear in an analytic hour, for example, they appear as current terrors. They are memories only in the sense that all transference reenactments repeat previous moments of devastation.

If blitzkrieg affects were verbal constructs, that is, merely the product of misunderstandings or concatenations of logical errors, they would yield to a purely rational re-education. In fact, they would be what Green calls "solid material" that finds a linkage to other significant material in the unconscious. If blitzkrieg affects are the core target of analytic work and they are not part of a chain of signification, a narrative metapsychology cannot be an exhaustive account of the analytic encounter. For narratives presuppose order, coherence, and thus pertain to the first class of affects, both Darwinian affects and culturally elaborated affects.

It is tempting to view blitzkrieg affects and defenses against them as private versions of public myths, which are another kind of narrative. Freud, and later Carl Jung, pointed out numerous ways in which patient's personal stories and their self-understandings parallel those found in the great public narratives of religion and other mythic forms. For example, Freud found surprising parallels between his painfully discovered feelings about his mother and father and the legend of a Greek mythic hero, Oedipus. Inspired by Freud's masterpiece, *The Interpretation of Dreams* (1900a), Jung expanded this part of analytic theory into a grand theory of world religions. In his first masterpiece and the book that marked his separation from Freud, *Symbols of Transformation* (1911–12), Jung advanced Freud's claims that a shared genesis in archaic thinking unites primitive myths, neurotic fantasies, and dreams of normal persons. While Freud rejected religion and Jung admired it, they shared a general claim that personal and public narrations, private dreams and public myths, are basically alike. In favor of this claim is a hundred years of applied psychoanalysis. Against it, at least against a strict claim of parallel ontological status, is a counterclaim that blitzkrieg affects and pathogenic beliefs create entities *unlike* those produced by public myths. Using Green's terms, we might say that in general public myths are semantically consistent entities. They are narrations, stories, theologies, and other accounts that may describe horrific events but, like Dante's great poem, also constrain affects. True, in most contexts the world "myth" denotes falsity, but false beliefs and make-believe are not chaotic in the special way that blitzkrieg affects are.

More pertinent to the question of analysis as a distinctive science are the intellectual costs of pursuing a narrative strategy. In an extreme version, if all we do as analysts is compare and contrast narratives, we ought to read more literary criticism and less psychiatry. For literary critics have had some three hundred years to develop a critical vocabulary for ascertaining the structure and methods of narratives. If we grant Aristotle standing as a critic, one might say that literary criticism precedes the rise of modern science by fifteen hundred years. The narrative strategy is fascinating and may prove to be the better route. However, clinicians deal with blitzkrieg affects and their effects upon living people who wish to be dead. If we accept Green's description of blitzkrieg affects they cannot be expressed in any verbal formula. This means that all narratives about them are incorrect. Although awkward, Freud's libido theory as least posits a nonnarrative set of forces about which the analyst can reason.

In contrast to Freud's model of the mind as shaped by the demands of instinctual forces, a purely narrative metapsychology leaves us no third thing against which to judge the merits of an analytic intervention, much less analytic reconstruction. Wilma Bucci (1985) put the problem clearly: "In the terms of these authors, we are left with no means of verifying analytic interpretations, no criteria for validating the accuracy of the inference from words to mental representations of the past; we are in fact led to question whether this is a meaningful pursuit. The propositions of [narrative] theory refer to psychic rather than material reality; therefore they cannot be validated by reference to historical facts. Evaluation of psychoanalytic propositions in terms of pragmatic or esthetic considerations leaves the issue of validation out of account, and thus removes psychoanalysis from the scientific, hypothesis-testing domain" (574).

Bucci's complaint is that constructivists like Roy Schafer (1976) and Donald Spence (1982) fail to note that (probably) verbal entities are encoded and stored in a mode quite separate from perceptual and affective memories: "In terms of dual coding, the problem is not that the nonverbal representations are vulnerable to distortion by words, but that the words that pass back and forth between analyst and patient will not affect the nonverbal schemata at all" (Bucci 1985, 605).

This nonverbal schema counts as a third thing about which both patient and analyst can propose interpretations. Since it has an ontological status independent of narrations about it, we can hope for validation: "Thus an interpretation may be characterized as valid if there is evidence that it has connected to the nonverbal schemata, i.e., if the referential links have been activated. This evidence may be found in the subsequent material the patient brings in. Reports of actions and emotions, experiences of them in the session itself, or descriptions of images, fantasies, and dreams in concrete and specific terms, would be evidence that the analyst's words had activated a nonverbal schema in the patient's mind. More abstract and general verbalizations would indicate that such representations had not been tapped" (1985, 601–2).[9]

### RAT MAN: THE OMNIPOTENCE OF THOUGHT AND BLITZKRIEG AFFECTS

As I said in chapter 2 I defend my picking and choosing of various analytic concepts by virtue of the proposal I am affirming, that the objects of analysis are not "real things" per se. They are neither ordinary, natural entities, like waterfalls and prairie dogs, nor are they ordinary cultural entities, like songs, stories, and myths. Rather, the objects of psychoanalytic investigation are a third kind of thing; products of pathogenic beliefs about what "mind" is and, I am suggesting, responses to blitzkrieg affects. These objects, which earlier psychoanalysts might have named neurotic fantasies, are not merely erroneous. Nor are they "mythic"; they are inchoate. In contrast to them we can categorize Rev. Dimmesdale's affects as either Darwinian or secondary and Dimmesdale's religious "theory" of his mind as consistent even if we do not share it. Dimmesdale's urge to flee from his circumstances is understandable as Darwinian affect (probably fear), as was his sexual attraction to the woman entrusted to his care. Dimmesdale's guilt, a secondary affect, no matter how painful, occupies a well-delineated place within the matrices of his religion. Its sacred texts had long ago categorized experiences named lust, guilt, sin, and remorse as secondary affects. For example, King David merits the titles of great leader, author of immortal psalms, and grievous sinner without losing his exalted status in Jewish and Christian traditions.[10]

Again, contrary to the investigation of Dimmesdale's guilt or David's sin, when we attempt to discern the structure of the objects of analysis we do not find patterned entities. If this is correct, then to the degree to which a patient's affects are of either type one (Darwinian) or type two (culturally elaborated) they are not among the ultimate objects of analytic inquiry. For while *psychotherapy* may pertain to both Darwinian and cultural affects, the *analytic process*, which is the uncovering and investigation of a deeper irrationality, pertains to something else, to another kind of affect and another kind of object. These objects are not like cancer which, while terrible in its effects, is fully natural in its relentless patterns of growth, attack, and destruction. Why is this? How might we understand, even by analogy, this odd feature of the analytic process?

When I discussed Freud's famous patient, Rat Man, I cited Freud's claim that his patient exhibited an extreme version of the "omnipotence of thought" and this cognitive error contributed to Rat Man's struggles. I demurred and suggested we should locate Rat Man's struggles not solely within himself, but between him and his father's moments of terrifying rage. His father demonstrated that even a manly, robust and idealized person could not master his anger, nor, for that matter, other feelings, like fear and loss that typically precipitate uncontrolled anger. Following these in vivo demonstrations, I suggested, Rat Man then perceived the same incapacity in himself. A genuine conflict emerged between one part of himself, his affective life (which classical theory views as based upon drive derivatives) and another part, his poorly formed capacity to express and to contain strong affects without also experiencing overwhelming danger.

Here I parted company with traditional Freudians and cast my lot with contemporary authors, especially developmentalists like Daniel Stern (1985), Stanley Greenspan (1997a, 1997b), and D. W. Winnicott (1971a; 1971b). For while traditional Freudians illuminate the ubiquity of the "omnipotence of thought," the latter three give more persuasive accounts of its genesis. An example of traditional theory is a much-cited study, *Shame and Guilt* (1953), by Gerhart Piers and Milton Singer. They generalize about the cycles of dread, anticipation, and repetition that typify neurotic life: "The basic dread is that of the external event (catastrophe) which, coming without the individual's knowledge, timing, or control, questions the omnipotence to which the neurotic hangs on precariously. To assert this 'omnipotence of thought,' the neurotic will resort to 'imaging the worst'" (1953, 42).

By grade school, many children have learned the value of the pessimistic style: to avoid disappointment, hope for nothing. It is difficult to think of a severe form of character pathology in which the patient does not focus obsessively upon controlling themselves and others often through what we label "magical thinking." However, as an explanation of neurotic suffering I find this wanting. For, paradoxically, it locates the neurotic's fears in *external* events and catastrophes, not in *internal* processes. While this may match a patient's manifest self-understanding, for example, "If my wife were prettier then I'd be happy," it does not explain why the patient continues to live in dread.

Many patients who manifest "omnipotent thoughts" and other grandiose attempts at self-mastery favor action, not thinking. They do not sit and contemplate, nor do they employ imagination, another form of thinking, to decrease their suffering. On the contrary, they divorce frequently, change jobs, take up fad diets, start affairs, or work too much. These are all external devices and modes designed to ameliorate external events.

I have suggested we focus upon *internal* catastrophes typical of children (and adults) who realize that they cannot control an internal cascade of emotions. They believe correctly that if unchecked their dread of their own feelings may lead them to harm themselves or other people they love. They do not merely imagine that their wishes will get them in trouble. They know with a high degree of certainty that their narcissistic wishes, for example, frighten them because they do not know how to sustain feelings of pride for very long before they crash and burn. To avoid this (correctly) anticipated horror they shortchange themselves or, if need be, humiliate themselves. As Piers and Singer say, this cycle occurs regularly and is repeated, naturally, in transference reenactments.

More subtle are infants' experiences of themselves and their affects. Daniel Stern notes that modern infant psychiatry is just beginning to appreciate the extraordinary depth of communication that occurs between infant and caretakers and the extraordinary attunement infants show toward the emotional states of adults, especially mothering objects. For example, B. K. Amsterdam and Morton Levitt (1980) support Freud's earliest reflections (1895a) upon the development of shame out of response to an original genital pleasure, what we would name a primary affect of pleasure: "The child learns to inhibit genital sensation and exploration in the presence of others at precisely the same time as he also experiences affective self-consciousness before the mirror. It is important to note that both these behaviors follow the onset of walking, the pleasurable and unselfconscious exhibition of the naked body, and the intentional touching of the genitalia" (78).

This statement is both plausible and exceedingly complex, as are many psychoanalytic reflections upon affect (or emotionality). If Amsterdam and Levitt are correct, then the following statements must be valid:

1. At about fourteen months, infants record and recognize their internal bodily sensations, distinguishing between genital sensations and others.
2. They also perceive, record, and can recall parental emotional responses, especially responses that occur outside the parents' conscious control.
3. When the parents' emotional signals are aversive and threatening, the infant learns to inhibit the recording or recall of pleasurable genital sensations.
4. Self-consciousness, a painful and often pervasive, self state derives, in part, from these early interactions with parents.

Regarding this kind of analytic description Jacob Arlow (1977) adds an important warning: "For the most part, judgements concerning the propriety of affects are made automatically, that is, intuitively. Unless the analyst has some defensive need to feel omnipotent (Lewin 1958), he can expect to be surprised regularly by his patient's patterns of affectivity. In such instances, the analyst's affective response enters into the process of judging the patient's emotions" (159).[11] Hence, we should add to this list of assumptions:

5. Through objective means we can distinguish the presence of one kind of affect, here named aversive, from another with the opposite valence.

This last requirement may seem to nudge psychoanalytic issues into a foreign camp of behaviorism or other objectivist accounts, thus obviating the value of an intrapsychic focus. However, Arlow's bona fide standing as a psychoanalyst cannot be questioned. His warning is salient because it underscores the tentativeness of analytic formulations about patients' emotions. Given the central Freudian assumption of unconscious processes, especially those that pertain to negative affects, initial claims about any person's affective state are provisional. Depending upon the data that emerge from subsequent psychoanalytic process, we may revise our first evaluation. Data that emerge later, from within the analytic frame, count as objective in this sense: "Since the most significant ideas are often unconscious, it is also important to remember that a patient's own label is by no means always reliable. It may be or it may not be. Only a successful application of the psychoanalytic method can decide" (Brenner 1974, 543–44). Stern says parents who are otherwise competent can diminish their children's abilities to connect one part of their internal world with another part. When this occurs there is no original linkage between an infant's inner experience of profound anxiety, say, and a fully responsive Other. What was never present in a child's mind cannot be discovered via retrospective interrogation. The labor expended by patient and analyst to evoke and transform blitzkrieg affects into language is novel, frightening, and constructive. This makes even the most precise analytic work a heuristic enterprise.

## ATTUNEMENT, AFFECT CURVES, AND THE TAMED BEAST

> That is to say, we have yet to tackle the question of what life itself is about. Our psychotic patients force us to give attention to this sort of question. . . . It is the self that must precede the self's use of instinct; the rider must ride the horse, not be run away with.
>
> —D. W. Winnicott

When Winnicott says psychoanalysts must consider what "life itself" is about, he recognizes that these are not scientific terms. In fact, they tilt precariously toward cliche. Yet, they capture a common experience of patients who experience psychotic moments. Regardless of the cause of their psychotic states, with deep eloquence they often describe an inner experience of "deadness" that is so painful anything seems preferable. They have no harmonious "self." They feel driven by parts of themselves (what Winnicott here calls instincts), by other people, or by disembodied voices. They are "run away with" and seek help desperately. To the degree that some of these states are the products of developmental and interpersonal conflicts over the rise of blitzkrieg affects we can say something useful about them. For when Stern (1985) describes parents' interactions with their children, he assumes we can denote failures of attunement and link them plausibly to subsequent psychopathology. Using his vocabulary, Stern describes "misattunements"[12] which occur when a mother (or other maternal object) just misses matching fully a child's emotional state: "The amount by which this match fails to occur packs the wallop" (211). While his accounts, like the following vignette, are highly suggestive, their plausibility depends upon our agreeing with the five statements above and accepting Stern's claim that we can denote accurately the degree of emotional matching present in such encounters.

His vignette concerns a mother who matched her ten-month old son's initial state of excitement up to a certain point and then withheld full approval: "[W]hen he evidenced some affect and looked to her with a bright face and some excited arm-flapping, she responded with a good, solid, "Yes, honey" that, in its absolute level of activation, fell just short of his arm-flapping and face-brightness" (211). Stern's claim about this mother's misattunement depends upon a prior claim that he and his colleagues can designate correctly what full-attunement looks like, namely, an aesthetic matching that follows, contour for contour, the infant's experience of his own internal sensations. Granting Stern this point, at least granting it plausibility, the next part of his account is especially interesting. The research team asked the boy's mother her thoughts about her interactive style. She agreed that she tended to undermatch her son because, "She felt that he tended to lose his initiative if she joined fully and equally and shared with him" (212). This worried her; she feared that her son was in danger of growing up to be like his father, her husband, whom she felt was too passive: "She was the initiator, the spark plug in the family" (211). Stern notes that if this mother pursues this strategy and remains consistently misattuned to her son's full affective expression, she will create exactly what she did not wish: a "lower-keyed child who was less inclined to share his spunk. The mother would inadvertently have contributed to making the son more like the father, rather than different from him" (212–13).

Stern's vignette about an anxious mother and her "passive" child can help us understand why parents who wish to *control* their children's affective lives *increase* the likelihood of psychopathology. The mother will produce the opposite of what she intended not because she wishes to harm her son but because she wished to shape his emotional responses, to improve them by withholding a complete mirroring response to him. To prevent him from becoming like her husband, whom she disdains, the mother fabricates a plan to alter her son's emotional expressiveness.

Stern's assessment of this woman's errors entails the notion of activation contour and similar concepts derived from contemporary child psychiatry and psychoanalysis. For both sciences address the domain of a person's internal experience of the rise and fall of tension states that we call affects or emotions (Gay 1992). I have followed Stern by emphasizing the exquisite ways children assess their parents' emotions and by noting the consequences when parents try to control the rise and fall of ordinary tension states. In a similar way when a parent is chronically distressed about a child and then punishes the child we would expect to find increasingly pathological consequences. Evidence from scientific studies of the effects of corporal punishment, such as spanking, supports consistently developmental theory. Parents who consistently inflict pain upon their children increase dramatically the likelihood that those children will themselves turn to violence, abuse, and other extreme forms of chaotic emotional expression.

These studies, like the values I employ in this book, are secular and scientific: if research evidence shows consistently that spanking children tends to harm them then a rational, modern adult should—according to these values—refrain from spanking and seek to stop others as well. Indeed, according to some researchers, the only arguments for corporal punishment come from conservative Christians who label themselves fundamentalist and inerranentists. The latter titles refer to the conviction that every word of the Bible (both Hebrew and Christian scriptures) is without error. Given this claim, the line of authority favoring corporal punishment is clear for one can cite Scripture, like Prov. 13:24 "He who spares the rod hates his son, but he who loves him is careful to discipline him" and similar texts (Prov. 22:15, 23:13, and 29:15). People favoring corporal punishment are serious and no doubt dedicated to their children and the children of their communities. With cautious zeal they punish children in part because they have seen with their own eyes that older children in their community will be unruly and insolent unless parents lay down the law. One spokesperson says that parents should distinguish between spanking (good) and abuse (bad) by noting their moods when they punish their children and by the length of time spent spanking them: "If your corporal discipline is leaving marks on the body which are still visible after thirty minutes, you may be involved in physical abuse, not corporal discipline."[13]

Stern's laboratory observations support Winnicott's clinical intuitions: that a parent can reshape a child's emotional development by chronically withholding attunement for a few seconds in a particular emotional exchange. If so, we doubt that there is any length of time during which corporal punishment is a good thing. On the contrary, if we can speak about another person's affective experience, we might imagine the ten-month-old boy perceiving *within* himself a slowly gathering tension marked by arm-flapping, smiles, and numerous other physical manifestations. At the same time, in the presence of the good-enough mothering Other, the child experiences his internal (private) state mirrored and thus made external and "real" by the mother's attunements. A completed experience of strong affects then requires both the perception and recording of internal sensations, and recognizing, through some form of mirroring, its substantiality by the actions of another, real, person. In good enough parenting we expect to find a preponderance of attunements and therefore experiences of the complete pattern of rise, peak, and diminution of affect.

In less ideal parenting, even in mild instances like that described in Stern's vignette, this does not occur. The child's internal experience of the activation contour is that it will not turn down and resolve "in due time." Because his mother intervened and stopped full expression, the boy could not learn somatically that his feelings have a natural end point. The trajectory of his tension states, especially those in which he felt exuberant, or self-involved, was not toward eventual, peaceful resolution but towards eventual catastrophe. Like this little boy and like Rat Man, many patients describe moments of success that we, as outsiders, imagine should be pleasurable. Yet, for these patients happiness or joy means only that they will soon be miserable. They, not we, are correct, for their internal experience is that such states will increase in intensity until an external catastrophe intervenes. As Kohut (1971, 1977) documents, for many persons too much of a good thing, like praise or joy in oneself, issues in anxiety. To defend themselves against this eventual suffering, patients find ways to deny themselves the original pleasure that marks the beginning of the cycle.

In contrast to this common neurotic pattern, Stern's descriptions of activation contours echoes descriptions of musical masters, like Mozart, who are able to contain extremely strong affects within the bounds of their art. Because I am not a musicologist I rely upon Charles Rosen (1971), who describes Mozart's work, such as his piano concerto K. 271 (No. 9 in E flat). Of the Andantino Rosen says, "As an expression of grief and despair, this movement stands . . . almost alone among Mozart's concerto movements; not until the Andante con moto of Beethoven's G major Concerto is the same tragic power recaptured" (211). Rosen adds: "What is most striking . . . about the opening phrase of the Andantino is its masterly architecture: the accents on the low AI (repeated in canon by the second violin) prepare the climax on an AI and octave higher in measure 4 . . ." (212). Rosen summarizes his evaluation of this piece by using a metaphor drawn from architecture: "The whole phrase is like a great arch, its classical rise and fall controlling and mastering the span of tragic grief from the canonic beginning to the climax and then to the halting, almost stammering end" (212).

This analysis echoes Rosen's earlier comments on Mozart's "sublime economy." By maintaining an overall pattern of stability, Mozart could range over a heretofore unimagined range of harmonic experiments. He says of the E flat Quartet, K. 428, "The opening measure is an example of Mozart's sublime economy. It sets the tonality by a single octave leap (the most tonal of intervals), framing the three chromatic measures that follow. The two EI's are lower and higher that any of the other notes, and by setting these limits they imply the resolution of all dissonance within an E flat context. They define the tonal space . . ." (186). To define tonal space is to establish a bounded universe. By offering listeners an initial, well-defined frame, Mozart makes the dissonant chords that follow tolerable. Indeed, Rosen suggests that having established the upper and lower reaches of our experience, Mozart transforms dissonance, which is typically unpleasant and tense, into an essential part of the music's beauty, for by the end our tensions are resolved.

To use psychoanalytic terms, Rosen's description of the E flat Quartet parallels Ernst Kris's (1956a) famous description of the "good hour." Like this quartet the good hour begins typically with dissonance. Neither patient nor analyst knows what is going on, only that the patient's affects are muddled and the patient feels uneasy. Kris says this dissonant opening requires the analyst to tune in and this "leads to the experience on which analytic therapy in its ideal case rests, to the experience of insight, in which the cognitive elements are merged with a particular kind of assurance. In this assurance the multiple elements which have led to conviction or comprehension tend to reverberate. Many a time we can watch the progressive establishment of this state of mind, when what was at first 'intellectual', 'flat', 'two-dimensional', becomes 'real', 'concrete', 'three-dimensional', to use expressions we all have heard from patients; expressions which seem all to refer to rather specific archaic modes of experience" (448). While these modes of experience are "rather archaic," according to Kris, because they draw upon somatic models, not purely intellectual ones generated through insight alone they are also "progressive" in an aesthetic sense because they are complete, direct, and immediate.

To use the language of romantic poetry, good music, good poetry, and the "good hour" match fully intense affective experience: "A child at play by itself will express delight by its voice and motions; and every inflexion of tone and gesture will bear exact relation to a corresponding antitype in the pleasurable impressions which awakened it . . ." (Shelley [1821] 1921, 24). To use terms from Stern's developmental theory, Mozart's music evokes and realizes a complete activation contour. Like the well-parented child who experiences strong, even violent affects, we hear in Mozart similar feelings without falling into abject misery. We recognize and "have" these strong feelings but do not surrender to chaos and depression.

Faithful to his scientific project, the integration of a theory of libidinal economics with ego psychology, Kris stresses the degree to which integrative processes occur beneath the surface: "This might well remind us how much remains unknown about the conditions under which the ego does its silent work" (453). This silent work includes "insight," which, contrary to common usage, does not mean to become consciously aware: "A connexion has been established, but before insight has reached awareness (or, if it does, only for flickering moments), new areas of anxiety and conflict emerge, new material comes, and the process drives on: thus far-reaching changes may and must be achieved, without the pathway by which they have come about becoming part of the patient's awareness" (452).

The parallels I noted between my patient, whom I named Reverend A, Chertoff's patient, and Freud's "Rat Man" find an unexpected echo in Stern's vignette. Speaking of Rat Man, I note a similar case involving a young professional man for whom any narcissistic tension, such as presenting an excellent piece of work to his students, was unbearable. Any hint of joy evoked instantly a sense of "shittiness" about himself. Dreams, jokes, associations, daydreams, waking fantasies, and his sexual life all centered on evacuating his feelings as quickly as possible. This, naturally, was colored by an anal sense of life: you stuffed yourself with good things, only to see them turn quickly into dirt. One source of this profound pessimism, which he shared with his older sister, was his mother. She was probably psychotic much of his life due to an undiagnosed bipolar illness. She could not tolerate her children's boisterousness, especially at the end of the day when they were "too excited" and she was probably near the end of her patience. When her kids were just on the verge of their greatest pleasure, when the game was in the last inning, or just before the tie breaker, she would insist they come inside and rest. Indeed, she sometimes insisted that they go to the toilet since, she said, *that* was the source of their restlessness.

I believe this patient's story resembles Stern's vignette, which, in turn, resembles that of Rat Man. Each illustrates a certain kind of pathogenesis. The anxious or distressed parent seeks to control a child's expression of primary affects, both negative, like anger, and positive, like joy. These efforts, like my patient's mother squelching her children and explaining to them that their excitement was the product of stopped up bowels, succeed in one sense: the child no longer experiences the tension state associated with the original affect. These efforts also tend to create the consequences that the parents wished to prevent. For by stopping the rise of affect *prior* to its resolution in a natural mode, the overcontrolling parent gives the infant or child no experience of its safe resolution. This means that strong, naturally occurring primary feeling states, like anger, sadness, fear, and joy, evoke anxiety in the child because the child has few experiences of their complete and benign resolution.

Children raised in these circumstances cannot rely upon their culture's institutional memory to contain fully these affects and transform them into art. They cannot share with John Keats, for example, those moments of joy in sadness and sadness in joy or, if Christian, the solace offered in Jesus' promises, especially the beatitude "Blessed are they that mourn" (from the Sermon on the Mount, Matt. 5:4).

With honest expression comes, of course, the danger of exposure and derision that often greets passionate feelings. Popular comics make easy fun of operas in which the heroine, for example Violetta in *La traviata* (by Giuseppe Verdi in 1853), sick with consumption, sings with vigorous abandon as she dies upon the stage. Opera makes itself an easy target for ridicule. Yet, in defense of Mozart at least, we note that the joy he imparts lies in his capacity to marry a libretto that talks about despair with his wonderful music. *The Marriage of Figaro* (presented in May 1786), while officially a comic opera (opera *buffa*), is a politically risky story about the diminishment of aristocratic privilege. It turns on reversals, covering and uncovering, of masking and unmasking Count Almavia who has renounced his traditional right of *ius primae noctis,* that is, the right to violate lower-class women under his jurisdiction prior to their wedding night. However, the count's sexual appetite (his id we might say) has not kept up with his political zeal (his superego), since he intends nevertheless to seduce his chambermaid, Susanna, the bride-to-be of Figaro. In lesser hands this would be merely a story of buffoonery, or an angry political message, or a lesson in propriety. But with Mozart it is more; the glorious music he gives to each character, such as the countess who plots revenge against her scheming, adulterous husband, demarcate each as striving toward a higher nobility, a union of thought and feeling that Mozart names love. We might name it a form of beguiling eroticism: "It is the primal forces of eroticism which constantly light up Mozart's music from within . . ." (Csampai 1992, 21). This is eroticism in Freud's sense, a primal urge toward unity and reconciliation of opposites. The vast range of popular songs, especially the blues, gospel, country, and now rap, are contemporary illustrations of the same artistic capacity to capture, name, and control affects that would otherwise be chaotic and overwhelming. These range from utter despair, to anger, to joy, to mourning.[14]

According to a general psychoanalytic developmental point of view, infants and children must accommodate themselves to drives like sexuality, aggression, and attachment. We assume that they take part in potentially stable, but imperfect systems. If parents or a dominant culture cannot tolerate the appearance of these expectable variations they will seek to control them. This unrealizable demand for perfection must then issue in increased aberrations. Naturally, these aberrations prove the existence of heretofore unseen forces of evil and destruction. In the face of these threats parents commonly *increase* their efforts to coerce their children and to control their emotional experiences.

As reflections of disorganization, rather than intentionality, one cannot trace in these unconscious fantasies an unbroken line of feeling or conceptualization. In Green's terms, one cannot find in explosive blitzkrieg moments type one affects which are limited and designated by semantic rules. Rather, blitzkrieg affects evoke irrational and self-harming behaviors.

These behavioral consequences are irrational in a strong sense of that term for both patients and analysts realize patients do not wish harm themselves; they have no choice. When they attempt to understand why they must cut their skin, for example, they happen upon all manner of stories and explanations. Because these are both founded upon pathogenic beliefs and responses to blitzkrieg affects, these accounts cannot comply with ordinary logic and sense. Rather, they are irrational; if graphed or put into causal narratives they yield contradictions and confusion. These stories will not yield to prediction except the weak claim that they will reveal no fixed pattern. A drunken pathway may lead home every so often but usually it will not.

Indeed, because persons subjected to blitzkrieg affects necessarily fail, these undesired outcomes evoke even stronger efforts to control the aberrant behavior. When a "bad" child fails to match a perfectionistic parent the parent makes more efforts to control the child. From these kinds of interactions children acquire two devastating beliefs: strong feelings are dangerous and even when subjected to painful "control" they will return with such force and irrational compulsion they feel like a blitzkrieg attack. Indeed, this suggests why fantasies of eternal easiness, heaven, and eternal horror, hell, are so plausible, especially to persons raised with perfectionistic ideals. For example, a two-year-old girl, whose musculature and nervous system work in a normal way, operates as a stable system. Sometimes she drops her food, sometimes she does not. If her instructor, say her father, upholds pathogenic beliefs, he concludes that she can do better and reach, eventually, perfection. Hence, he redoubles his efforts to control the aberrant child. According to pathogenic beliefs 1 and 2 ("Everything she does is caused and intentional," and "There must be ways to control her") the girl drops her food intentionally. Thus, her father "knows" that her behavior is willed. Failures to comply with his requests signify the sin of stubbornness. To combat this sin the girl's father punishes her, then exhorts, and then bribes her.

If the child is doing the best she can, given her developmental level and other ego functioning, then at the conclusion of each interaction she will exhibit new errors. For each of her father's actions, whether punishing or rewarding, adds additional randomness to an otherwise stable system. Aberrations increase and the cycle of failure, control, and "error" repeats. The little girl will always fail eventually. She and her father will have many battles down the road; each battle will confirm her father's original premonition: "She's a bad child." For example, by concentrating upon holding the spoon just right, the child may no longer drop her food. Instead, because she cannot control every part of her musculature, she soils her pants. If the child's father is consistent and dedicated to the job of improving her, he draws one conclusion: increase punishment and increase efforts to control the girl's new, deviant behavior. If he tires (or passes out or gets drunk), he will cease trying to control his child, for the moment. Later, sparked on by the wish to do the right thing, he will try again to improve upon his daughter's performance.

Every so often the girl will randomly (that is, accidentally) exhibit the behavior her father demands. These apparent successes provoke father to another round of exhortation and attack: indeed, his daughter's every-so-often successes serve as intermittent reinforcements for the father. For each supports the father's conviction that his demands, threats, and seductions caused his child to "get the point." After all, she obeyed him once: this proves that obedience is a matter of "will power." Of course, after trying to comply and "be good" the child may perceive, dimly, that even if she gets it right every so often, this too eventually yields to chaos and becomes another instance of failure. At this and other moments of despair, she will become distressed; she had been good for a moment but then, inexplicably, failed to maintain her virtuous self. Evoking a set of pathogenic beliefs and other forms of perfectionism, she reasons that having been good (or lovable) she abandoned her good self; hence, her badness is evident to all. Because these are aversive emotions the child defends herself against their reappearance. To defend herself against despair, for example, she may discover the benefits of denying that she loves her father, or she will discover ways to make herself unconscious, or, in extreme instances, she will discover ways to destroy herself.

Because the child focuses upon his moods especially if they portend punishment, the father's spurts of reward and punishment systematically increase randomness within his daughter's self-system. Each cycle of exhortation, failure, and punishment multiplies the child's burdens. Accepting her father's perfectionism and knowing that he hurts her when she is "bad," the child will try to deduce why she was bad one moment and good at another. But because there is *no* reason, that is, discernible pattern, for her every-so-often successes, *all* her answers will be wrong. This means that every new "theory" offered as to her evil nature will increase randomness and increase chaos and incoherence. These evoke, naturally, from father and child increased despair and more punishment. If a Christian the father may cite Scripture and so align God and Jesus with terror and despair. These proclamations about love will neither match the child's initial expectations nor will they match her internal sense of her rising terror. None of her efforts to predict her father's actions will be accurate enough to prevent her inevitable failures and none will prevent his eventual explosion. Indeed, her father predicted these failures; if not directly then indirectly through the distrust he communicated when he assumed the task of controlling her behavior, including, naturally, her thoughts and feelings.

Children need to be sensible and need to comprehend their worlds, especially the minds of their caretakers. Their failures to do so become yet another sign that they are inadequate. Like persons living on the side of active volcanoes, children of alcoholic parents, for example, stay alert to every indicator of imminent disaster. That they cannot use those indicators to predict exactly the next disaster only means they must keep on searching. In other words, they institute an obsessive-like routine, driving themselves to discern evidence that does not exist.

## MISATTUNEMENT, BLITZKRIEG AFFECT: THE OBJECTS OF PSYCHOANALYSIS

Psychoanalysts wish their discipline to be scientific but this wish is not always granted. In chapter 2 I summarized many of the traditional criticisms of psychoanalytic method and theory made by both analysts and non-analysts. While acknowledging the merit of these criticisms, I nevertheless argued that we can account for our disappointments, in part, by noting that the objects of analysis, these odd theories of mind and attendant terrors, are not substantive entities. Diabetes, for example, is a terrible disease but it is a substantial entity. It is caused by a complex series of biological events that determine its appearance and its course. Eventually, normal science, as T. S. Kuhn (1962) defines a well-defined research tradition, will master its intricacies. Then physicians will provide ways to interfere with the genesis of diabetes or at least ameliorate its effects.

That many patients get better through psychoanalytic experience and that psychoanalysis cures, does not prove that its objects are rational or capable of rational deconstruction. On the contrary, that neurotic suffering yields to psychoanalytic labor does not prove that analysis is therefore the investigation of rational entities. With its roots in Freud's profound insights into transference repetition, analytic technique permits us to comprehend our patient's inner experiences and their sense of their past through the drama of transference reenactment, not by solving intellectual puzzles. When he seeks to explain why Rat Man feared the return of his dead father, Freud does not give "reasons" in an ordinary sense of that term. Rather, Freud and his patient had to endure numerous struggles with Rat Man's violent feelings and violent attacks.

Freud and his patient lived through these attacks. That persistence, along with Freud's intense commitment to his patients, the brilliance of his proffered interventions, and his good will all manifested his faith that there was a way out of the Rat Man's terrors. This route required them both to experience these powerful affects between themselves. Freud's bravery permitted him to convert his and his patients' blitzkrieg affects into affects linked to words and then to memories of their joint agonistic drama. This adult, therapeutic enactment reproduces the schemata of good enough parent and child. Saying that a person has expressed fully an affect, in Stern's sense, means that the person has lived through an intense emotion *in the presence* of another, real, person capable of mirroring the intensity of that emotion and its patterns. This demonstrates an otherwise unavailable and invisible reality: that one can live through intense anger, for example, without destroying the relationship or having to dissociate from one's affective experience. Freud says Rat Man "had thought that if there were murderous impulses in [Freud's] family, [Freud] would fall upon him like a beast of prey to search out what was evil in him" (1909d, 285). Having said this and having learned that Freud would not attack him Rat Man proceeded to the next act in the drama of his therapy.

This drama was made possible by Freud's stage setting and by his use of the rule of free association. The brilliance of Freud's "basic rule" requiring free association is that he did *not* require patients to produce meaningful, connected discourses about themselves. By asking patients to report the flow of their experience, he made possible subsequent psychoanalytic discoveries. For the basic rule requires patient (and analyst) to *not* impose narrative sense upon the stream of thoughts and feelings that emerge in the analytic process. While analysts take seriously patients' experiences of Darwinian and culturally prescribed affects, especially guilt and shame, their ultimate goal is to uncover those deeper terrors that are responses to overwhelming and uncontrolled affects. Upholding the basic rule makes the invisible visible; it asks the patient to bring into the hour the host of devices, split selves, defensive techniques, and externalized parts of the patient's self with which the patient has learned to exist in a nether world.

In this netherworld live the patient's split off experiences, which are best described in the language of folk religion: as ghosts and spirits driven to reunite with those who see them. For example, George Atwood and Robert Stolorow (1981) describe a child who learned to survive with the help of ghosts: "A sense of profound personal disunity had haunted the patient all her life, appearing even in her earliest recollections. For example, she recalled from her fourth year an obsession with the issue of how it could be that her mind controlled the movement of her body. A disturbance of mind-body unity was also indicated by quasi-delusional journeys outside of her body that began during that same year. These journeys commenced on the occasion when she was visited by the benevolent ghosts of two deceased grandparents. The ghosts taught her to leave her body and fly to a place she called the field, "a peaceful expanse of grass and trees somewhere far removed from human civilization" (201). We are not surprised to learn that she was repeatedly abused by both her mother and father; we are surprised to learn the sad truth that she felt closer to her father than her mother "because when he whipped her he always had a reason. The mother's attacks on her were unpredictable and extremely violent" (201).

I have also stressed the pathogenic features of these kinds of random attacks. For by being unpredictable the mother made it impossible for her daughter to comprehend why she was suffering and how to prevent it by "being good." In Shelly's beautiful words, poetry can sometimes help create within us a "being" that resides with us as part of our sense of self. The antithesis of this happy occurrence is a child, like this girl, who seeks desperately to find companions from a netherworld when no one in this world proves adequate.

By holding the basic rule constant the analyst creates a grid of comparative memory and expectation against which to judge the presence or absence of authentic emotional expression. From the beginning of his reflections upon technique Freud realized that he had to use words to set the frame of analysis, to offer interpretations, and to carry out discourse about psychoanalysis. However, these words are always secondary to the psychoanalytic set up, as Winnicott terms it. There, in the analytic frame, reappear procedural memories, the origins of the transference, and the affect storms that are the heart of psychoanalytic experience. More primary than analytic speaking is analytic listening, because by listening we discover the ebb and flow of affects, especially their crescendos and their deformations through defense. More so, by holding open a frame of expectation and by tolerating the efflorescence of transference, analytic technique makes possible analytic process; the gradual revelation of the patient's response to overwhelming affects that "advance in force towards the heart of the ego."

Technique, training, tradition, craft, and other arts give the good enough analyst ways to assay and navigate these emotional storms, not simply examine patterns of discourse. At the same time or a little bit later, the analyst must disentangle the patient's internal narrative about these events. These internal narratives typically revolve around a core of pathogenic beliefs. These entrenched pathogenic beliefs together with horror of their strongest feelings make up these patients' experience of dread and anxiety. Because intense anxiety obliterates joy, their lives are not joyful. Any strong affect, positive or negative, makes them feel out of control; instead of joy, they feel narcissistic tension, instead of sadness they feel depression.

Accordingly, children raised in chaotic and perfectionistic environments experience blitzkrieg affects daily. Because these are irrational they fit no narrative. Their efforts to reason about their suffering

lead only to failure. Failure to locate their suffering in plausible discourse validates these children's worst fears about themselves and
reinforces their pathogenic beliefs. As adults they cannot imagine
benign resolution of conflicts with their analyst because there are
none (or few) in their past. Hence, their internal experience is that
strong feelings are chaotic and irredeemably harmful. While they
naturally tell themselves stories about their suffering and their sense
of failure the linkages between their suffering and these stories is like
the path of a drunk who meanders aimlessly. The inner connections
we hope to find linking one part of our patient's feelings with memories of the safe diminution of those feelings are *not* present. There is
no pattern (and thus no narrative continuity) linking the experience
of blitzkrieg affects with experiences of interpersonal safety. Rather,
these patients' internal worlds are dominated by chaos. From this
derives their conviction that life cannot be other than constant
struggle, shame, and defeat. If the pathogenic rules of the games
taught them in childhood remain in force this belief is unhappily
correct. Because of self-object inversions, seductions, and partial
successes that issue in intermittent reinforcement, the child's and
adult's pathogenic beliefs are reinforced daily. These beliefs become
entrenched: life becomes a series of anxious battles followed by catastrophes and ever more dangerous risks.

    If through good fortune the child discovers a culturally sanc-
tioned form of retreat and reparation, like that afforded in monastic
institutions, these battles may diminish or even disappear. Alternatively, if a child happens to resonate with the child's culture and its
institutions of emotional expression another partial victory may appear. To cite Shelley ([1821] 1921) again, "But poetry defeats the
curse which binds us to be subjected to the accident of surrounding
impressions. In addition, whether it spreads its own figured curtain,
or withdraws life's dark veil from before the scene of things, it equally
creates for us a being within our being. It makes us the inhabitants
of a world to which the familiar world is a chaos" (56). I have suggested that Shelley's intuition is correct. Those happy few who find
relief in art can confront an internal world of chaos, engendered by
pathogenic beliefs and overwhelming anxiety, and keep it at bay.
The rest of us need other ways. One of these other ways was first
discovered by Sigmund Freud.

# CHAPTER 6

# The Objects of Psychoanalysis

## THE OBJECTS OF PSYCHOANALYSIS:
## PATHOGENIC BELIEFS, BLITZKRIEG AFFECTS

I have suggested that among interesting problems for psychoanalysis is that of identifying its subject matter, what I have termed its "objects." Indeed, to offer a clear definition of its objects is to make a theoretical claim subject to many counterclaims. Entering the fray, I have suggested that the objects of analysis are a peculiar combination of beliefs about two important pieces of human psychology: the nature of mind (and its attendant questions) and the nature of chaotic feelings, what I have termed blitzkrieg affects. Our objects, then, are patients' idiosyncratic beliefs about minds, especially their caretakers' minds, and beliefs (convictions, fantasies) about how to control feelings, particularly blitzkrieg affects. When these beliefs emerge in childhood and when caretakers are disorganized and demand caretaking from the child, they become deeply rooted and pathogenic. They are pathogenic because they give rise to self-harming actions that are reinforced constantly and thus become a way of life. I suggested that these beliefs are analogous to plausible but erroneous management theory. Like managers who insist upon controlling employees whom they mistrust, children raised by disorganizing parents "know" that everything will fall apart unless they step in and make it right.

Beginning with Freud, psychoanalysts have explored and mapped these idiosyncratic beliefs. I have emphasized that they operate like entrenched ideologies: every possible outcome validates them. If, on Monday, a child believes she lessened her mother's depression this proves that this is her special calling and her destiny. If she fails to control her mother's mood sufficiently to prevent mother from becoming depressed on Tuesday, this means she should work doubly hard on Wednesday, Thursday, and Friday. Eventually mother's mood will change. If it improves, this change validates the child's struggles and reinforces her pathogenic beliefs: "I am special because I have saved mother." If mother's mood worsens and issues in a suicide gesture, for example, then the child's deepest fear about herself—that she will prove inadequate—reemerges, as if announced by God. J. T. Curtis (1988) cites a patient who recognized how much her depressed mother relied upon her and that if "somebody makes me feel guilty, my God, I'd go out and move a whole mountain for her."[1]

Children raised in these circumstances simulate relationships: they become adept, sometimes brilliantly so, at anticipating the moods of their caretakers. If they are talented artistically, they may transform their losses into poetry, or music, or stories. If they are intellectual, they substitute "reasoning," an action fully under their control, for nonexistent benign relationships. (When this fails, they often attack their body and thus, in "mastering" their pain, control the self.) Driven by anxiety they fabricate "trust" and other ego states that require one to depend upon the good will of others. This they cannot do actually, for trusting another means (1) losing their fantasy of dominance and self-control, and (2) an inevitable slide into terror and disorganization. Curtis's patient discovered that she would move mountains to help her mother and thus avoid guilt, a strong secondary affect. We add that while guilt propelled her to remain tied to her mother and thus avoid independence, pride drove her to rescue others. Discovering that she could govern her mother's feelings was also part of this grand seduction: she was "mother's favorite" (Curtis et al. 1988, 259); "she has been, and continues to be, the family member closest to her mother" (260).

I suggested that we can supplement this version of cognitive psychoanalytic theory by noting that these seductions and reinforcements dominate a child's affective life. This means, in turn, that all later object relations occur within a grid of unstable affects and increasingly terrified response to them. Guilt is a "cultural affect," constructed out of Darwinian affects and shaped by cultural rules. To sustain its full and complete expression requires one to tolerate an affect curve that, from the inside, feels precipitous, and, in the most frightening instances, unending. To tolerate this curve of feelings and to not short circuit them (by primitive defenses or by action-discharge) typically requires the presence of another, real person who can stand as a guarantor of a benign outcome. Benign does not mean ideal, for we recognize that persons die and that they can achieve dignity in death if they are also loved and are not alone when they say good-bye. I have followed Daniel Stern and other developmentalists to suggest that when an affect curve is destroyed the interior experience shifts from "flow" to blitzkrieg-like chaos.

Analysts, again, have long recognized this terrifying dimension of their patients' experience. According to his students, Elvin Semrad, a noted Boston analyst, often said, "[M]uch of individual clinical work has to do with acknowledging, bearing, and putting into perspective intolerable affects."[2] We note that, as usual, this wise counsel seems manifestly false: we cannot tolerate intolerable affects. Of course, Semrad means that therapists must first learn to tolerate the patient's story, identify with the patient's intense, often eroticized, experience, and then recognize how the patient (and therapist) defends against the latter, especially overstimulation. When working with patients who have suffered physical and sexual abuse it is particularly difficult to recognize but not assume the heroic powers patients imagine are necessary to help them. Because therapists are usually benign and skilled, the contrast between them and the patient's abusive parents, for example, are striking and we are not surprised that patients idealize their therapists. However, beyond this ordinary feature of therapy lies the "strange attractor" of blitzkrieg affects: like medieval portraits of Hell, they are fascinating. Like the image of Satan frozen in Hell, they are repugnant, but also fascinating because they define the outer limits of our conceptual worlds. They denote the edge of our tolerable experience and we fear them. Although they are frozen in ice, like other split-off parts of the self, they might break free and pull us toward them.

When therapists ask patients to encounter these affects and challenge their occult powers, patients project onto their therapists the mantle of hero. In *Memories, Dreams, Reflections* (1961) Carl Jung describes blitzkrieg affects and mythic battles during his painful separation from Freud. A typical dream is "I was with an unknown, brown-skinned man, a savage, in a lonely, rocky mountain landscape. It was before dawn; the eastern sky was already bright, and the stars fading. Then I heard Siegfried's horn sounding over the mountains and I knew that we had to kill him" (180). Siegfried is the German hero around whom thirteenth-century bards wove the *Nibelungenlied,* from which Richard Wagner created his epic *Der Ring des Nibelungen.* That Jung must kill Siegfried signifies Jung's sense that his calling was to confront a pre-Christian European myth and to replace it with a mythology adapted to the twentieth century. Freud's metaphors for therapeutic process, including resistance and cathexis, often derive from battle imagery and other forms of agonistic struggle (Gay 1997).

Between two opposing forces or between two extremes is, by definition, the "middle ground." This region emerges in traditional character theory and in psychoanalytic characterology as the ideal place. For common sense and traditional psychological theory affirm Aristotle's dictum:

> That moral virtue is a mean . . . a mean between two vices, the one involving excess, the other deficiency, and that it is such because its character is to aim at what is intermediate in passions and in actions, has been sufficiently stated. (*Nicomachean Ethics* 2.9.1–4)

Those whom moderns might label "well adjusted," Aristotle calls "moral": they discover balancing points midway between polar extremes. Psychoanalysts who write on character development make a similar point when they extol a golden mean as the best outcome of developmental struggles. Erik Erikson's (1962, 1963) master theory of ego development rests upon the metaphor of ego development as a building under construction. Each new stage is foundational to the next and each presents to persons at its threshold a nuclear conflict. Erikson gives each conflict a dramatic title like "Autonomy vs. Shame and Doubt" and "Initiative vs. Guilt," which generations of college students have now memorized. Collapsing into either pole of these conflicts is, by definition, a sign of psychopathology. Like Freud, Erikson does not denigrate either pole of these conflicts, for example shame and guilt; he merely requires them to be balanced off with their counterparts. This occurs when a child enjoys the grace of "mutual regulation."

Like other psychoanalysts and moralists, Erikson offers concepts like "mutual regulation" to overcome what seem to be conceptual contradictions. These are "both p and not-p" terms that recognize, in this case, that both parents raise children and children raise parents, that the ideal of a good relationship is not a world of domination where one person regulates another. On the contrary, Erikson notes that the nursing pair of happy mother and happy nursing infant, for example, is paradigmatic of benign human relationships because neither party dominates. Both regulate the other's body, self-state, and form a social "pair." In the same way, he proposes to solve the problem of the concept of "reality" in psychoanalytic discourse by distinguishing it from "actuality." The first term refers to the world investigated by ordinary scientific methods; the second term refers to "the world of participation, shared with a minimum of defensive maneuvers and a maximum of mutual activation. Mutual activation is the crux of the matter; for human ego strength while employing all means of testing reality depends, from stage to stage, upon a network of mutual influences within which the person actuates others even as he is actuated, and within which the person is 'inspired with active properties,' even as he so inspires others. This is ego actuality; largely preconscious and unconscious, it must be studied by psychoanalytic means" (1962, 462).

Robert Wallerstein (1987, 1988) followed Erikson's lead when he revised classical ego psychological formulations and redefined ego functioning. Because it was difficult to define "defense" mechanisms, Wallerstein substituted the concept "psychological capacities." These are "low-level (experience-near) theoretical constructs" (1988, 255) like self-esteem. Each capacity has two poles: self-esteem, for instance, has the poles "Grandiosity" and "Self-depreciation." The desired location is the "so-called 'normal' or optimal ideal point" (247) between these polar extremes. Wallerstein and his colleagues assign to empathy, another psychological capacity, two polar extremes: too much empathy is "Emotional Absorption" and too little empathy is "Emotional Blunting" (256). Another psychological capacity, "Reciprocity," has two poles: when too much it merits the label "Exploitation of Others," and when too little it merits the label "Surrender of Self" (256).[3]

Wallerstein's criticism, that traditional psychoanalytic terms are difficult to operationalize, recalls our earlier concern about the language of psychoanalysis. Often it appears that psychoanalytic terms are best efforts to designate an assumed "thingness" to what are, minimally, complex behaviors. Yet, these objects are more than mere behaviors: psychoanalytic terms are more than recitations of complex patterns, named "Borderline Personality," for example. We assume that terms like "ego function" and "ego defense" are useful and validatable. Wallerstein suggests that the latter is not easy to show, hence his recommendations. We may agree with this recommendation and accept his substitutes. However, even these substitute terms reveal their origins in theory, rather than observation, for they replicate, uncannily, the patterns of Aristotle's discourse on ethics.

That Wallerstein's terms, like Erikson's famous "Eight Stages" of human life, are *typical* suggests we are dealing with definitions, not empirical discoveries. Like Aristotle, these authors name as ideal a balance point between two polar extremes: "This much then is clear; that it is the middle disposition in each department of conduct that is to be praised." Aristotle adds a bit of advice, "but that one should lean sometimes to the side of excess and sometimes to that of deficiency, since this is the easiest way of hitting the mean and the right course" (*Nicomachean Ethics* 2.9.9). This is exactly what neurotic persons *cannot* do. They cannot lean sometimes to the side of excess and then to the side of deficiency because to lean either way is to begin a long slide into painful feelings, cataclysmic behaviors, and unnamable dread. Christian fundamentalists, as we shall see, who declare all dancing dangerous do not suggest a child lean toward "too much eroticism" and then back toward "too little" eroticism because they know that all eroticism is poisonous and of the devil.

Freud let us disagree with another of Aristotle's dicta: "Men [*sic*] deficient in the enjoyment of pleasures scarcely occur, and hence this character also has not been assigned a name, but we may call it Insensible" (*Nicomachean Ethics* 2.7.4). After Freud, we can say that *many* persons are deficient in the enjoyment of pleasure and we call this state neurosis or character pathology. Neurotic and other persons typically diagnosed as character pathological are *not* emotionless robots, nor are they insensible. On the contrary, patients labeled as borderline personality disorder (BPD) show frequent expressions of rage, grief, and acute depression. These constitute part of modern diagnostic. Severely impaired patients, labeled as "character pathological," always struggle with the expression of affects in the presence of others.

Typically, they reveal both too much (hyperemotionality) and too little (hypoemotionality). These wild gyrations are puzzling to themselves and to persons around them. The "too much, too little" pattern suggests that a system that ought to be self-regulated has gone haywire. Lacking genuine experiences of mutual regulation (Erikson 1963), children who attempt to control their parents' affects have no "lived experience" of the natural resolution of *their* strong affects in interpersonal safety. Therefore, they attempt to control their feelings and those of important others, especially their therapists. When these patients are giving, parenting, teaching, and caring for others they control the interaction and thus do not face blitzkrieg affects in themselves. To persist through the entire cycle of blitzkrieg affects requires one to depend upon the good will of another person. This they cannot do: they can love, but not be loved. They cannot bear to hope that others will become active and do for them what they do so well for others.

## FROM THE GOLDEN MEAN TO THE CONTROL STATE; FROM ARISTOTLE TO DEMING

In *Nicomachean Ethics* Aristotle says that it is not easy to be good:

> For in everything it is no easy task to find the middle, e.g., to find the middle of a circle is not for every one but for him who knows; so, too, any one can get angry—that is easy—or give or spend money; but to do this to the right person, to the right extent, at the right time, with the right motive, and in the right way, that is not for every one, nor is it easy; wherefore goodness is both rare and laudable and noble. (2.9.1–4)

Aristotle's recommendations verge upon tautology: to be good one must do the right thing in the right way. We can save Aristotle from appearing simplistic if we note that his concept of "moral" action is very similar to what Deming called the "control state." Once Deming has hammered it home, the idea of "control state" is straightforward. It means that a system is functioning at its most efficient level and that all "errors" or deviations from the desired outcome are due to chance, not to correctable behaviors on the part of any actor. However, establishing when a given system is in control is not easy. On the contrary, it is a difficult, empirical task that requires one to discover what counts as too much and what counts as too little.

We cannot accurately use the term "control state" until we have assessed the system and found its failure points. We have no instantaneous way to designate the system's limits and to establish the "control state" of the system. If one has an ideology in place *prior* to assessment one cannot learn from the system. This preexisting ideology renders subsequent observations useless; if they affirm our ideology they are privileged, if they contradict it then we should redouble our efforts. Ideological formulae, therefore, give no empirical basis to our method and no way to alter our actions based on the outcome of trial and error. (We note how Freud, in contrast to caricatures of him, altered his clinical theorems when they failed, a spectacular instance being his failed analysis of Dora [Freud 1905e]).

An alternative to discovering the control state (through trial, error, and honest evaluation) is provided by perfectionism and other ideologies. Religious ideologies, like political ideologies, are attractive to persons who feel themselves in crisis. They live on slippery slopes. Like a nation at war, persons operating with ideologies suspend ordinary rules of civility and openness. Some conservative Christians, for example, who feel beleaguered by a culture of permissiveness, condemn dancing in all its forms. Like other ideologues, they know in advance that "that way lies sin," hence they need not locate the boundaries that separate decent from indecent dancing. "The atmosphere of the dance, its provision for close physical contact between opposite sexes, the soft lights, and langorous [*sic*] music are all calculated to stimulate unlawful thoughts and purposes." Once stimulated these unlawful, that is, sexual, thoughts swiftly lead to "a coarsening of character if not a tragic ruining of life."[4]

So too, ideological relativists, their political counterparts, lazily ignore the reality of indecency and "sin" or "crime." Like the authors of the treatise against dancing, ideological relativists sidestep the struggle to find the actual contours of adolescent struggles. "Anything goes" is not a recipe for success. Unless parents enjoy the comfort of an absolutistic ideology, they struggle to find a good enough way to raise adolescents with increasing freedom and increasing responsibility.

The "art" of analysis, like other arts, consists of acquired expertise: one learns how to learn from one's materials. Like ironworkers who learn from iron its limits, the therapist as artist must learn from his or her errors and mistakes. Because we operate within a moral and psychological universe constrained by polar concepts we sometimes oscillate and sometimes lurch between them. In fantasies about art (TV movies, for example) this lengthy apprenticeship rarely appears: instead, artists expropriate visions granted them, which they reproduce in their media. The painting or the symphony appears and the artist merely copies it down. However, in real life, art is not pretty. The sweat and tears that go into making ballet look effortless, for example, are hidden in numerous dress rehearsals. Naturally, TV and other imaginary renditions of psychoanalysis are, usually, equally fantastic.

Another way to describe Aristotle's dictum, that becoming good means alternating between the "too much" and "too little," is "oscillation" (Gardner, 1991, 1994). This term designates a capacity to go back and forth between conceptual polar extremes, something children raised by infantile parents *cannot* do. They cannot oscillate between polar images of their parents' minds without falling into despair. These children bring to their version of adulthood the same imaginative zeal we bring to watching *Amadeus*. We leave the theater or switch off the VCR and idealize Mozart safely, knowing that we need not compose an exquisite piece of music that night. Children raised by infantile parents cannot do this: they are called upon daily to perform their imagined roles. Indeed, given the usual selfobject inversions in such families and the pathological reward systems in place, their parents share this expectation.

Such children cannot escape back into "reality" because the only contrast they have to the imaginary is hopelessness. Sometimes alcohol or other drugs offer manic highs but these are followed by remorse and more dread. Because the alternative to fantasy is a dreadful, chaotic mess, these children cannot learn from their parents. They fall back upon images of adulthood constructed during their childhood. From these images they create guidelines, rules, and such for being strong (or "good," or "manly," or "feminine," or "Christian"). These they write out in diaries or other private journals. From our point of view, these rules establish grandiose expectations that their authors eventually fail to match. As Kohut noted (1966, 1971), this can spur significant achievement, but at the costs of inner doubt and emptiness.

From pieces of their parents, siblings, teachers, coaches, other real-life persons, and imaginary persons like the mother in *Little Women* or thinkers like Nietzsche and Freud, or rebels like alcoholic poets or gun-toting rap singers, they fabricate "how to" guides. In contrast to older children and adolescents who construct various versions of adult life as trial runs at adulthood, children raised by infantile parents use their fabricated guides to "run" themselves and to control their affects. Because they correctly reject their parents as plausible self-objects, they fall back upon their constructions to raise themselves. Compelled to put into words, like ardent philosophers, they search for essential truths about feelings, behavior, and the mind. This is a task they and Aristotle cannot solve, a game that cannot be won.[5]

However, I have suggested that children raised in chaotic homes cannot enjoy this kind of optimism. To explore this fact I have followed out one line of analytic thought begun by Freud, then extended by Melanie Klein, D. W. Winnicott, and Andre Green, among many others. This is a focus upon patients' experience of feelings that are so overwhelming that Green terms them blitzkrieg affects. In defense against these affects, patients typically act; they must do something, usually something that either makes them lose consciousness (for example, the teenager who sniffs glue) or dissociate (using a variety of altered states of consciousness) or displace their focus from their suffering (sexualization, thrill seeking, masochism). If these affects arise in conjunction with parents' chaotic treatment, children try to prevent their reoccurrence by "reasoning." Hoping to control their parents' aberrations, they manufacture private "theories" of what causes psychopathology. Typically, these theories are some form of pathogenic belief.

To know existentially that it is safe to express feelings, including anger and sexual passions, patients must discover a resilient, but empathic, boundary. This merely restates classical transference theory and affirms that we, as therapists, continuously fall into errors. We will not grasp fully the specific nature of our patients' lived experiences except when we fail the first dozen or so times. For transference theory presumes, I am suggesting, that we value genuinely our patients' efforts, as children, to comprehend adult psychopathology and other processes constrained by human fallibility and by randomness. How can we, ensconced in our adult offices and drawing upon years of experience, know for sure how much of a person's actions, say a drunken father's brutality, was "caused" by his conscious mind, his unconscious mind, and by randomness?

We cannot easily answer these questions. Indeed, great artists and philosophers cannot answer them either. As I note below, Greek and Elizabethan tragic poets, for example, as well as Freud, struggled with the same questions: not accidentally, their answers, like those of the analyst, evolve over the course of drama. Their characters' stories become compelling to us when they portray the too much, too little reality of agonistic struggles. Hamlet, for example, becomes irreplaceable to us when he articulates his nearly disabling self-doubts and when he fails miserably to match his self-demands. He tries to answer unanswerable questions; waits until he can be sure of being "correct," and then fails nobly. Recognizing this dimension of human finitude and the task of acting upon poor or nonexistent facts has long been the province of dramatic art.

## ROMANTIC POETRY, BLITZKRIEG AFFECTS, AND AFFECT CURVES

English romantic poets, like John Keats and Percy Bysshe Shelley, and an American romantic novelist, Nathaniel Hawthorne, have appeared throughout this book. This may seem eccentric since the book is about a discipline, psychoanalysis, that claims to be scientific. Of course, it is odd only if one believes that artists are merely entertainers, hired to give scientists and scholars relief from serious work. I believe that artists are more than this. For example, I find that poets and novelists describe better the nature of "joy" (and agony) than do academic psychologists. In chapter 5, I cited Shelley's defense of poetry because he articulated well the common features of the happy child and happy adult. Yet psychoanalysts deal with people who cannot be joyful, and we recognize that to understand them we must look beyond the insights of romanticism. Freud admired the great romantics, like Johann Wolfgang von Goethe and others who championed the individual against the stultifying control of the group and its religion. He did not share their optimism that nonelite groups would rescue art from its staleness. We would not expect Freud to agree with William Wordsworth and Samuel Taylor Coleridge, who wrote in the preface to the second edition of *Lyrical Ballads* (1800): "The majority of the following poems are to be considered as experiments. They were written chiefly with a view to ascertain how far the language of conversation in the middle and lower classes of society is adapted to the purposes of poetic pleasure."[6]

Freud acknowledged continuously the superior intuition of artists who saw deeper than did ordinary persons, including ordinary scientists. He acknowledged also that "life imitates art," but he could not grant to art exhaustive authority as arbiter of psychological truths. The latter had to be established through scientific methods, which included the discipline of psychoanalytic process. For example, like many German educated readers, young man Freud admired Goethe's novel *The Sufferings of Young Werther* (1774), and during his passionate pursuit of his beloved Martha he recalled the tragic story of young Werther and his doomed pursuit of his beloved Lotte. Later, after his self-analysis, Freud offered a psychoanalytic interpretation of the novel. Martin Bergmann (1980) cites records from a meeting of the Vienna Society when Freud asserted that "Love is said to be irrational, but its irrational aspect can be traced back to an infantile source: the compulsion in love is infantile. Such a condition of love found a very beautiful expression in Goethe's *Werther* when young Werther enters the room and immediately falls in love with the maiden. He sees her buttering slices of bread and is reminded of his mother" (56). Bergmann notes that this insight is Freud's, not Goethe's, for Freud traced the young man's irrepressible love for the unavailable young woman back to earlier, now subterranean, feelings. In other words, Werther's yearnings for his beloved Lotte stemmed from an erotic, maternal transference. This Freudian insight presupposes the theory of the Oedipus complex and the Freudian topography: that we cannot know our minds in depth fully and directly. We must wait for those depths to make themselves known. This radical, Freudian critique of narcissistic yearning always affronts us for it marks us permanently dependent upon correction by others, by supervisors, by spouses, by colleagues, and most of all, by patients. Being faithful to Freud's revolution means stepping back from idealization. This is another continuous task and is among those narcissistic resistances that Freud did so much to illuminate.

*Paradoxical representations of blitzkrieg affects*

A pre-Freudian example of idealization appears in Shelley's *Defence* when he proclaims the power of drama to detoxify aggression: "In the drama of the highest order there is little food for censure or hatred; it teaches rather self-knowledge and self-respect. Neither the eye nor the mind can see itself, unless reflected upon that which it resembles. The drama, so long as it continues to express poetry, is a prismatic and many-sided mirror, which collects the brightest rays of human nature and divides and reproduces them from the simplicity of these elementary forms, and touches them with majesty and beauty, and multiplies all that it reflects, and endows it with the power of propagating its like wherever it may fall" ([1821] 1921, 37). We may agree that drama is essential to a well-functioning culture, but to reduce drama to a prism, which shows only majesty and beauty, denies to aggression an ontological status equal to that of Eros and love.

If Shelley is correct, wise artists and wise psychologists will see that beyond hatred is love and forgiveness. This may be a theological truth; indeed, Shelley speaks immediately about "the poetry in the doctrines of Jesus Christ," but it is not compatible with Freud. Nor is it compatible with the phenomenology of chaotic experience proposed in the previous chapter. For if blitzkrieg affects have a chaotic core and if genuine art confronts all sides of human experience, then art must portray chaotic affects as well as love and other coherent feelings. Chaotic affects are not among the "brightest rays" of human nature. In Aeschylus and Shakespeare, we witness child murder, regicide, torture, and the destruction of fidelity.

Shelley was no fool. He recognized that Shakespeare, for example, explores dark themes and he cites (43) a few lines from *Macbeth:*

> the crow
> Makes wing to the rooky wood;
> Good things of day begin to droop and drowse,
> And night's black agents to their preys do rouse.

This passage is typically Shakespearean. Metaphors intermesh, overlap, and refract one another; each iteration reveals more clearly the character's internal contradictions. Confronting his wife, Macbeth calls her "chuck," a term of endearment derived from "chick" or "chicken." From this domain of domestic charm of farmyard birds he moves to the realm of tamed birds of prey, to falcons and hawks (we learn that "seeling" means to close the eyes of a hawk by stitching up its eyelids with a thread). "Scarf up" carries the force of repair or bandage, as well as to hide from terrible visions by covering one's eyes with a scarf. Macbeth's line, "Light thickens, and the crow makes wing to rooky wood," which entranced Shelley, sustains the theme of birds of prey and night ("rooks" are a kind of crow). The transformation of good into evil, of care and concern into malevolence, is

encapsulated in the oxymoronic metaphor that light thickens. Light
becomes heavy, and in becoming "more" brings on its opposite,
darkness. Within three lines Macbeth transforms these homely and
kindly metaphors into a prayer that night destroy a good thing, his
fealty to his king, a "bond" that keeps him pale, here meaning staunch
in his sacred oaths and afraid of violating them.

These lines are Macbeth's response to Lady Macbeth who asked,
"What's to be done?" Having inaugurated evil, they realize that they
must continue to kill and so Macbeth evokes visions of himself as
one of "night's black agents." This is wonderful poetry and if we
cannot love Macbeth, we can relish these incantations announced
with such beautiful economy. A deeper and more complete reading
of these lines would reveal their relationship to Macbeth's character
and the play's empathic examination of the greatest crime that
Shakespeare can imagine, regicide, an attack upon the heart of the
state.

Yet, these lines do not disclose the blitzkrieg affects aroused in
Macbeth's victims when they realize they are being murdered. In
fact, we do not witness Macbeth kill Duncan, nor do we see Duncan's
face. This happens offstage. Preceding it is Macbeth's meditation
upon the evil forces evoked by night, which are witchcraft, night-
mares, wolves, and crime:

> *Macbeth:* It is the bloody business which informs
> Thus to mine eyes. Now o'er the one half-world
> Nature seems dead, and wicked dreams abuse
> The curtain'd sleep; witchcraft celebrates
> Pale Hecate's offerings; and wither'd Murther,
> Alarum'd by his sentinel, the wolf,
> Whose howl's his watch, thus with his stealthy pace,
> With Tarquin's ravishing strides, towards his design
> Moves like a ghost.
>
>                                    (act 2, scene 1)

Immediately following the murder comes Shakespeare's great hymn
to sleep:

> *Macbeth.* I heard a voice cry, "Sleep no more!
> Macbeth does murther sleep"—the innocent sleep,
> Sleep that knits up the ravel'd sleave of care,
> The death of each day's life, sore labor's bath,

> Balm of hurt minds, great nature's second course,
> Chief nourisher in life's feast—
>
> > (act 2, scene 3).

Scholars might object when the latter three lines are wrenched from their context and used by lesser writers as hymns to sleep. Yet, they are beautiful and convey a poetic fullness that rounds out the experience of night and sleep begun in the play's first scenes when dark, non-Christian powers of fate, the three witches, prefigure the play's actions. The witches, whom Macbeth calls "secret, black, and midnight hags," have already shown us they can destroy sleep. These later lines about sleep portray the natural cycle of sleep as balm: sleep reknits the unraveled affects of each day and is the central nourisher, the loving and generous maternal presence given us through the great circadian cycle of sleep, wake, and sleep. Again, with more time and space a sympathetic reader could find in these few lines refractions in the rest of the play, and in other Shakespearean drama. That Macbeth can utter them makes it impossible to view him as merely ambitious, a moral monster; so we are dragged, against our will, to admire him even as we loathe his actions.

For his action, murdering a king in his bed, has overturned the natural order of the state that is akin to the natural order of sleep and wakefulness. Macbeth has murdered sleep, in this sense, and that he will sleep no more is a fit punishment; he has forfeited his natural rights to its balm. Even this punishment, which is terrible, is fitting and so another instance of a universe which rights itself. While regicide, a moral monstrosity, disturbs the order of things, it does not destroy the great engines of moral equilibrium. They respond to grave disorder by evoking inescapable responses from nature (God?) which will not tolerate these deformations forever. Malcolm's speech, at the play's end, emphasizes restitution and balance: he will call back exiled nobles, found a new order of civil caste, and do "what needful else / That calls upon us, by the grace of Grace / We will perform in measure, time, and place" (act 5, scene 9). A similar appeal ends *Hamlet* when Fortinbras agrees to hear Horatio's summary of the treachery that killed Hamlet and then proclaims his place as rightful ruler: "Let us haste to hear it, / And call the noblest to the audience. / For me, with sorrow I embrace my fortune. / I have some rights of memory in this kingdom / Which now, to claim my vantage doth invite me" (act 5, scene 2).

It may be that Shakespeare's radical skepticism about the speed and sureness of divine justice does not prevent him from expecting something like a response from nature. If so, this may prevent him from portraying fully the irredeemable consequences of blitzkrieg affects. (Though this is a large claim to make about an artist of Shakespeare's scope.) For example, a parallel instance appears in Leo Tolstoy's reflections upon the face of death in *Anna Karenina* (1875–77). It exemplifies Winnicott's celebration of the "good-enough mother" to immunize a child against overwhelming despair, "The sight of his brother, and the nearness of death, revived in Levin that sense of horror in the face of the insolvable enigma, together with the nearness and inevitability of death, that had come upon him that autumn evening when his brother had come to him. This feeling was now even stronger than before; even less than before did he feel capable of apprehending the meaning of death, and its inevitability rose up before him more terrible than ever. *But now, thanks to his wife's presence, that feeling did not reduce him to despair.*"[7]

Shakespeare and Tolstoy describe the eventual triumph of order; parricide summons forth justice, rebellion provokes restoration, despair evokes love. In contrast to these are portrayals of murder and blitzkrieg affects to which there is no repair. Numerous instances appear in *The Brothers Karamazov* (1879–80) and other novels by Fyodor Dostoevsky when he describes people who perceive murderous impulses in themselves or in the eyes of another. While Shakespeare does not show us Duncan's face when he recognizes he is being murdered, Dostoevsky typically depicts these kinds of events with exquisite detail. For example, in *The Brothers Karamazov*, Dostoevsky describes horror and disbelief that generate actions, not poetic reflections. A young woman sees a murdered man's "motionless dead face" and runs screaming to her neighbors. She is speechless and can only gesture wildly for help.

Dostoevsky compels us to overhear the criminal mind and its battles with blitzkrieg affects. Throughout *The Brothers Karamazov*—and even more so in *Crime and Punishment*—Dostoevsky reconstructs scenes of terrifying affects that *precede* murder. In *The Brothers Karamazov,* Ippolit Kirillovitch, the prosecutor, says about the accused's (Dmitri's) state of mind: "His passion might well, for a moment, stifle not only the fear of arrest, but even the torments of conscience. For a moment, oh, only for a moment! I can picture the state of mind of the criminal hopelessly enslaved by these influences—

first, the influence of drink, of noise and excitement, of the thud of the dance and the scream of the song, and of her, flushed with wine, singing and dancing and laughing to him! Secondly, the hope in the background that the fatal end might still be far off, that not till next morning, at least, they would come and take him."[8]

In his well-known comments on Dostoevsky, Freud (1928b) argues that Dostoevsky's ambivalent response to the murder of his father, alongside his innate bisexual orientation and intense superego, made him identify with those who killed his father when Dostoevsky was eighteen. Dostoevsky then felt driven to anatomize this profound crime in two great novels, especially *The Brothers Karamazov*, in which he dissects the criminal mind: "Dostoevsky's sympathy for the criminal is, in fact, boundless; it goes far beyond the pity which the unhappy wretch has a right to, and reminds us of the 'holy awe' with which epileptics and lunatics were regarded in the past. A criminal is to him almost a Redeemer, who has taken on himself the guilt which must else have been born by others" (190).

### *"Her mouth twitched piteously, as one sees babies' mouths"*

Dostoevsky's identification with both murderer and victim are central to *Crime and Punishment* (1866). Conspicuous is his description of Raskolnikov, a young man who kills a wealthy woman, Alyona Ivanovna, then confronts her sister, Lizaveta: "In the middle of the room stood Lizaveta with a big bundle in her arms. She was gazing in stupefaction at her murdered sister, white as a sheet and seeming not to have the strength to cry out. Seeing him run out of the bedroom, she began faintly quivering all over, like a leaf, a shudder ran down her face; she lifted her hand, opened her mouth, but still did not scream. She began slowly backing away from him into the corner, staring intently, persistently at him, but still uttered no sound, as though she could not get breath to scream. He rushed at her with the axe; her mouth twitched piteously, as one sees babies' mouths, when they begin to be frightened, stare intently at what frightens them and are on the point of screaming." To be caught up in blitzkrieg affects is to be beyond words: to be stupefied, frozen, shaking, unable even to scream. In Dostoevsky's phrase, it is to be like an infant—to be "in-fans" without speech, reduced to speechless horror.

Later, Dostoevsky portrays Raskolnikov's view of the same moment when he confesses the murder to another woman, Sonia. As

Raskolnikov describes Lizaveta's face and her infantile gesture at self-defense, Dostoevsky shows us the effects of the story on Sonia: "'You can't guess, then?' he asked suddenly, feeling as though he were flinging himself down from a steeple. 'N-no . . .' whispered Sonia. 'Take a good look.' As soon as he had said this again, the same familiar sensation froze his heart. He looked at her and all at once seemed to see in her face the face of Lizaveta."

Concerning the "face" as a register of blitzkrieg affects, we can imagine a spectrum of responses and beliefs. This spectrum ranges from utter horror evidenced in Dostoevsky's portraits, to existential acceptance found in Joseph Conrad, to Winnicott's nonreligious but idealized portrait of the mother's gaze, to Tolstoy's personalized form of Christianity, to overt theological claims about the face of God, to outright petitions for immortality in the *Egyptian Book of the Dead*. Depending upon the analyst's religious convictions one of these responses may enthrall him or her more than the others. For example, one might affirm the heroic, existential emptiness of Kurtz in *Heart of Darkness* (1902), Joseph Conrad's study of evil and blitzkrieg affects. At the novel's conclusion, Marlowe reflects upon the death of the main character, Kurtz, and his last words:

> He had something to say. He said it. Since I had peeped over the edge myself, I understand better the meaning of his stare, that could not see the flame of the candle, but was wide enough to embrace the whole universe, piercing enough to penetrate all the hearts that beat in the darkness. He had summed up—he had judged. "The horror!" He was a remarkable man. After all, this was the expression of some sort of belief; it had candour, it had conviction, it had a vibrating note of revolt in its whisper, it had the appalling face of a glimpsed truth—the strange commingling of desire and hate.[9]

Marlowe, in pity, denies Kurtz's less-than-ideal response to death by lying to his fiancée, who demands to know the dying man's last words: "'Repeat them,' she murmured in a heartbroken tone. 'I want—I want—something—something—to—to live with.' I was on the point of crying at her, 'Don't you hear them?' The dusk was repeating them in a persistent whisper all around us, in a whisper that seemed to swell menacingly like the first whisper of a rising wind. 'The horror! The horror!' 'His last word—to live with,' she insisted. 'Don't you understand I loved him—I loved him—I loved him!' I pulled myself together and spoke slowly. 'The last word he pronounced was—your name.'" Marlowe, caught momentarily in a folk religious belief that God or the heavens will punish liars, hesitates at first to honor this wishful fantasy. He complies with her demand: "She was sure. I heard her weeping; she had hidden her face in her hands. It seemed to me that the house would collapse before I could escape, that the heavens would fall upon my head. But nothing happened. The heavens do not fall for such a trifle."

I have termed Marlowe's struggle against lying an existentialist (or modernist) response to this woman's pleas. For the scene contrasts what Freud most disliked about religion, its wish-fulfillment and "just so" stories, with a skeptic who doubts its replacement by ruthless objectivity (as Freud did in his occult moments). We may admire Freud's struggles against his proclivities to occult belief. Yet, we may doubt that these self-conscious struggles are adequate as response to another person's despair. We might share Freud's admiration for reason and share his hope that eventually it will replace religion (1927c, 1933a). However, evidence from developmentalists, like Stern, suggests that Marlowe's response, even if a lie, is more humane and accurate than truth-telling. For by lying to Kurtz's fiancée, Marlowe prevents the reappearance of the horror that Kurtz experienced at his death.

In contrast to this metaphysics of despair is another shared by some psychoanalysts, like Winnicott (1971a, 1971c), and some theologians, like Martin Buber (1919), Emmanuel Levinas ([1948] 1979, 1981), and Edward Farley (1990, 1996). Each asserts that face-to-face encounters between loving persons form the foundation of ethics and personal integrity, immunization against fragmentation anxiety. This theological claim may be extended to a developmental claim and also a biological claim: early encounters with the Other's face, usually the mothering person, are necessary to safeguard the child against blitzkrieg affects. Repeated and reliable experiences of a loving, mutually holding gaze make joy possible and help prevent hopelessness, what Winnicott calls primal agony: "The infant may then experience libidinal mutual gazing as maternal holding and sudden aggressive looking away as being suddenly dropped, bringing about the primal agony of falling forever" (Winnicott 1974, 103).[10]

This kind of agony, an overwhelming dread, is one of those feelings that, following André Greene, I have named a blitzkrieg affect. I cited Deming's brilliant model of management errors and applied it to the control of affects. I suggested that when children are raised in normal, expectable environments they learn over time that there is a natural ebb and flow to their affective experiences. This ebb and flow is what Daniel Stern and other psychoanalytic developmental psychologists refer to as affect curves. Because these are "natural" and show average expectable patterns, parental attempts to improve affect curves always increases randomness and this, in turn, makes emotional aberrations impossible to avoid. Self-fulfilling prophecies become entrenched: "bad" children require extra punishments; this induces additional extreme behaviors, and these evoke additional punishment. When rooted in a family system and supported by archaic religious traditions, these kinds of interaction constantly reinforce pathogenic beliefs, a common one being that children have no independent rights to lives of their own. If we are lucky, we engage in infantile behaviors like dreaming, fantasy, wishing, sexual tension and relief, and merger with beloved others frequently. To *not* do so is to be ill. Using the terms of Freud's structural theory, regression means that the organized part of the personality, the ego, finds itself threatened with massive disorganization and chaos.

Freud always views the mind as an evolving, hierarchical organ that must adapt to two sources of variability, the "inner world" and outer world. Both worlds impinge upon the mind with chaotic-like forces. Beginning in the "Project" of 1895 (1895a) and extending to his last piece of metapsychology, the "Outline of Psychoanalysis" (1940a), Freud recognized that a complete metapsychology would have to explain the role of "chance" in the generation of mind and its status as a chief problem for mind. Looking back to the Greeks, Freud granted to "chance" its proper Greek name, *tyche,* and to "character" another Greek name, *daimôn.* In a footnote to "The Dynamics of Transference" (1912b), he says: "*Daimon kai tyche* determine the fate of man; seldom, perhaps never, one of these powers alone. The relative aetiological effectiveness of each is only to be measured individually and in single instances. In a series comprising varying degrees of both factors extreme cases will certainly also be found. According to the knowledge we possess we shall estimate the parts played by the forces of heredity and of environment differently in each case, and retain the right to modify our opinion in consequence of new knowledge" (312).

This typically Freudian passage acknowledges that "constitutional" factors and "environmental" factors play shifting roles in the production of psychopathology. In contrast to polemical psycholo-

gists and polemical biologists, Freud does not reduce mental processes, including psychopathology, to either of these elemental forces.
By naming these forces *daimôn* and *tyche* Freud evokes the Greeks'
conviction that we cannot distinguish easily the boundaries that separate a person's "character" from a person's "fate" or happenstance.
In Homer, for example, *daimôn* can mean an individual god or god-
dess (*Iliad* 1.222) but also divine power (*Odyssey* 3.27). Related
meanings pertinent to *daimôn* are the inner souls of mortals, and
semidivine beings inferior to the gods. From this association it is not
far to the idea of *kata daimona,* which means "by chance" (Pindar,
*Odes* 8.67). Because the gods *(daimones)* desire particular ends and
have powers greater than most mortals, *daimôn* also evokes the idea
of "destiny." Thus Bacchylides, a Greek lyric poet, says *hoti daimones
thelôsin,* which means "what the Gods ordain" (l. 15.23).[11]

That persons might approach semidivine status and that gods
might become human were, according to Greek religion, possibilities regulated by character and by chance. Greek authors often delineate persons transformed from mere mortals into authentic *daimôn*s.
For example, in *Oedipus at Colonus,* which follows *Oedipus Tyrannus,*
Sophocles depicts Oedipus addressed by citizens of Colonus. Thun-
der breaks, and the chorus of citizens says: "Look! Look! Once again
the piercing din is divinity around us! Be merciful, divinity, [*ô daimôn*]
be merciful, if you are bringing anything of gloom for the land which
is our mother! May I find you well disposed, and may I not, because
I have cared for a man accursed, somehow obtain a favor without
profit! Lord Zeus, to you I cry!"[12] Oedipus could not achieve this
exalted status without having first passed through the crises of hubris and enlightenment afforded him in *Oedipus Tyrannus.* In this
sense, we recognize boundaries after the fact; sometimes after disasters like those that befell Oedipus's family. Like the three witches in
Macbeth, Oedipus was warned by occult powers whose uninterpret-
able conundrums he had to solve before he could comprehend them.
"Fate" or *tyche* names powers that cannot be controlled; even the
gods are subject to their force. Yet, we cannot know the limits of
our own powers except by challenging fate. If this is our characteristic, as it was Oedipus's, then our *daimôn* drives us to explore these
limits and, having reached them, provoke the wrath of *tyche. Macbeth*
begins with the three weird sisters, akin to Fates, tempting Macbeth
with promises of glory dependent upon chance *(tyche):* "If chance
will have me King, why, chance may / crown me / Without my

stir." (act 1, scene 3). Of course, Macbeth's *daimôn* drives him to challenge *tyche* and this ensures his destruction.


## Six or Seven Pathogenic Beliefs

Relying upon psychoanalytic developmental theory, I have focused upon the interactions between parent and child that seem to give rise to pathogenic beliefs. From other sources, beginning with Freud, we know that archaic ideas and even false ideas are not, in themselves, pathogenic. As I stressed above, since most of us for most of human history have not known (scientifically) how human beings think and feel, none of us has had a fully valid theory of the human mind. This universal lack has not produced a universal neurosis.

On the contrary, beliefs are pathogenic because, in conjunction with the appearance of primary affects, they yield blitzkrieg affects. I named five pathogenic rules or beliefs:

> *Belief 1. Everything that happens and that people do is caused by some form of intentionality.*
>
> *Belief 2. There must be ways to control these intentional, causal agents.*
>
> *Belief 3. Affects can be controlled by "willpower."*
>
> *Belief 4. Perfection is a worthy goal and entails controlling affects in self and others.*
>
> *Belief 5. Novelty is always bad.*

To these we can now add two more:

> *Belief 6. My suffering makes me special (in ways I would not otherwise be).*
>
> *Belief 7. My story, my narrative, describes accurately what "must have occurred."*

*Belief 1. Everything that happens and that people do is caused by some form of intentionality.*

Both psychoanalysts and religionists have long studied this belief in its private and public forms. In the latter, it had reached the level of a cliché already by Freud's time when he explored it in his essays on premodern people's religion (1912–13). There Freud compares this "primitive" belief and uses it to show what he claims is an essential unity between the thought processes of neurotic patients and the thought processes of primitive religious groups. In both circumstances, this belief reflects a primary narcissistic projection: that what I believe is true of my mind, that I can direct it sometimes, therefore I can direct it always, is projected onto nature. When disasters occur often people seek out the "reasons" for them and these are understood to be motivations: thus the standard refrain heard in anthropological accounts of so-called primitive religion.

Of course, no one believes in strict determinism and the omnipotence of thoughts all the time. That is, since this belief is one of many folk theories of psychology and human nature it coexists easily with contrary beliefs. It lies ready to hand (as Sperber [1974] says of similar modes of thought). When danger threatens or an especially uncanny event occurs then this belief springs back into life (Freud 1919h). More so, because folk beliefs derive from complex and subtle interactions, they need never enter conscious formulations. Just as we need no theory of gravity to know we should not step off into thin air, we need no consistent theory of ghosts or demons to get through our ordinary days. Unless, by ill fortune, we happen to stay in a spooky house.

This is *not* true of pathogenic beliefs. Because they are generated out of needs and anxieties that are constant, pathogenic beliefs require constant articulation. The inner voices that patients suffer under, describe, and which emerge eventually in the analytic encounter repeat pathogenic beliefs relentlessly. Because they are personal and private, one might conclude that pathogenic beliefs should feel seamless with other aspects of an individual's mental life. Yet, this seems not true. For the basic sense of "neurosis" is one of conflict and distress. Having exhausted all other forms of self-cure and relief, patients may end up in a long-term psychotherapy. The child has no distance from the child's mental creations: it is simply the way things are. So too, in the midst of a transference storm (or a countertransference storm) we do not feel "as if" the present is the past, we experience them as identical. Given a slight similarity between the analyst and a previous person with whom the patient is still entangled, analogical reasoning is sufficient for the patient to fill in the blanks and deduce that the analyst and the previous person are in essence the same.

As I noted above when discussing the basic rule, implicit in these apparently contradictory teachings is an analytic value, enunciated by Freud and subsequently by all major theoreticians, namely, that psychoanalysis is a process that cannot ignore the role of chance (Rangell 1986).

*Belief 2. There must be ways to control these intentional, causal agents.*

Parents need never articulate this second belief. Instead, through the thousands of interactions along multiple channels of communication, parents communicate to their children their aversion to particular features of their child's external and internal expression of strong affects. From these encounters springs the child's relentless demand to control, inhibit, or abort strong affects. As I noted above and as daily life teaches us, often people can shape the other person's emotional response. Indeed, this defines what it means to be in a relationship: we influence the other person's inner states.

Between this daily event and pathogenic belief no. 2 is the demand for total control. While I use words like "shape" or "influence," a child caught up in inverted self-object relationships with chaotic parents demands perfect "control." The work of the child is never done, because to control fully the other person's feelings one must be on constant alert; everyday is "Condition Red" day. Nothing can be left to chance, for without exacting and perfect attention to the other's moods all hell will break loose. Just as the U.S. defense experts cannot tolerate a "small nuclear exchange," so too children living within the world of inverted self-objects and chaotic affects cannot tolerate letting go of their role as master of the emotional universe.

*Belief 3. Affects can be controlled by "willpower."*

Again, there are multiple sources to this belief, but the primary inductions occur between parent and infant and parent and child. These primary lessons are paradoxical since the parent typically affirms belief no. 3 through either an idiosyncratic or a cultural form of perfectionism yet demonstrates its falsehood. For like Rat Man's father, parents admonish and remonstrate with a child over the child's lack of control and do so with such ferocity that the child perceives (correctly) that the parent is frightened about the parent's own affects.

If we follow Greene's standard distinction between type one and type two affects, that is affects contained fully by speech and affects that cannot be contained, this belief is validated by the child's experience of catastrophic affects. First, it is validated when the child's parents demand the child "show some self-control" and through some massive defensive effort the child's behavior changes or the child no longer experiences the affect that enraged the child's parents. This, as I noted above, seems to prove that the child can be obedient when she or he musters up the correct willpower. Second, it is validated when the repressed wishes and disowned affects return, this time having grown vastly in power, confronting the child with irrefutable evidence that sexual wishes, for example, are truly the work of the devil. This requires children to acknowledge that indeed dark powers run their lives, and that only a "higher willpower" can control them.

A common feature of working with patients who were sexually abused as children is to note how painful it was for them to discover themselves responding sexually to the abusive person's actions. Since these children typically affirm some version of belief no. 3, the appearance of sexual pleasure in the midst of terror or shame (depending upon their developmental stage and other features of abuse) can only mean that they lack willpower as well as other good things that would have prevented their suffering. Naturally, when similar sexual feelings arise in therapy they feel the original terror, and the original shame returns.

This becomes another sign of their worthlessness and sometimes precipitates severe regressions and threats to treatment or impulses to harm themselves. Deming's model of a system out of control lets us connect this common clinical finding with aspects of Kleinian thought, especially as reformulated by W. R. Bion and his colleagues. For, to the degree I understand them, the latter attend to patients' experience of the interface between their sense of organized self and the terror of "Nothingness, meaninglessness, chaos."[13]

*Belief 4. Perfection is a worthy goal and entails*
*controlling affects in oneself and others.*

Perfectionism is the demand a child feels that he or she should (and can) find a way to be exact and perfect in specific parts of their life: their bowels, sexuality, eating, or feeling, all of which are inherently in flux and therefore inexact. Not knowing what is normal and what behavior counts as natural and acceptable, these children (and their parents) strive to make the good into the better. They conclude that they are acceptable only when they are perfect, and unacceptable when they are not. Since they cannot be both perfect and spontaneous, creative and fully alive, children reject novelty: what is unknown is uncontrolled and what is uncontrolled frightens them. Being "too creative" means taking chances that threaten to overwhelm the self with blitzkrieg affects. (Of course, if later, as young adults, they cannot live without being creative, suicide offers them one way to control their fate.) At the center of these children's pathogenic beliefs is a tangled web of the grandiose self, and profoundly distressing affects, especially shame, doubt, and hopelessness. In response to devastating images of the self and the self's future are multiple defenses ranging from manic states, denial, drug use, promiscuity, ("If I cannot rule heaven then I shall rule hell") to reaction formation and identification with the aggressor.

The child will discover in the child's mind horrible images that seem to demonstrate the child's worthlessness. Or the child may engage in sudden outbursts of extreme behaviors, like hypersexualized encounters, which provide additional evidence that the child's mind is a pool of dark impulses ruled by frightening and overwhelming powers. As one patient put it, she sometimes felt that her mind was like a sewer pipe, containing all the refuse of her body and her family's secrets, secure only if undisturbed. If she dared to alter the way she thought about herself and looked more directly at her terrors, then her mind would split apart, like a sewer pipe smashed by a hammer or twisted apart by an earthquake. Like many other children she was raised to fear any expression of feelings that was not under her parents' control.

Over a long period of time and through multiple (small) errors and corrections we try to comprehend the patient's experience of the patient's worlds: the patient's body, the patient's self, and the patient's being in the "real world." This goal and the gradual mode of psychoanalytic learning run counter to all pathogenic beliefs. When taken together these beliefs create a demand for perfection in the governance of affects; this is the antithesis of psychoanalytic values. Just as Deming says the good employer learns from employees and their interactions, so too analytic technique has always required patient and therapist to learn the distinctive tone of their blended interactions. Even in schools of analysis that sharply criticize the other's metapsychological claims, one finds that the rules advanced by each include some version of the basic requirement.

*Belief 5. Novelty is always bad.*

This belief may be the most pernicious of all pathogenic beliefs. For it becomes a way of life, an ingrained habit that makes patients avoid new object relationships. It creates "watertight" illusions of the unity of the self and makes learning to learn impossible. All subsequent experiences of nonself forces (internal drive derivatives, other people's affects, "destiny," fate) are re-traumatizing and thus evoke defenses. These range from minor to major. Whether minor or major, each decreases the amount of novel information available to the patient. This, in turn, gives the child (and patient) less data about their current circumstances. This, in turn, decreases their ability to make informed judgments and decisions. A common feature of the narcissistic style, for instance, is to make guesses about this or that upcoming event. When successful, these guesses validate grandiose visions of the self. When unsuccessful they evoke deep shame and self-loathing.

Returning to Deming's discussion of management theory, we note that this kind of guessing and the avoidance of learning are another version of top down reasoning. With an ideology in place, each new encounter evokes one question: are you for me or against me? Does this request, by a spouse for example, diminish me or enhance me? These common questions are, technically, paranoid since they impose upon novel situations templates derived from previous battles. Hence, at each new interaction, which rarely goes well, novelty is feared and the pathogenic belief—that novelty is bad-—is affirmed. This creates new chaotic experiences and these validate the original paranoid hypothesis. Transference reenactments, especially negative transferences, illustrate such cycles in depth. (Even recognizing this, the well-intentioned analyst and the well-intentioned patient may not be able to overcome them.)

*Belief 6. My suffering makes me special*
*(in ways I would not otherwise be).*

This is pathogenic because it encourages patients to cling to their suffering as essential markers of their distinctiveness. It is also a partial truth. Indeed, some children and adults suffer in ways that can drive them to utter despair *and* they are "special." By pegging their deepest sense of themselves to these facts patients who affirm this belief resist challenges to their current self-understandings. Frequently, patients frame this belief within a primitive dichotomy: either my suffering is especially severe and makes me special or my suffering is ordinary and I am not special. To challenge this belief the analyst must solve this dilemma and neither deny the patient's genuine pain nor deny that the patient (like all human beings) is indeed special.

*Belief 7. My story, my narrative, describes accurately what "must have occurred."*

This belief is pathogenic in at least three ways. First, it is pathogenic because it entails the error of post facto reasoning: because one thing happened after an event the two events *must* be causally related to one another. Like other pathogenic beliefs, this is plausible because sometimes causes precede effects and looking backward (from effect to those things that occurred before) permits us to denote the "cause." The task, as usual, is to discern the facts as best we can. Does smoking cause cancer? Does burning fossil fuels cause global warming? Do rain dances cause rain? These are important questions upon which much depends and which often require years of dedicated scientific effort to answer. Children cannot afford to be judicious and wait for science to tell them its current truths: like any mammal caught in a dangerous moment, children act immediately to decrease their suffering. That mother or father "got better" after sexually using the child proves that the child can control the parent's needs and moods. Sometimes the child's prayer, for example, that a despised sibling die, or that a drunken father not come home, is answered. This proves, naturally, to the child that thoughts really can be omnipotent. Since the narcissistic style necessarily fails, if not today, then tomorrow, a healthy dose of pessimism becomes part of a self-fulfilling prophecy.

Second, it is pathogenic to claim that my narrative describes accurately what "*must* have occurred" because it throws the child back into the obsessional whirlpool surrounding the validity of memory. Even before the recent media attention to "false memory" claims, psychoanalytic patients recognized with Freud that it is often difficult to know for sure that their recollections are accurate and exact. Given another dichotomy—either you remember perfectly or you are a liar—such patients fluctuate between perfectionistic demands upon themselves (and their therapists) and denunciations of their worthlessness and moral decrepitude.

Third, this belief is pathogenic because it denies the omnipresence of chance in human lives. Like ancient religious prophets, children who affirm this belief deny that mere chance can arrange our lives. Even the Greeks, who idealized reason, affirmed a causal nexus between character and fate. Somehow, what took place between Oedipus and his parents was destined: it *must* have occurred precisely as it did. By adolescence many children have wakened to the realization that "being here" in their lives and not another persons, or indeed, being alive, are peculiar events and evoke peculiar questions, such as "Why am I here?"

While these are wonderful questions and typical of many adolescents wakening into the world of abstract thought, they admit no answer. They are like the questions that spring to mind when a local tragedy occurs: "Why did the drunk driver lose control just as the pregnant woman crossed the street?" Similarly, when tragedies that are more massive and crimes that are more grotesque occur, such as the Nazi war against the Jews, one naturally asks, "Why did *these* people die and not *those?*" As Michael Bernstein puts it, we must ask these kinds of questions about the Shoah, for example, "in which so much is at stake, humanly as well as epistemologically, in the simultaneously impossible and unavoidable debate about its meaning" (1994, 14).

I think this gets close to the heart of the traumatized child and our responses to the child's dilemmas. As therapists, we respect the child's need to ask such questions and we recognize that they are unavoidable. Yet, we also recognize that these questions and the childhood answers they engender are pathogenic and that children (and our adult patients), when caught up in transference storms, cannot comprehend this fact. To grasp this truth one must fail many times as an adult and as a therapist. That painful way seems necessary if we are to understand how these questions are impossible to answer fully. We can claim lucidity about the boundaries of our private and collective suffering only *after* we have discovered the limits to our understanding. This means that we must experience various degrees of narcissistic pain, ranging from brief slivers of shame that we can shake off with humor or good will, to attacks upon our sense of the "natural" and sometimes humiliation, that we were wrong, completely wrong.

## Conclusions

I have tried to raise what I claim is a central question for psychoanalysts: *what* do we talk about and what do we investigate? I have suggested one set of answers; that we deal with the origin, structure, and cost of pathogenic beliefs engendered in response to blitzkrieg affects. This restates, in part, Freud's earliest claim that neurotic suffering is the result of traumata. I find that undeniable, but also incomplete. For while everyone suffers in some ways, not everyone becomes neurotic. To expand upon Freud's thoughts and to evaluate contemporary analytic discourse, I have suggested that by suffering in silence, in the private theater of the inner world, children are forced to recapitulate the history of the philosophy of mind with all its ambiguities and to solve puzzles about Self that may be unsolvable. Unlike philosophers who can debate conceptual niceties, and then go home in peace, children raised in homes with massively aberrant parenting cannot put their labors aside and take them up when class begins again. Their struggles are continuous; their fear that at any time chaos may return is permanent; they know that, inevitably, suffering will return.

The rejection of the claim that rationality is at the center of human being implies a particular form of freedom. Returning to the language of affect theory, by ascribing to human being an irreplaceable mammalian heritage, the source of Darwinian affects, Freud dethrones Reason with a capital "R," an ego function, from a commanding status over the whole of the personality.[14] Freud grants to reason a role in the construction of the self and the rise of science, and a unique status as the "quiet voice," as he calls it (1927c). Yet, Freud always says that reason is circumscribed by process, "reasoning" about a patient's suffering must occur within the working through of analysis over a long period of time.

This form of acceptance and trust, I have suggested, an abused child cannot emulate. The child must find a way to survive, and to survive the child must fabricate immediate, plausible, and memorable solutions. Like someone caught in a snowstorm alone, children caught in severely depriving environments must lash together affects with ideas and create a habitude: the set of pathogenic beliefs with which they control themselves, especially blitzkrieg affects.

These efforts at self-definition are bound to fail because, up to this point at least, the mystery of human being is not solved. Therefore, *no* set of articulated formulas, or dicta, or rules, including those engendered in childhood, can be correct. Because the object of these predictions, the behavior of human beings engaged in complex exchange, is shaped by randomness and multiple, unknowable variables, all such predictions are wrong. Thus, "fully rational answers" that require correct consciousness are always wrong. These kinds of answers are precisely what frightened or traumatized children fabricate in the bowels of their suffering. The six or seven pathogenic beliefs I named as typical are, as a set of claims, conscious rules of "procedure" and attempts to predict and control human behavior.

Because they cannot rely upon their essential others to help contain and shape their strongest feelings, children prone to neurosis take that job upon themselves. Impelled to control their feelings, especially affects that might evoke punishment, they find ways to quash them using both primitive and advanced ego defenses. Among primitive defenses are somatization, regression, splitting, and denial. Among advanced ego defenses are rationalization and intellectualization, the two modes that give rise to pathogenic beliefs. These attempts to control a natural, regular and self-limiting process, in turn, create blitzkrieg affects whose appearance, long predicted by their caretakers and anticipated in their most anxious moments, proves that life is basically horror followed by boredom followed by more anxiety.

Because neurotic children and neurotic adults cannot trust another person to help regulate the rise and fall of affects, they demand rules, signs, methods, devices, and modes of "fully conscious" control over their inner worlds. This quest is doomed to failure and, consequently, a life that should move from joy to mourning, and back to joy remains fixed in anxious dedication to controlling everything.

# Notes

## Introduction

1. All citations of *Washington Square* are from Electronically Enhanced Text © Copyright 1991–94 World Library, Inc.

## Chapter 1. Neurotic Suffering as the Absence of Joy

1. See recent issues of major psychoanalytic journals devoted to this topic: *International Journal of Psychoanalysis* 75, nos. 5 and 6 (1994) and *Journal of the American Psychoanalytic Association*, vol. 41 (1993), supplement.

2. A process that began in American Psychiatric Association 1980 and continued in American Psychiatric Association 1994. On the debate about the term "neurosis" in DSM III and DSM III R see Gillman 1986 and Wallerstein 1987.

3. For example, Houdini showed the gullible Doyle that he could "remove" his thumb and then put it back on again. This grade-school sleight of hand left Doyle speechless with praise for Houdini's amazing ability to alter his fleshly body, not for Houdini's trick. See Silverman 1996, 277.

4. See, for example, research efforts in Miller et al. 1993.

5. See Shevrin 1978.

6. This brief paper generated a series of studies by psychoanalysts and religionists about the nature of "illusion" and religion. For, as Winnicott notes, there are uncanny parallels between his notions of how infants use objects and Christian religious behaviors such as the Eucharistic meal and other forms of symbolic presence. Like Bateson (1972), Winnicott notes that the traditional debate between Catholic and Protestant interpretations of the wafer as the body of Christ or as merely a symbol turns on theological reasoning about a thing, the wafer, that occupies a status for believers analogous to that of the transitional object for the infant. Among major responses to this paper are Rizzuto 1979, Pruyser 1983, McDargh 1983, Gay 1983, Meissner 1984, and Jones 1991.

7. See comments on "anasemia" in Abraham and Torok 1994; regarding "meaning," see Dan Sperber's (1974) critique of Lacan, Lévi-Strauss, and Freud.

8. See Alexander 1979, 19.

9. See literary representations of similar events, e.g., C. S. Lewis's autobiography, *Surprised by Joy* (1955).

10. Alexander and I might be criticized as restating, in architectural language and psychological terms, the biases and worldview of the English experience at its most elite. For example, we can show Alexander's core values, especially his celebration of the village and its nonhierarchical community, have as their ideals the English town and English university.

11. From: http://www.library.utoronto.ca/utel/rp/poems/wordswor25.html

12. On Revisiting the Banks of the Wye During a Tour July 13, 1798.

13. Emerson continues: "Epicurus relates that poetry hath such charms that a lover might forsake his mistress to partake of them. And the true bards have been noted for their firm and cheerful temper. Homer lies in sunshine; Chaucer is glad and erect; and Saadi says, 'It was rumored abroad that I was penitent; but what had I to do with repentance?' Not less sovereign and cheerful,—much more sovereign and cheerful, is the tone of Shakespeare. His name suggests joy. . . ." From: http://www.jjnet.com/emerson/shak.htm

14. Freud discusses but does not endorse the idea that dreams may also be joyful. He cites the poet Novalis (Friedrich von Hardenberg, 1772–1801), who says "The dream is a bulwark against the regularity and commonplace character of life, a free recreation of the fettered phantasy, in which it intermingles all the images of life and interrupts the constant seriousness of the adult by the joyful play of the child. Without the dream we should surely grow old earlier, so that the dream may be considered, if not precisely as a gift from above, yet as a delightful exercise, a friendly companion on our pilgrimage to the grave" (Freud 1900a, 83). Freud cannot endorse this naive celebration of joy in dreams for it bears no evidence of an underlying biological reality, which Freud's theory tells him must drive all such manifest expressions of joy. Hence, Freud concludes this section on joyous dreams with reference to childhood games of being tossed in the air and other forms of libidinal excitement.

15. From Electronically Enhanced Text (©) Copyright 1991–1994 World Library, Inc.

16. From Electronically Enhanced Text (©) Copyright 1991–1994 World Library, Inc.

17. From Electronically Enhanced Text (©) Copyright 1991–1994 World Library, Inc.

18. A great modernist statement that recognizes these losses, especially the loss of Wordsworthian nature, remains beautiful and joyful, such as Matthew Arnold's *Dover Beach* (1867).

19. To account for these stagelike processes Turner advanced his well-known concepts of "separation, transition, and incorporation." See Turner 1969 and 1982.

20. Turner (1982, 73) cites a diagram from Richard Schechner (1977) that describes a continuity between social dramas, such as political strife, and stage dramas that mirror them and thus permit a culture to understand itself with increased consciousness. See also Myerhoff and Moore 1977.

21. Based on the novel *Rasho-Mon* by Ryunosuke Akutagawa (1915).

22. See Oliner and Oliner 1988.

23. Karl Popper devotes half of his two volume study of the philosophy of power to Plato and his view that the true philosopher, possessed of wisdom, "does not love, as ordinary people do, sensible things and their 'beautiful sounds and colours and shapes,' but he wants 'to see, and to admire the real nature of beauty'— the Form or Idea of Beauty" (1962, 1:14).

24. Holst-Warhaft documents a dramatic shift in the valuation of mourning: in contrast to the heroic period, it becomes unmanly, barbarian, and un-Greek (1992, 119).

25. On "frames," compare the narrow, technical sense of the rules of engagement that Robert Langs has helped clarify (Langs 1985) with the broader, general sense of the stage or "set" proper to the analytic attitude noted, for example, by Spruil (1989). On psychoanalysis as drama see Freud (1916d and 1942a) and McDougall (1985) and reviews of her book by Larsson (1987), and Kalinich (1994). On psychoanalysis and the mind as theater, see Castelnuovo-Tedesco (1989) and see especially Modell (1988) and Loewald (1975).

26. Text from: http://eldred.ne.mediaone.net/nh/hmind.html

## CHAPTER 2. MEDICINE AND PSYCHOANALYSIS: MODELS OF PSYCHOLOGICAL DISEASE

1. Philosophic debates about the meaning of the term "cause" and its proper use abound. But within workaday science the idea of causation is uppermost. See below, my discussion of Grünbaum (1988), Lumsden and Wilson (1981), and Kuhn (1977).

2. See also Cloninger 1986.

3. It does appear that once the decision has been made that a set of symptoms arise from "mere" social or interpersonal deficits, the malady in question becomes less interesting to the elite. This is a question for the anthropological or sociological study of the medical elite (NIH, AMA, hospitals) in this country. See additional references in Taussig (1980) and Gergen (1994).

4. This form of agnosticism seems to be the rational for DSM III and DSM IV. See also Benjamin (1993).

5. See Homans (1989) and Ricoeur (1991) and their references to hermeneutics.

6. For example, as Cloninger (1986) does in his detailed conjectures about the neural-mental-self structures that interact to form the human personality.

7. See Teller and Dahl (1986); Flanagan (1992); Meehl (1994); Spruiell (1993) on the rapidity of "natural" intelligence processing and the computational power required to carry out these cognitive tasks.

8. See Cohen and Stewart (1994): "We don't even know how our own memories work, though we do have a lot of evidence to suggest that the brain has at least three different memory mechanisms . . ." (169).

9. See Freud's newly discovered "lost" paper on metapsychology, *A Phylogenetic Fantasy* (1987). A notorious instance of Freud's zeal to accomplish this kind

of task is his "historical novel," *Moses and Monotheism* (1939a). See also Yerushalmi 1991.

10. See Brenner (1982) for examples.

11. See Freud's earliest training in the Viennese academies and research centers. Each rejected vitalism with a sometimes religious fervor. The most famous leader of these circles was Hermann von Helmholtz (1867, 1877) whom I cite in my study of sublimation (Gay 1992). Franz Brentano (1838–1917), another celebrated Viennese scientist, impressed Freud (McGrath 1986, 100–102) with his erudition but Freud committed himself to the "godless empiricism" of Ernst Brücke and Carl Claus. McGrath's discussion is especially detailed; see also Amacher (1965) and Ernst Jones (1953) for lengthier discussions of Freud's early schooling.

12. "There was nothing unscientific about the astrologer's explanation of [predictive] failure. Nevertheless, astrology was not a science. Instead it was a craft, one of the practical arts, with close resemblances to engineering, meteorology, and medicine as these fields were practiced until little more than a century ago. The parallels to an older medicine and to contemporary psychoanalysis are, I think, particularly close" (Kuhn, 1977, 275).

13. A virtue of Kuhn's focus upon puzzles is that he need not distinguish the psychology of the astrologer from the psychology of the astronomer: there need be no difference in their personalities, only a difference in their practice. Many astronomers, including Tycho Brahe (1546–1601) and Johannes Kepler (1571–1630), studied astrology, just as Isaac Newton (1642–1727), the archetype of European science, studied many disciplines that we would now consider occult religion, not science. Another virtue of Kuhn's notion of "puzzle" is that we can ask: Are the neuroses structured like puzzles? To put the same question into a developmental frame: Are the emotional problems with which a child struggles structured like puzzles? If they are, then with sufficient labor neuroses and similar problems should yield to reasoning. If they are not, then no amount of thinking (worrying and planning) will solve them.

14. The human genome project depends completely upon the computerization of science: both the root metaphor and organizing principles of the operative theory (the 3 billion base pairs are conceived of as "bits") and the machinery require computer manipulation.

15. "I reject materialism and monism as well. The deep mistake is to suppose that one must choose between these views" (Searle 1992, 28).

16. Or Masterson's terms, "Rewarding Object Relations Part-Unit" (RORU) and "Withdrawing or Aggressive Object Relations Part-Unit" (WORU). These designate the internalized representations of parents, evident, he says, in the borderline patient. See Masterson 1976, esp. 57–68.

17. Searle 1992, 71.

18. See Charles Brenner's lifelong efforts to articulate the concept of "compromise formations" as part of a general analytic theory in Brenner 1959, 1982.

19. Eissler 1971, 410. Compare Donald Winnicott's "prayer," that he be alive when he died, cited in Phillips 1988, 19.

20. Citing Freud 1930a, 124, Weiss (1986) notes, "A child must come to fear any motive or behavior that he infers would seriously hurt a parent, provoke severe punishment from a parent, or seriously threaten him with the loss of the parent's love" (69).

## CHAPTER 3. PATHOGENIC BELIEFS, PERSONAL AND PUBLIC SPECIMENS

1. "The asocial nature of neuroses has its genetic origin in their most fundamental purpose, which is to take flight from an unsatisfying reality into a more pleasurable world of phantasy. The real world, which is avoided in this way by neurotics, is under the sway of human society and the institutions collectively created by it. To turn away from reality is at the same time to withdraw from the community of man" (Freud 1912–13, 74).

2. From Darwin 1859: gopher://gopher.vt.edu:10010/02/69/2.

3. As Norman O. Brown noted in his chapter on "The Excremental Vision" (1959, 179–201).

4. For additional materials and sources see: http://emporium.turnpike.net/C/cs/. See also Creationist criticisms of geology, paleontology, and indeed all the natural sciences that deal with geological time scales.

5. With predictable results: "A department had failed miserably for months to produce enough items for the market. The general manager . . . found . . . inspectors overpowered with fear. They had taken the ideas into their heads that if the customer found an item to be faulty, the inspector that passed the item would lose his job. As a consequence, the inspectors held up almost the total output" (Deming 1982, 61).

6. Deming (1982) reiterates an insight that Freud announced before him: "People naturally suppose that if something happened here and now, there must be something special at the spot where it happened. The usual reaction of almost everyone, when an accident happens, is to attribute it to somebody's carelessness or something unusual about the equipment used. It is unwise to jump to this conclusion" (478).

7. Lest the reader think I exaggerate the diminution of women in a some contemporary religions, see the Southern Baptist Seminary's web page at http://www.founders.org/back.html. Fundamentalism asserts that an Eternal Truth is an essential truth and hence Baptists, for example, should convert Jews since the latter fail to see that their immortal souls are at stake. One more tiny step leads to the Nazi conclusion: Jews have refused to take part in an Eternal Good and thus threaten, as diseased organisms, the health of everyone else.

8. When engaged in political battles with Creationists, Darwinians are also liable to fundamentalism. Michael Behe (1996) notes that these battles have led some biologists to downplay the quite real problems that Darwinians face when trying to account for biochemical structures that are essential for survival but seem not to have evolved piecemeal.

9. See *The Martin Luther King, Jr., FBI File*, ed. David J. Garrow, 16 reels, 35mm microfilm (ISBN: 0-89093-678-1). See also Garrow's book (1981).

10. Hence, Milosz adds, "Fear of the indifference with which the economic system of the West treats its artists and scholars is widespread among Eastern intellectuals. They say it is better to deal with an intelligent devil than with a good-natured idiot" ([1953] 1990, 39).

11. Emphasis mine, from: *Selected Works of Mao Tse-tung*, vol. 9, from André Malraux: *Anti-Memoirs*. Downloaded 8.15.98. http://www.blythe.org/mlm/

12. "To sum up, violent revolution is a universal law of proletarian revolution. This is a fundamental tenet of Marxism-Leninism. It is on this most important question that Khrushchov [*sic*] betrays Marxism-Leninism." From: "The Proletarian Revolution and Khrushchov's Revisionism—Comment on The Open Letter of The Central Committee of The CPSU (VIII) by the Editorial Departments of Renmin Ribao *(People's Daily)* and Hongqi *(Red Flag),* March 31, 1964" (Peking: Foreign Languages Press, 1964). http://www.blythe.org/mlm/

13. Greenson 1965, 135. See also Greenson 1967.

14. See Hayek 1944, chap. 6, "Planning and the Rule of Law." See also the classical defense of process in science in Popper 1962.

15. Milosz continues: "I alone know that the assent to the world in the first poem masks much bitterness and that its serenity is perhaps more ironic than it seems. And the disagreement with the world in the second results from anger which is a stronger stimulus than an invitation to a philosophical dispute. But let it be, the two poems taken together testify to my contradictions, since the opinions voiced in one and the other are equally mine." From "Introduction to the Readings," two poems by Czeslaw Milosz. *http://sunsite.unc.edu/ipa/milosz/milintro.html,* downloaded 8/11/98.

## CHAPTER 4. PATHOGENIC BELIEFS, PERFECTIONISM, AND THE PRODUCTION OF PSYCHOPATHOLOGY

1. And for this reason ancient philosophers, like Aristotle in *Poetics,* and modern psychologists, like Richard Lazarus, emphasize the dramatic, interpersonal process of emotional events: "An emotional encounter is an unfolding event that is typically characterized by many complex and fleeting cognitive, motivational, emotional, and coping processes in consequences of which change takes place in the person-environment relationship for *each* participant" (Lazarus 1991, 111, emphasis his.) Citation from Marilyn McCabe, Ph.D.

2. "I was ten when they buried you. / At twenty I tried to die /And get back, back, back to you. / I thought even the bones would do." From the poem "Daddy" in Plath 1981, 224.

3. From Strachey's footnote in Freud 1926d, 108. Though Freud retains a version of the drive theory, even in this late work, he reformulates the notion of signal anxiety as an expression of cognitive processes. I am taking, obviously, the latter point of view.

4. Cited in McWilliams 1994, 334ff.

5. In a masterful account of his work and efforts to clarify "MPD," I found no place where Ross cites scientific literature on memory even though, with his customary concern for scientific values, Ross acknowledges disputes about MPD and its iatrogenic sources.

6. See citations in Showalter 1997. On erroneous memory and errors of reconstruction, see Brenneis 1996, Loftus 1979, and Roediger 1995.

7. Gottlieb cites important papers by Jacob Arlow (1959, 1984).

8. The more famous case is Judge Schreber and his father, Dr. Daniel Gottlieb Moritz Schreber (1808–61), about whom a great deal is now known.

9. See Freud 1909d, 234 n. 1. Freud cited this anecdote in his essay on the uncanny (1919h).

10. Freud, of course, prosecutes the metapsychology of this period of his thought when he traces his patient's mixed feelings and archaic beliefs back to "his remote childhood" (1909d, 237) and those instinctual forces that "built up this neurosis" (237).

11. See Griffiths 1997, 52–53

12. See Lazarus et al. 1966, cited in Griffiths 1997, 53.

13. This passage comes verbatim from Gay 1992.

14. For example, Yeats offered an elaborate, philosophic explication of the "gyre" as symbol of the human soul a few years later in *A Vision* (1925). See Jeffares 1989, 572–74.

15. Since one can see transference events as repetitions of previous ruptures in child-parent interaction, her six types pertain also to types of intervention.

16. Stern (1985) makes a parallel point when he offers nuances between types of attunement and their relationship to "intersubjective disjunctions." He notes: "These appear to be analogous to the spectrum of nonattunement, misattunements, selective attunements, and communing attunements" (219–20).

## CHAPTER 5. AFFECTS: DARWINIAN, CULTURAL, AND BLITZKRIEG

1. For reflections upon the concept of Darwinian affects and their pertinence to psychoanalytic theory see Amsterdam and Levitt (1980); Arlow (1977); Brenner (1974); Gaensbauer (1982); Green (1977); Jacobson (1994); Knapp (1987); and Schwartz (1987).

2. Carl Jung, more than Freud, explored the numerous parallels that obtain between traditional "medicine" healing, religious rituals, magic, and psychoanalysis. Literary portraits of a (Jungian) analytic process appear in Robertson Davies's novels, especially *The Manticore* (1972) and in Hermann Hesse's famous novel, *Der Steppenwolf* (1927). Hesse uses the magic show as the vehicle for his hero's self-examination and transformation. My thanks to Peter W. Gjevre, Vanderbilt German Department, for pointing out the latter.

3. That "courage" is more than a primary emotion, yet based upon them, Aristotle also says: "And so, if the case of courage is similar, death and wounds will be painful to the brave man and against his will, but he will face them because it is noble to do so or because it is base not to do so. And the more he is possessed of virtue in its entirety and the happier he is, the more he will be pained at the thought of death; for life is best worth living for such a man, and he is knowingly losing the greatest goods, and this is painful" Book 3, chapter 9, Electronically Enhanced Text (©) Copyright 1991–94 World Library, Inc.

4. Aristotle, *Rhetoric* 1381a. Source: http://www.perseus.tufts.edu.

5. Hawthorne cites are from ftp://sailor.gutenberg.org/pub/gutenberg/etext92/scrlt11.txt.

6. ftp://sailor.gutenberg.org/pub/gutenberg/etext92/scrlt11.txt

7. ftp://sailor.gutenberg.org/pub/gutenberg/etext92/scrlt11.txt

8. Using a superb website from Tufts University (*http://hydra.perseus.tufts. edu/*) we see illustrated the complex task of articulating fully one culture's secondary affects and "values" into terms and concepts pertinent to another. When we ask their search engines to locate all Greek texts whose English translations might include the word "virtue" we find instantaneously *sixteen* Greek terms.

9. To put this another way, "According to the approach proposed here, the nonverbal representations in the patient's mind are the "facts" by which the interpretation must be tested. The observer can "know" them only by indirect means. The scientific effort should be directed toward developing objective operational measures to demonstrate that nonverbal representations have been aroused" (Bucci 1985, 603).

10. See 2 Kings 11–13.

11. The full reference is Lewin 1958, 6:389.

12. Concepts parallel to Stern's are "synchrony, pseudosynchrony, and dissynchrony." See Field and Fox 1985 and Bernieri et al. 1988.

13. From: http://www.gelservices.com/spank.html. Downloaded 1/19/98.

14. On the blues see http://www.island.net/~blues/

## CHAPTER 6. THE OBJECTS OF PSYCHOANALYSIS

1. From Curtis et al 1988, 260.

2. Simon and Bullock 1994, 1261. For example, a sophisticated analyst writes about loving, even passionate, feelings towards patients, "One function of our clinical theory is to help us with our discomfort in the analytic setting by providing us with a therapeutic legitimization of such uncomfortable feelings" (Coen 1994, 1109).

3. Wallerstein notes that persons may fail to find this midpoint and err in both directions at once, "since it is in the nature of human psychological functioning that deviations can be in the "hyper" and the "hypo" directions simultaneously . . ." (1988, 257). Wallerstein names 26 psychological capacities. A different set of research questions might well name different capacities. See below where I discuss six or seven pathogenic beliefs.

4. Even square dancing and barn dancing are forbidden, for once smitten by these activities some people feel encouraged "to participate in their baser companion—the modern dance." All citations are from "The Christian and the Dance," a pamphlet from Twentieth-Century Christian Bookstore, November 1963, 6–7. On its cover is a large, white spiral that evokes the famous spirals in Alfred Hitchcock's film, *Vertigo* (1958): a spiral that begins with barn dancing and leads, inevitably, to fox trot and swing and then to hell.

5. This is a puzzle with which Aristotle struggles and fails to solve. For example, we note that while Aristotle's comments in *Nicomachean Ethics* are interesting, they do not escape the pull of metaphorical gravity. To explain how one finds the middle way he says one must approximate it just as one finds the center of a circle. This is attractive since it suggests (1) there is a middle ground, (2) that it is "natural," in the way a circle is natural, and (3) there is a heuristic method that, if followed, will bring us to the center point.

6. Text from: http://etext.lib.virginia.edu/cgibin/browse-

7. Text from: http://sailor.gutenberg.org/etext98/nkrnn10.txt

8. All citations of Dostoevsky texts are from Electronically Enhanced Text (©) Copyright 1991–94 World Library, Inc.

9. Text from: http://sailor.gutenberg.org/etext95/hdark10.txt

10. See Buber [1919] 1970; Winnicott 1974; Hand 1996; Farley 1990 and 1996; Levinas [1948] 1979 and 1981.

11. A nephew of the poet Simonides, Bacchylides was "born on the island of Ceos near the end of the sixth century B.C. and lived at least until the middle of the fifth century. Like his contemporary Pindar, Bacchylides wrote in a variety of lyric genres (e.g. hymns, paeans, encomia), but the bulk of his surviving works consists of epinician odes for victors in the Panhellenic games." From: http://hydra.perseus. tufts.edu/cgi-bin/text?lookup=encyclopedia+Bacchylides.

12. Lines 1480–85. Text and translation from: http://ra.perseus.tufts.edu/ cgi-bin/engindex?author=&lookup=oedipus+at+colonus&partial=1&.submit= Search&.cgifields=case&.cgifields=partial.

13. See Grotstein 1990.

14. The rationalist tradition, exemplified by Descartes and socialist and collectivist theory, tends to disdain social institutions that have *merely* evolved. See Hayek 1948, 8.

# References

JOURNAL ABBREVIATIONS

| | |
|---|---|
| *Contemp. Psychoanal.* | *Contemporary Psychoanalysis* |
| *Int. J. Psycho-Anal.* | *International Journal of Psycho-Analysis* |
| *Int. Rev. Psychoanal.* | *International Review of Psychoanalysis* |
| *J. Amer. Psychoanal. Assn.* | *Journal of the American Psychoanalytic Association* |
| *Psychoanal. Quart.* | *Psychoanalytic Quarterly* |
| *Psychoanal. St. Child* | *Psychoanalytic Study of the Child* |

WORKS

Abraham, Nicolas, and Maria Torok. 1994. *The shell and the kernel.* Chicago: University of Chicago.

Akutagawa, Ryunosuke. [1915] 1954. *Rashomon and other stories.* Translated by Takashi Kojima. Tokyo: C. E. Tuttle Co., 1954.

Alexander, Christopher. (1979). *The timeless way of building.* New York: Oxford.

Amacher, Peter 1965. *Freud's neurological education and its influence on psychoanalytic theory.* New York: International Universities Press.

American Psychiatric Association. 1980. *Diagnostic and statistical manual of mental disorders.* 3d ed. Washington, D.C.

American Psychiatric Association. 1994. *Diagnostic and statistical manual of mental disorders.* 4th. ed. Washington, D.C.

223

Amsterdam, Beulah Kramer, and Morton Levitt. 1980. Consciousness of self and painful self-consciousness. *Psychoanal. St. Child* 35:67.

Aristotle. 1991–94. *Nicomachean ethics.* Book 3, chapter 9. © Electronically Enhanced Text .

———. 1950. *The poetics.* Translated by W. Hamilton Fyfe. Cambridge: Harvard University Press.

———. *Rhetoric.* Source: http://www.perseus.tufts.edu.

Arlow, Jacob. 1959. The structure of the déjà vu experience. *J. Amer. Psychoanal. Assn.* 7:611.

———. 1977. Affects and the psychoanalytic situation. *Int. J. Psycho-anal.* 58:157–59.

———. 1984. Disturbances of the sense of time—with special reference to the experience of timelessness. *Psychoanal. Quart.* 53:13.

Atwood, G., and R. Stolorow. 1981. Experience and conduct. *Contemp. Psychoanal.* 17:197.

Bateson, Gregory. 1972. *Steps to an ecology of mind.* New York: Ballantine.

Behe, Michael J. 1996. *Darwin's black box: The biochemical challenge to evolution.* New York: The Free Press.

Benjamin, Lorna S. 1993. *Interpersonal diagnosis and treatment of personality disorders.* New York: Guilford.

Bergmann, Martin. 1980. On the intrapsychic function of falling in love. *Psychoanal. Quart.* 49:56.

Bernieri, F. J., et al. 1988. Synchrony, pseudosynchrony, and dissynchrony: Measuring the entrainment process in mother-infant interactions." *Journal of Personality and Social Psychology* 54, no. 2:243–53.

Bernstein, Michael A. 1994. *Forgone conclusions: Against apocalyptic history.* Berkeley: University of California Press.

Bion, W. R. 1967. *Second thoughts.* New York: Aronson.

Bird, Brian. 1972. Notes on transference: Universal phenomenon and hardest part of analysis. *J. Amer. Psychoanal. Assn.* 20:267–301.

Blatt, S., and C. Maroudas. 1992. Convergences among psychoanalytic and cognitive-behavioral theories of depression. *Psychoanalytic Psychology* 9:157–90.

Bradshaw, Graham. 1987. *Shakespeare's scepticism.* Ithaca: Cornell University Press.

Brenneis, C. Brooks. 1996. Memory systems and the retrieval of trauma. *J. Amer. Psychoanal. Assn.* 44:1165.

Brenner, Charles. 1959. The masochistic character: genesis and treatment. *J. Amer. Psychoanal.* Assn. 7:197–226.

———. 1974. On the nature and development of affects: A unified theory. *Psychoanal. Quart.* 43:532–44.

———. 1982. *The mind in conflict.* New York: International Universities Press.

Breuer, Joseph, and S. Freud. 1893a. On the psychical mechanism of hysterical phenomena: Preliminary communication. In Freud 1966–74, vol. 2.

———. [1895]. 1955. *Studies on hysteria.* London: Hogarth Press.

Brown, Norman O. 1959. *Life against death: The psychoanalytic meaning of history.* Middletown, Conn.: Wesleyan University Press.

Buber, Martin. [1919] 1970. *I and thou.* Translated by Walter Kaufmann. New York: Scribners.

Bucci, Wilma. 1985. Dual coding: a cognitive model for psychoanalytic research. *J. Amer. Psychoanal. Assn.* 33:571–74.

Castelnuovo-Tedesco, Pietro 1984. Fear of change as a source of resistance in analysis. *The Annual of Psychoanalysis* 14:259–72.

Castelnuovo-Tedesco, Pietro. 1989. *Change and therapeutic effectiveness in psychoanalysis and psychotherapy.* Special issue of *Psychoanalytic Inquiry* 9:1.

Chadwick, John. 1958. *The decipherment of Linear B: The key to the ancient language and culture of Crete and Mycenae.* New York: Vintage.

Chertoff, Judith M. 1989. Negative oedipal transference of a male patient to his female analyst during the termination phase. *J. Amer. Psychoanal. Assn.* 37:687.

Cloninger, C. Robert. 1986. A unified biosocial theory of personality and its role in the development of anxiety states. *Psychiatric Developments* 3:167–226.

Coen, S. J. 1994. Love between patient and analyst. *J. Amer. Psychoanal. Assn.* 42:1107.

Cohen, Jack, and Ian Stewart. 1994. *The collapse of chaos: Discovering simplicity in a complex world.* New York: Penguin.

Csampai, Attila. 1992. *Le nozze di Figaro.* Sony Classical Music. Zubin Mehta, conducting. No. 3K 53286.

Curtis, J. T., et al. 1988. Developing reliable psychodynamic case formulations: An illustration of the plan diagnosis method. *Psychotherapy* 25, no. 2:256–65.

Darwin, Charles. [1859.] *The origin of species by means of natural Selection, or The preservation of favoured races in the struggle for life*: 6th ed. gopher: // gopher.vt.edu:10010/02/69/2. New York: Collier Books.

———. 1872. *The expression of the emotions in man and animals.* London: J. Murray.

Davies, Robertson. 1972. *The manticore.* New York: Viking Press.

Dawkins, Richard. 1986. *The blind watchmaker.* New York: Norton.

———. 1996. *Climbing Mount Improbable.* London: Viking.

Deming, W. Edwards. 1982. *Out of the crisis.* Cambridge: MIT Press.

Demos, V. 1984a. A perspective from infant research on affect and self-esteem. In *The development and sustenance of self-esteem,* edited by S. Aablon and J. Mack, 45–76. New York: International Universities Press.

———. 1984b. Empathy and affect reflections on infant experience. In *Empathy,* edited by J. Lichtenberg et al., 2:9–34. New York: Analytic Press.

Dolan, Frances, ed. 1996. *The taming of the shrew.* By William Shakespeare. Boston: St. Martin's.

Edelson, Marshall. 1986. Causal explanation in science and in psychoanalysis: Implications for writing a case study. *Psychoanal. St. Child* 41:89–127. New Haven: Yale University Press.

Eissler, Kurt. 1971. *Discourse on Hamlet and Hamlet: A psychoanalytic inquiry.* New York: International Universities Press.

Ekeland, I. 1993. *The broken dice and other mathematical tales of chance.* Translated by Carol Volk. Chicago: University of Chicago Press.

Ekman, Paul; E. Richard Sorenson; and Wallace V. Friesen. 1969. Pan-cultural elements in facial displays of emotion. *Science* 164, no. 3875 (April): 86–88.

Erikson, Erik H. 1962. Reality and actuality. *J. Amer. Psychoanal. Assn.*10:451–73.

———. 1963. *Childhood and society.* 2d ed. New York: Norton.

Farley, Edward. 1990. *Good and evil: Interpreting a human condition.* Minneapolis, Minn.: Fortress Press.

———. 1996. *Divine empathy: A theology of God.* Minneapolis, Minn.: Fortress Press.

Fenichel, Otto. 1945. *The psychoanalytic theory of neurosis.* New York: Norton.

Field, Tiffany M., and Nathan A. Fox, eds. 1985. *Social perception in infants.* Norwood, N.J.: Ablex.

Flanagan, Owen. 1992. *Consciousness reconsidered.* Cambridge: MIT Press.

Fodor, Jerry A. 1983. *Modularity of mind: An essay on faculty psychology.* Cambridge: MIT Press.

Freud, Anna. [1936] 1946. *The ego and the mechanisms of defence.* Translated by Cecil Baines. Reprint, New York: International Universities Press.

Freud, Sigmund. 1966–74. *The standard edition of the complete psychological works of Sigmund Freud.* Edited by James Strachey. 24 vols. London: Hogarth Press and The Institute for Psycho-Analysis.

———. [1891b] 1953. *On aphasia.* London: Imago.

———. 1893c. Some points for a comparative study of organic and hysterical motor paralyses. Reprinted in Freud 1966–74, 1:157.

———. 1895a. A project for a scientific psychology. In *The origins of psychoanalysis,* translated by Eric Mosbacher and James Strachey, 347–445. New York: Basic. Revised and reprinted in Freud 1966–74, 1:175.

———. 1895d. *Studies on hysteria.* Reprinted in Freud 1966–74, vol. 2.

———. 1900a. *The interpretation of dreams.* Reprinted in Freud 1966–74, vols. 4–5.

———. 1901b. The psychopathology of everyday life. Reprinted in Freud 1966–74, vol. 6.

———. 1905d. *Three essays on the theory of sexuality.* Reprinted in Freud 1966–74, 7:125.

———. 1905e. Fragment of an analysis of a case of hysteria. Reprinted in Freud 1966–74, 7:3.

———. 1909d. Notes upon a case of obsessional neurosis. Reprinted in Freud 1966–74, 10:155.

———. 1911e. The handling of dream-interpretation in psycho-analysis. Reprinted in Freud 1966–74, 12:89.

———. 1912b. The dynamics of transference. Reprinted in Freud 1966–74, 12:99.

———. 1912d. On the universal tendency to debasement in the sphere of love. Reprinted in Freud 1966–74, 11:179.

———. 1912-13. *Totem and taboo.* Reprinted in Freud 1966–74, 13:1.

———. 1913c. On beginning the treatment: Further recommendations on the technique of Psycho-Analysis, I. Reprinted in Freud 1966–74, 12:121.

———. 1913i. The disposition to obsessional neurosis. Reprinted in Freud 1966–74, 12:313.

———. 1914g. Remembering, repeating, and working-through. Reprinted in Freud 1966–74, 12:147–56.

———. 1915e. The unconscious. Reprinted in Freud 1966–74, 14:161.

———. 1916d. Some character types met with in psycho-analytic work. Reprinted in Freud 1966–74, 14:311

———. 1917c. On transformations of instinct as exemplified in anal erotism. Reprinted in Freud 1966–74, 17:127.

———. 1917d. A metapsychological supplement to the theory of dreams. Reprinted in Freud 1966–74, 14:219.

———. 1917e. Mourning and melancholia. Reprinted in Freud 1966–74, 14:239.

———. 1919h. The "uncanny." Reprinted in Freud 1966–74, 17:219.

———. 1923a. Two encyclopaedia articles. Reprinted in Freud 1966–74, 18:235.

———. 1923b. *The ego and the id*. Reprinted in Freud 1966–74, 19:3.

———. 1925d. *An autobiographical study*. Reprinted in Freud 1966–74, 20:3.

———. 1926d. *Inhibitions, symptoms, and anxiety*. Reprinted in Freud 1966–74, 20:77.

———. 1927c. *The future of an illusion*. Reprinted in Freud 1966–74, 21:3.

———. 1928b. Dostoevsky and parricide. Reprinted in Freud 1966–74, 21:175.

———. 1930a. *Civilization and its discontents*. Reprinted in Freud 1966–74, 21:59.

———. 1933a. *New introductory lectures on psycho-analysis*. Reprinted in Freud 1966–74, 22:3.

———. 1939a. *Moses and monotheism*. Reprinted in Freud 1966–74, 23:3.

———. 1940a. *An outline of psycho-analysis*. Reprinted in Freud 1966–74, 23:141.

———. 1942a. Psychopathic characters of the stage. Reprinted in Freud 1966–74, 7:305.

———. 1987. *A phylogenetic fantasy: Overview of the transference neuroses*. Edited by I. Grubrich-Simitis. Cambridge: Harvard University Press.

Friedman, Lawrence. 1997. Ferrum, ignis, and medicina: Return to the crucible. *J. Amer. Psychoanal. Assn.* 45:21–45.

Gaensbauer, Theodore. 1982. The differentiation of discrete affects—a case report. *Psychoanal. St. Child.* 37:29.

Gardner, M. 1991. The art of psychoanalysis: On oscillation and other matters. *J. Amer. Psychoanal. Assn..* 39:851.

———. 1994. Is that a fact? Empiricism revisited, or a psychoanalyst at sea. *Int. J. Psycho-Anal..* 75:92.

Garrow, David J. 1981. *The FBI and Martin Luther King, Jr.: From "Solo" to Memphis*. New York: Norton.

Gay, V. P. 1979. Against wholeness: the ego's complicity in religion. *Journal of the American Academy of Religion* 47:539–55.

―――. 1983. Winnicott's contribution to religious studies: The resurrection of the culture hero. *Journal of the American Academy of Religion* 51, no. 3:371–95.

―――. 1989. *Understanding the occult: Fragmentation and repair of the self.* Minneapolis, Minn.: Fortress Press.

―――. 1992. *Freud on sublimation: Reconsiderations.* Albany: State University of New York Press.

―――. 1996. "Ritual and psychotherapy: Similarities and differences." In *Religious and social ritual,* edited by V. De Marinis and M. Aune, 217–34. Albany: State University of New York Press.

―――. 1997. "Interpretation interminable: Agonistic in psychoanalysis." In *Agonistics: Arenas of creative contest,* edited by J. Lugnstrum and E. Sauer, 111–28. Albany: State University of New York Press.

Gergen, Kenneth J. 1994. *Realities and relationships: Soundings in social construction.* Cambridge: Harvard University Press.

Gibbs, W. 1994. Software's chronic crisis. *Scientific American,* September, 86–95.

Gillman, Robert D. 1986. Review of *Severe personality disorders: Psychotherapeutic strategies,* by Otto F. Kernberg. *Psychoanal. Quart.* 55:502.

Goethe, J. W. [1774] 1970. *The sufferings of young Werther.* Translated by Harry Steinhauer. New York: Norton, 1970.

Gottlieb, Richard. 1997. Does the mind fall apart in MPD? *J. Amer. Psychoanal. Assn.,* 45:907.

Green, André. 1977. Conceptions of affect. *Int. J. Psycho-Anal.* 58:129.

Greenson, Ralph R. 1965. The working alliance and the transference neurosis. *Psychoanal. Quart.* 34:135.

―――. 1967. *The technique and practice of psychoanalysis.* New York: International Universities Press.

Greenspan, Stanley. 1997a. *The growth of the mind: and the endangered origins of intelligence.* Reading, Mass.: Addison-Wesley.

―――. 1997b. *Developmentally based psychotherapy.* Madison, Conn.: International Universities Press.

Griffiths, Paul E. 1997. *What emotions really are: The problem of psychological categories.* Chicago: University of Chicago Press.

Grotstein, James. 1981. *Splitting and projective identification.* Northvale, N.J.: Jason Aronson.

―――. 1990. Nothingness, meaninglessness, chaos, and the "black hole" I—the importance of nothingness, meaninglessness, and chaos in psychoanalysis. *Contemp. Psychoanal.* 26:257.

Grünbaum, Adolph. 1988. The role of the case study method in the foundations of psychoanalysis. *Canadian Journal of Philosophy* 18:623-658.

Hand, Seán, ed. 1996. *Facing the other: The ethics of Emmanuel Lévinas.* Richmond, U.K.: Curzon.

Hawthorne, Nathaniel. [1850.] *The scarlet letter.* Library of the Future ® Series Third Edition, Windows ™ Ver. 3.1.

Hayek, F. A. 1944. *The road to serfdom.* Chicago: University of Chicago Press.

———. 1948. *Individualism and economic order.* Chicago: University of Chicago Press.

Heller, Joseph. 1974. *Something happened.* New York: Ballantine Books.

Helmholtz, Hermann von. 1867. *Handbuch der physiologischen Optik.* Leipzig: L. Voss.

Helmholtz, Hermann von. [1877] 1954. *On the sensations of tone as a physiological theory of music.* Translated by Alexander J. Ellis. New York: Dover.

Henschen, Folke. 1989. News, notes, and queries: On the term diabetes in the works of Aretaeus and Galen. In *Diabetes: Its medical and cultural history,* edited by Dietrich Von Engelhardt, 120–24. London: Springer-Verlag.

Herman, Judith. 1992. *Trauma and recovery: The aftermath of violence— From domestic abuse to political terror.* New York: Basic .

Hitler, Adolf. [1925] 1971. *Mein Kampf.* Translated by Ralph Manheim. Boston: Houghton Mifflin.

Hoffman, Irwin Z. 1987. The value of uncertainty in psychoanalytic practice. *Contemp. Psychoanal.* 23:205.

Hofstadter, D. 1979. *Gödel, Escher, Bach: An eternal golden braid.* New York: Vintage.

Homans, Peter. 1989. *The ability to mourn: Disillusionment and the social origins of psychoanalysis.* Chicago: University of Chicago Press.

Homer. 1962. *The Iliad.* Translated by Richmond Lattimore. Chicago: University of Chicago Press.

Holst-Warhaft, Gail. 1992. *Dangerous voices: Women's laments and Greek literature.* London: Routledge

Hughes, Ted, ed. 1981. *Sylvia Plath: Collected poems.* London: Faber and Faber.

Hume, David. 1739. *A treatise of human nature.* London.

Jacobson, Jacob. 1994. Signal affects and our psychoanalytic confusion of tongues. *J. Amer. Psychoanal. Assn.* 42:15.

James, William. 1902. *The varieties of religious experience.* New York: Collier Books.

Jeffares, A. N. 1989. *Yeats's poems*. London: Macmillan.

Jones, Ernest. 1953. *The life and work of Sigmund Freud*. Vol. 1, *The formative years and the great discoveries, 1856–1900*. New York: Basic.

Jones, James. 1991. *Contemporary psychoanalysis and religion: Transference and transcendence*. New Haven: Yale University Press.

Jung, Carl G. [1911–12] 1956. *Symbols of transformation*. The Bollingen Foundation. Princeton: Princeton University Press.

———. 1961. *Memories, dreams, reflections*. New York: Random.

Kalinich, L. 1994. Review of *Theaters of the body*, by Joyce Mcdougall. *J. Amer. Psychoanal. Assn.* 42:258.

Kant, Immanuel. [1788] 1991–94. *Critique of practical reason*. © Electronically Enhanced Text.

———. [1796] 1964. *Groundwork of the metaphysic of morals*. Translated by H. J. Patton. New York: Harper and Row.

Keats, John. 1973. *The complete poems*. Edited by John Bernard. London: Penguin.

Klein, Donald F. 1974. Endogenomorphic depression. *Archives of General Psychiatry* 31, no. 4 (October): 447–54.

———. 1981. Anxiety reconceptualized. In *Anxiety: New research and changing concepts*, edited by Donald F. Klein and Judith G. Rabkin, 235–63. New York: Raven Press.

Knapp, Peter H. 1987. Some contemporary contributions to the study of emotions. *J. Amer. Psychoanal. Assn.* 35:205

Kohut, Heinz 1966. Forms and transformations of narcissism. *J. Amer. Psychoanal. Assn.* 14:243–73.

———. 1971. *The analysis of the self*. New York: International Universities Press.

———. 1977. *The restoration of the self*. New York: International Universities Press.

Kramer, Peter D. 1992. *Listening to Prozac*. New York: Viking.

Kris, Ernst. 1956a. On some vicissitudes of insight in psychoanalysis. *Int. J. Psycho-Anal.* 37:445.

———. 1956b. The personal myth: a problem in psychoanalytic technique. *J. Amer. Psychoanal. Assn.* 4:653.

Kuhn, Thomas S. 1962. *The structure of scientific revolutions*. Chicago: University of Chicago Press.

———. 1977. *The essential tension: Selected studies in scientific tradition and change*. Chicago: University of Chicago Press.

Lacan, Jacques. [1953] 1979. The neurotic's individual myth. *Psychoanal. Q.,* 48:405

Langs, Robert. 1985. Making interpretations and securing the frame: Sources of danger for psychotherapists. *International Journal of Psychoanalytic Psychotherapy* 10:3–23.

Larsson, B. 1987. Review of *Theater of the mind, illusion, and truth on the psychoanalytic stage,* by Joyce McDougall. *psychoanal. Q.* 56:693.

Lazarus, Richard S. 1991. *Emotion and adaptation.* New York: Oxford University Press.

Lazarus, Richard; Edward Opton; Masatoshi Tomita. 1966. Cross-Cultural study of stress-reaction patterns in Japan. *Journal of Personality and Social Psychology* 4, no. 6:622–33.

Levinas, Emmanuel. [1948] 1979. *Le temps et l'autre.* Reprint, St. Clement: Fata Morgana.

———. 1981. *Otherwise than being, or Beyond essence.* Translated by Alphonso Lingis. The Hague: Martinus Nijhoff.

———. 1987. *Time and the other.* Translated from the French by Richard A. Cohen Pittsburgh: Duquesne University Press.

Lewis, C. S. 1955. *Surprised by joy: The shape of my early life.* London: G. Bles.

Lewin, Bertram D. 1958. Education or the quest for omniscience. *J. Amer. Psychoanal. Assn.* 6:389.

Loewald, H. W. 1975. Psychoanalysis as an art and the fantasy character of the psychoanalytic situation. *J. Amer. Psychoanal. Assn.* 23:277–99.

Loftus, E. 1979. *Eyewitness testimony.* Cambridge: Harvard University Press.

Luborsky, Lester. 1973. Forgetting and remembering (momentary forgetting) during psychotherapy. In *Psychoanalytic Research,* edited by M. Mayman. New York: International Universities Press.

———. 1984. *Principles of psychoanalytic psychotherapy.* New York: Basic.

Lumsden, Charles J., and E. O. Wilson. 1981. *Genes, mind, and culture: The coevolutionary process.* Cambridge: Harvard University Press.

Maclean, Norman. 1976. *A river runs through it, and other stories.* Chicago: University of Chicago Press.

McDargh, John. 1983. *Psychoanalytic object relations theory and the study of religion: On faith and the imaging of God.* Lanham, Md.: University Press of America.

McDougall, Joyce. 1985. *Theater of the mind, illusion, and truth on the psychoanalytic stage.* New York: Basic Books.

McGrath, W. 1986. *Freud's discovery of psychoanalysis: The politics of hysteria.* Ithaca: Cornell University Press.

McWilliams, Nancy. 1994. *Psychoanalytic diagnosis: Understanding personality structure in the clinical process.* New York: Guilford Press.

Mahler, Margaret, and M. Furer. 1968. *On human symbiosis and the vicissitudes of individuation.* New York: International Universities Press.

Mahler, Margaret; F. Pine; and A. Bergman. 1975. *The psychological birth of the human infant.* New York: Basic.

Marble, Alexander. 1989. John Rollo. In *Diabetes: Its medical and cultural history,* edited by Dietrich Von Engelhardt, 229–34. London: Springer-Verlag.

Masterson, James F. 1976. *Psychotherapy of the borderline adult: A developmental approach.* New York: Brunner/Mazel.

Meehl, Paul. 1994. Subjectivity in psychoanalytic inference: The nagging persistence of Wilhelm Fliess's Achensee question. *Psychoanalysis and Contemporary Thought,* 3-82.

Meissner, W. W. 1984. *Psychoanalysis and religious experience.* New Haven: Yale University Press.

Miller, Nancy E., et al., eds. 1993. *Psychodynamic treatment research: A handbook for clinical practice.* New York: Basic.

Milosz, Czeslaw. [1953] 1990. *The captive mind.* Translated by Jane Zielonko. Reprint, New York: Vintage.

Modell, Arnold H. 1965. On having the right to life: An aspect of the superego's development. *Int. J. Psycho-Anal.* 46:323–31.

———. 1971. The origins of certain forms of pre-oedipal guilt and the implications for a psychoanalytic theory of affects. *Int. J. Psycho-Anal.* 52:337.

———. 1980. Affects and their non-communication. *Int. J. Psycho-Anal.,* 61:259.

———. 1983. Self-preservation and the preservation of the self. In *Narcissism, masochism, and the sense of guilt in relation to the therapeutic process,* 1–11. The Psychotherapy Research Group, Department of Psychiatry, Bulletin no. 6. New York: Mount Zion Hospital and Medical Center.

———. 1988. The centrality of the psychoanalytic setting and the changing aims of treatment. *Psychoanal. Q.* 57:577.

Müller, Reinhold F. G. 1989. The urinary flux of the ancient Indians, Pramcha (with special reference to the Carakasamhita). In *Diabetes: Its medical and cultural history,* edited by Dietrich Von Engelhardt, 160–200 London: Springer-Verlag.

Myerhoff, Barbara, and Sally Moore, eds. 1977. *Secular ritual.* Amsterdam: Royal van Gorcum.

Oliner, Samuel P., and Pearl M. Oliner 1988. *The altruistic personality: Rescuers of Jews in Nazi Europe.* New York: Free Press.

Phillips, Adam. 1988. *Winnicott.* Cambridge: Harvard University Press.

Piers, Gerhart, and Milton B. Singer. 1953. *Shame and guilt: A psychoanalytic and a cultural study.* Springfield, Ill.: Thomas.

Plath, Sylvia. 1981. *Sylvia Plath: Collected poems.* Edited by Ted Hughes. London: Faber and Faber.

Plato. 1963. *The collected dialogues.* Edited by Edith Hamilton and Huntington Cairns. Bollingen Series, 81. New York: Bollingen, 1963.

Popper, Karl. 1962. *The open society and its enemies.* 5th ed. 2 vols. Princeton: Princeton University Press.

Popper, Karl 1972. *Objective knowledge: An evolutionary approach.* London: Oxford University Press.

Porkert, Manfred. 1989. Epistemological fashions in interpreting disease. In *Diabetes: Its medical and cultural history,* edited by Dietrich Von Engelhardt, 143–59. London: Springer-Verlag.

Pruyser, Paul. 1983. *The play of the imagination: Toward a psychoanalysis of culture.* New York: International Universities Press.

Putnam, H. 1963. Brains and behavior. In *Analytical philosophy,* edited by R. Butler. Oxford: Basil Blackwell.

Rangell, L. 1986. The executive functions of the ego—an extension of the concept of ego autonomy. *Psychoanal. St. Child.* 41:1.

Rapaport, David. 1960. *The structure of psychoanalytic theory.* New York: International Universities Press.

Ricoeur, Paul. 1991. *From text to action.* Translated by Kathleen Blamey and John B. Thompson. Evanston, Ill.: Northwestern University Press.

Rizzuto, Ana-Maria. 1979. *The birth of the living God: A psychoanalytic study.* Chicago: University of Chicago Press.

Roediger, Henry L., et al. 1995. *Psychology.* Minneapolis, Minn.: West/Wadsworth.

Rosen, Charles. 1971. *The classical style: Haydn, Mozart, Beethoven.* New York: Norton.

Ross, Colin A. 1989. *Multiple personality disorder: Diagnosis, clinical features, and treatment.* New York: Wiley.

Schadewaldt, Hans. 1989. Paracelsus and the Sugar Disease. In *Diabetes: Its medical and cultural history,* edited by Dietrich Von Engelhardt, 201–8. London: Springer-Verlag.

Schafer, Roy. 1968. *Aspects of internalization.* New York: International Universities Press.

———. 1976. *A new language for psychoanalysis.* New Haven: Yale University Press.

———. 1980. Action and narration in psychoanalysis. *New Lit. Hist.* 12:61-85.

————. 1992. *Retelling a life: Narration and dialogue in psychoanalysis.* New York: Basic.

Schechner, Richard. 1977. *Ritual, play, and performance.* New York: Seabury.

Schwartz, Andrew. 1987. Drives, affects, behavior—and learning: approaches to a psychobiology of emotion and to an integration of psychoanalytic and neurobiologic thought. *J. Amer. Psychoanal. Assn.* 35:467.

Searle, John R. 1992. *The rediscovery of the mind.* Cambridge: MIT Press,

Shapiro, Theodore, and Robert N. Emde, eds. 1995. *Research in psychoanalysis: process, development, outcome.* Madison, Conn.: International Universities Press.

Shelley, P. B. [1821] 1921. In *Peacock's Four ages of poetry, Shelley's Defence of poetry, Browning's Essay on Shelley,* edited by H. F. B. Brett-Smith. Oxford: Basil Blackwell, 1921.

Shengold, Leonard. 1988. *Halo in the sky: Observations on Anality and Defense.* New York: Guilford.

Shevrin, Howard. 1978. Semblances of feelings: the imagery of affect in empathy, dreams, and unconscious processes—a revision of Freud's several affect theories. In *The human mind revisited,* edited by Sydney Smith, 263–94. New York: International Universities Press.

Showalter, Elaine. 1997. *Hystories: Hysterical epidemics and modern media.* New York: Columbia University Press.

Silverman, Kenneth. 1996. *Houdini!!!; The career of Ehrich Weiss.* New York: HarperCollins.

Simon, B., and C. Bullock. 1994. Incest and psychoanalysis: Are we ready to fully acknowledge, bear, and understand? *J. Amer. Psychoanal. Assn.* 42:1261.

Spence, Donald. 1982. *Narrative truth and historical truth: Meaning and interpretation in Psychoanalysis.* New York: Norton.

————. 1987. *The Freudian metaphor: Toward a paradigm change in psychoanalysis.* New York: Norton.

————. 1994. *The rhetorical voice of psychoanalysis: Displacement of evidence by theory.* Cambridge: Harvard University Press.

Sperber, Dan. 1974. *Rethinking symbolism.* Translated by A. L. Morton. Cambridge: Cambridge University Press.

Spruiell, Vann. 1989. The future of psychoanalysis. *Psychoanal. Q.,* 58:1.

————. 1993. Deterministic chaos and the sciences of complexity: psychoanalysis in the midst of a general scientific revolution. *J. Amer. Psychoanal. Assn.* 41:3–44.

Stern, Daniel. 1977. *The first relationship: Infant and mother.* Cambridge: Harvard University Press.

———. 1985. *The interpersonal world of the infant: A view from psycho-analysis and developmental psychology.* New York: Basic.

Stern, Donnel. 1983. Unformulated experience—from familiar chaos to creative disorder. *Contemp. Psychoanal.* 19:71.

Szasz, Thomas S. 1961. *The myth of mental illness: Foundations of a theory of personal conduct.* New York: Hoeber-Harper.

Taussig, Michael. 1980. *The devil and commodity fetishism in South America.* Chapel Hill: University of North Carolina Press.

Teller, Virginia, and Hartvig Dahl. 1986. The microstructure of free association. *J. Amer. Psychoanal. Assn.* 34, no.:763–98.

Terr, Lenore. 1990. *Too scared to cry: Psychic trauma in childhood.* New York: Harper & Row.

Tomkins, S. 1962. *Affect, imagery, consciousness.* Vol. 1: *The positive affects.* New York: Springer.

———. 1963. *Affect, imagery, Consciousness.* Vol. 2: *The negative affects.* New York: Springer.

———. 1980. Affect as amplification: Some modifications in theory. In *Emotion, theory, research, and experience,* edited by R. Plutchik and H. Kellerman, 1:141–64. New York: Academic Press.

Turner, Victor. 1969. *The ritual process: Structure and anti-structure.* Ithaca: Cornell University Press.

———. 1982. *From ritual to theater: The human seriousness of play.* New York: Performing Arts Journal.

Vaillant, George E. 1993. *The wisdom of the ego.* Cambridge: Harvard University Press.

Von Engelhardt, Dietrich, ed. 1989. *Diabetes: Its medical and cultural history.* London: Springer-Verlag.

Wallerstein, Robert. 1987. Psychoanalytic contributions to psychiatric nosology. *J. Amer. Psychoanal. Assn.* 35:693.

———. 1988. Assessment of structural change in psychoanalytic therapy and research. *J. Amer. Psychoanal. Assn.,* supp., 36:241–61.

Weiss, Joseph, and Harold Sampson. 1986. *The psychoanalytic process: Theory, clinical observation, and empirical research.* New York: Guilford.

Wellman, H. 1990. *The child's theory of mind.* Cambridge: MIT Press.

Winnicott, D. W. 1971a. *Playing and reality.* London: Tavistock.

———. 1971b. *Therapeutic consultations in child psychiatry.* New York: Basic.

———. 1971c. Mirror role of mother and family in child development. 1967. Reprinted in *Playing and Reality*, 111–18. New York: Basic.

———. 1974. Fear of breakdown. *Int. Rev. Psychoanal.* 1:103–7.

Wittgenstein, L. 1953. *Philosophical investigations*. Translated by G. E. M. Anscombe. 3d ed. New York: Macmillan.

Wollheim, Richard. 1971. *Sigmund Freud*. New York: Viking.

Yerushalmi, Yosef Hayim. 1991. *Freud's Moses: Judaism terminable and interminable*. New Haven: Yale University Press.

# Index